CAMPANA BROTHERS
COMPLETE WORKS (SO FAR)

Rizzoli
NEW YORK

New York · Paris · London · Milan

ALBION

CAM

COMPLETE WORKS

PAN

(SO FAR)

A

BROTHERS

First published in the United States of America in 2010 by
RIZZOLI INTERNATIONAL PUBLICATIONS, INC.
300 Park Avenue South
New York, NY 10010
www.rizzoliusa.com
ALBION
Registered address:
Stuart House
55 Catherine Place
London SW1E 6DY
www.albion-gallery.com

ISBN-13: 978-0-8478-3326-9
Library of Congress Control Number: 2009929566
ISBN-13: 978-1-900829-29-8
A catalogue record for this publication is available from the British Library, London
© 2010 Rizzoli International Publications, Inc.
© 2010 Albion, London
© 2010 Estudio Campana, São Paulo
All texts © 2010 by their respective authors
Distributed to the U.S. trade by Random House, New York
Printed and bound in China
2010 2011 2012 2013 2014 / 10 9 8 7 6 5 4 3 2 1

Every effort has been made to seek permission to reproduce those images for which the copyright does
not reside with the Estudio Campana, Albion or Rizzoli, and the partners are grateful to the individuals
and institutions that have assisted in this regard. Any omissions are unintentional and the details should
be addressed to Rizzoli, New York.
Designed by Herman Lelie and Stefania Bonelli, London
Edited by Matt Price, Dung Ngo, and Lelia Arruda
New photography by Stefan Jonot, Fernando Laszlo, and Ed Reeve
Cover designed by Humberto and Fernando Campana, with Herman Lelie

Collages:
pp. 6–9 by Fernando Campana
pp. 10–13 by Humberto Campana

CONTENTS

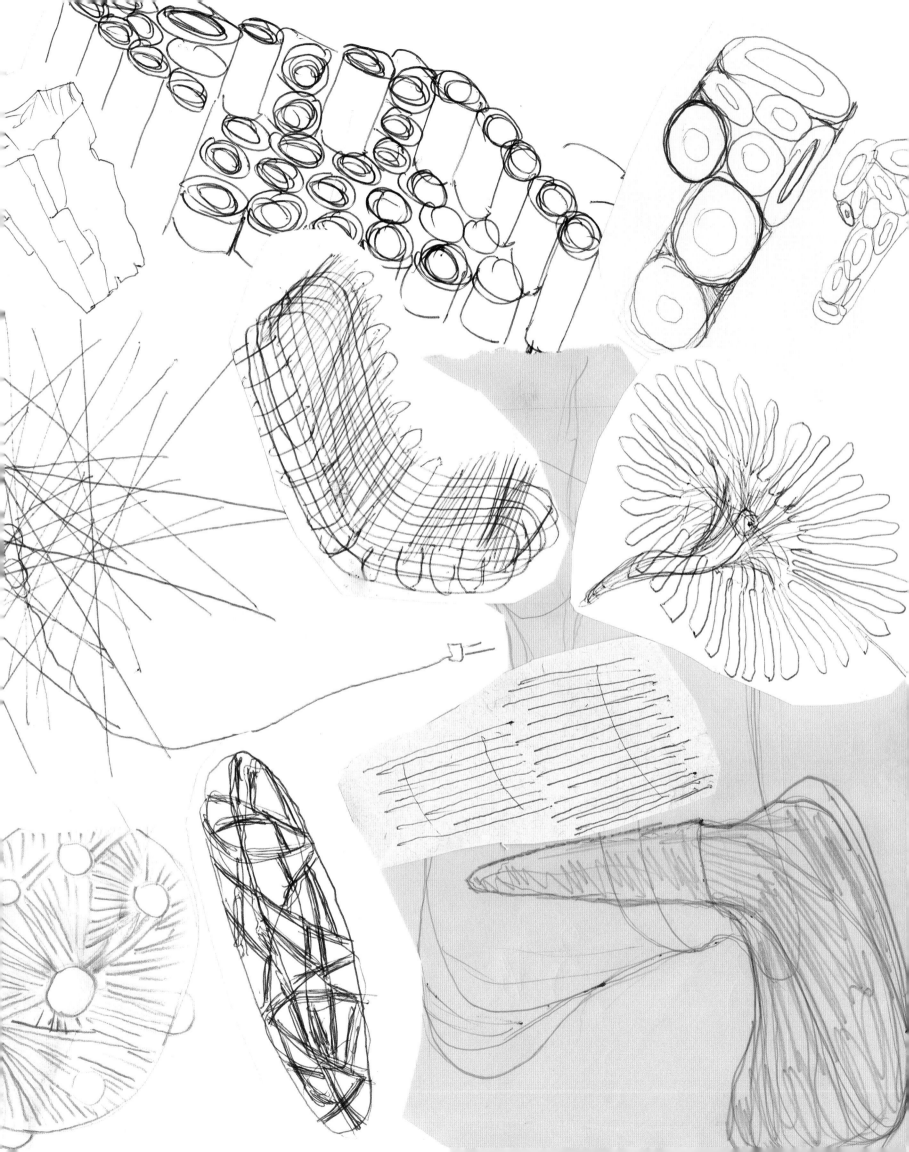

Li Edelkoort

Campana Culture

When five hundred meters of bright red rope are wound like *tagliolini* around a modest metal structure, one ponders whether the object before us is in fact a sculpture, a performance or a meticulous display of artisan craft? It is however a chair…

Hundreds of wooden chips that look like offcuts and discarded planks from a lumber workshop are actually a domestic installation resembling both a futuristic sketch and an ideal archaic dwelling—it is however a house…

Ninety meters of upholstered fabric that twist like a giant serpent into a new form of seating may seem to originate from a kindergarten, an undiscovered jungle, or indeed another planet—it is however a couch…

This is design and it comes from the world of Campana, a place where chaotic creativity is distilled into potent and explosive creations that have animated the design scene over the past two decades in the same way that the Campana brothers themselves have lit up openings, seminars, exhibitions, and workshops with their gregarious Latin energy and sense of humor.

The work of Fernando and Humberto Campana speaks an international language of transformation and reinvention, of pluralism and hybridization. Although the brothers travel profusely, it is their native Brazil that ignites their unique ideas: concepts, prototypes, and editions developed in their laboratory and studio in São Paulo, a city that is a spectacular collage of juxtaposed extremes, an accumulation of urban by-products as numerous as they are colorful, violent, boisterous, and engaging.

Yet it is important to know that the boys grew up in the countryside, where a barefoot Humberto built rock pools by hand and Fernando discovered his innate talent for architecture when constructing tree houses. The neighboring forest floor stimulated a wealth of imagination for the children—a sense of imagination still present in their current and at times naïve approach to form.

The foreign movies they grew up watching in the 1960s and '70s were eye-opening windows to the world. Fernando once dreamed of becoming an astronaut while Humberto's attachment

15

to the indigenous Indians was embedded in his heart. Such early differences between the brothers lightheartedly illustrate a recipe of contrasts inherent to their philosophy; in this case, a merging of techno and ethno and later, the fusion of technology and craft, the tension between order and chaos, the measured application of form and color, the embracing of the natural as well as the synthetic. It's not surprising that their resulting body of work is concerned with defining the transient space between city and country; fitting snugly into a new millennium where the frontiers between urban and rural are becoming blurred, resulting in a greener and slower city and a wired and contemporary countryside.

The two brothers started working together at a time of rapturous change in Brazil; the delayed arrival of postmodernism in a post-dictatorship country on the eve of a global post-minimalist decade, a moment of abolishment mirroring the end of communism and the deconstruction of clothing explored by Japanese and Belgian fashion designers. While business and expansion in Brazil were not concerned with preserving local flavor or a folkloric identity, the Campanas caught wind of the early beginnings of a new ecological movement and the emerging arts and crafts revival that reacted to the information revolution. The more virtual the world was becoming, the more tactile it had to be. Consumers of the future would be interested not only in industrial objects, but also by handmade ones, and designers were starting to investigate how serial production could be unique at the same time. The birth of autonomous form became a new discipline in design.

Craft has positioned itself to become one of the major movements of the future. Fear of a boring global market and the virtualization of society inspires designers and artists to offer work that is linked to the important humanization of the making process, eventually inviting the consumer to become a cocreator. Craft is able to speak of personalization, collaboration, and folklore, the sharing of ideas and the return of production to our doorstep through flourishing cottage industries and local workshops. It promotes the survival of important and endangered hand-crafts that have been passed on for centuries over generations. Evermore educated and mature consumers will soon expect that sustainable ideologies become invisibly ingrained into production methods and the well-being movement at large will have long-lasting and far-reaching effects on the way we live.

The Campana brothers started to work together long before other siblings, twins, couples, and groups teamed up in the recent mood for collective creation. A prophetic brotherhood that heralds the comeback of family values and the power of the individual within the context of a group. Their working together seems effortless and without agony; they actually finish off each other's sentences in the same way they complete each other's ideas in a fusion of thoughts about creation. Although they become one in work and word they are distinctly different and complementary, each bringing valuable assets to their studio and creative development. Theirs is a distinctly twenty-first century creative process.

Products of the future will be universal as well as individual; the local will feed back to the global and will animate world brands to become fervently interactive and reactive. As unofficial ambassadors of Brazil, the Campanas have continually embodied this current, working with artisan specialists to bring handmade techniques with Brazilian charm to products exported and produced around the planet. The brothers speak passionately about these experiences, acknowledging a communal sense of creation and the improvised and emotional freedom that these collaborations bring to their work. This relinquishing of the designer's ego that is typical of their open mentality is the beginning of a new phase for design. Others will follow.

Perhaps it was this visionary sense of freedom that Paola Antonelli perceived when in 1998 she invited the relatively unknown Campanas to exhibit with the design luminary Ingo Maurer. This sizzling coupling of creative forces at MoMA's exhibition demonstrated how the designers shared the use of innovative or unconventional materials and optimistic wit; the show was an important introduction of the brothers' work to an international audience.

Perhaps it was this improvised sense of fantasy that Massimo Morozzi recognized when he called Fernando about their work, before embarking on a courageous decade-strong commitment to presenting their talent at Edra, taking huge commercial risks at each step and requiring dedicated production programs that had to be designed from scratch. The Campanas' use of materials such as plush velvet, polished mirror, golden rope, shimmering fabric, faux fur, and alligator-printed leather reflected the shine of the times prominent at the turn of this century.

The need for shine still thrives as designers everywhere continue to be fascinated by lustrous alloys and surfaces, although the metals are now more matte, brushed, or rusted—patinas tarnished like our world amidst a severe global financial crisis. Unlike several past crises, society is unwilling to become completely reclusive and avidly enjoys healthy doses of hedonism and especially eccentricity. The lessons learnt from this current crisis show us that old methods of doing and being are no longer valid. The world will witness a moment of concentration and consensus, a cultural renaissance through which we will focus on producing less in better ways in compact and robust monolithic form, honing our skills on what we do best—a sculptural and abstract movement. Another decade in favor of the forceful Campana culture of sharing skills and social critique lies ahead.

To answer the growing global resistance to constant renewal and limitless expansion, the humanity and integrity found in the Campanas' work are also qualities requested for the years to come. It is time to empower products with a new dimension: their own character, an invisible energy locked into the design process.

Design will be able to make the object, concept, or service come alive to be our partner, pet, or friend, and to relate to us on a direct and day-to-day level. Only when design is empowered with an almost human emotion will we be able to create a new generation of things capable of promoting and selling themselves—products that will have acquired an aura to seduce even the most hardened consumers on their own terms. Only then will design have acquired soul.

The realization that we have to cease destroying our planet has made young designers adamant to produce sustainably and locally, thus creating fewer polluting proposals and turning to timber, fur, skin, textile, ceramic, and glass to express themselves. Getting in touch with the more animistic side of man, archaic inspirations have fostered a new aesthetic of bold organic form and natural materials dancing to a shamanistic beat. The Campanas' Prived Oca chandelier that was commissioned for Swarovski by Ilse Crawford in 2003 was an incarnation of how the brothers have been early observers of this return to primitivism and fetishism from within Brazil, itself a center of ancient rituals and blended cultural extracts from Africa and Europe and its own indigenous Indian heritage.

Recently the brothers have started to use botanical and animal references that are part of a bigger picture that seems to indicate a new and contemporary form of art nouveau is starting to bloom. Designers of this century will be interested in representing another vision of nature by integrating advanced technologies into the mimicry of biology to create hybrid states of nature, or "post-nature" as it may be known. The day will come when even design will be grown, cloned, and developed, able to be harvested in the same way we harvest our crops and livestock today.

Biosynthesis will become the model for new scientific, industrial, and philosophical development. Our rational human thinking will be subject to evolution; we will think bio-logically, intuitively and act fluidly. An exciting era of fusion in which the Campanas and their contemporaries will explore new terrains to encapsulate the soul of a product and the life cycle of design.

Digging deeper into their landscape, the Campanas have incorporated organic inspirations from the rain forest into the shapes of their chairs and seating. Shown in the spring of 2007 at London's Albion Gallery, "TransPlastic" is a seminal series of morphing silhouettes woven from Brazilian wicker that illustrates the power of nature to take over and destroy all human culture; reclaiming territory with a vengeance from an overwhelming plastic industrial expansion. The Campanas have also integrated geological crystals and minerals in the Diamantina and Cristalina works that are an extension of the same collection; these crystalline shards that carry spiritual values could have been discovered on one of the many sabbaticals the brothers take at remote deserts, lost volcanic lakes, and secluded forests, yet they were actually sourced through an inspiring dealer located not far from the designers' studio in the heart of the urban metropolis.

Though travel and adventure are important to both brothers to rest from their super-nomadic existence, it is the hectic inner city and its jungle of juxtaposed rags and dolls, tools and crates, fences and colorful plastics that represent the major anthropological values in their work so far. The found object as a source for creation and political observation.

A street vendor's kiosk filled to the brim with teddy bears becomes a chair design icon of our time, illustrating our dire need for tactility and tenderness; rag doll souvenirs from the streets of northern Brazil are collected to become another iconic chair, representing the bustle of multi-cultural society but also reflective of human struggle; our history makes us ask whether it represents a container of refugees, victims of a tsunami, slaves being transported, or a voodoo ceremony… ? And the layered multicolored displays of textile found at the market become a recycled piece of furniture fit for our interiors; recycling being part of their idiom from the beginning and taking on more and more sophisticated applications as their careers progress.

This constant source of improvised life, such as that found in the *favelas*, is music to their ears, bringing movement to their bodies that like to dance, extreme values to their eyes that like to wander, and taken as a token of dignity and desire for change on the world stage. Like their Italian namesake—Campana means "bell"—and the ingenious collaboration with Venini once commissioned by Murray Moss, the brothers truly ring bells in our minds, provoking joy while also instilling awe and reflection—representing the world as one global *favela* while fighting fear, industrialization, and poverty. An exciting melting pot of a chaotic culture ready to boil over and spill.

Stephan Hamel

A Modernist Carnival:
The Campana Brothers and Brazil

Campana is an Italian family name from Ferrara and means "bell." Church bells are among the most potent marketing tools ever devised. Every hour they remind Christians of their earthly duties and of the Passion Christ suffered for their redemption. With each toll, they enter a discussion with their conscience and, every quarter or half hour, they register that the time of judgment grows nearer. The Christian faithful know that they must work for their salvation and to gain a place in paradise. If they are interested in negotiation, they can always confess their secrets and sins. As with church bells, confession has also been used as a brilliant marketing strategy through which to communicate the Church's ideas to the public.

The Campana brothers were born into a similar Catholic environment—that of Brazil. Humberto was born in 1953 in Rio Claro, an area of São Paulo, and Fernando in 1961, in Brotas, a small town in the middle of the state of São Paulo. Most of the families in the area come from the same town in Italy and have known each other since they arrived, although most no longer speak Italian. A very special kind of community results from such migrations. In this case, the cultural challenges of immigration resulted in a form of island in which Italian traditions and language became merged with Brazilian customs, creating a unique mix of cultures. From wonderful food to distinctive architecture, the Italian influence is evident and easy to trace. But it was perhaps the cinema in Brotas that brought them closest to Italy and to the Italian way of perceiving art. The brothers would often watch Italian neorealist films there—something that had a considerable influence on their thinking and outlook on the world. The preoccupation of such films with poverty and real life clearly struck a cord for the brothers with the Brazilian context within which they grew up. Neorealism is still part of the drama of the brothers' lives and fundamental to the irony of their style.

The Campanas grew up in an idyllic landscape amid lush vegetation, interspersed with vast waterfalls that instill a sense of purity and peace. The region's climate and tropical breezes, as well as the jungle with its vast array of plant species, have also had a strong influence on the work of the Campanas. It is easy to imagine the brothers playing house as children and furnishing their improvised shelter in much the same

Exterior view of the Igreja Matriz da Cidade (First Church of the City) in Brotas, where Humberto used to attend Mass every week

Young Humberto Campana with his father and the local priest leading a procession in Brotas with a model of Oscar Niemeyer's Cathedral of Brasília

way as would later generate their adult works. From banana leaves to a multitude of flowers, an exotic natural history is evoked and can be seen today in their use of synthetic materials: plastic piping becomes like vines, cardboard is used as if wood, polished aluminum bars treated as if bamboo. In the end, natural and artificial elements are so mingled as to be transformed into a new and distinctive entity.

A country like Brazil is a melting pot with an incredible history and an even more incredible social reality. In a region that is as populous as Europe or the United States, you find Amazon Indian tribes living in an ancestral way in close proximity to the wealthiest 'modern' people— the kind of people who use helicopters to avoid the monstrous traffic jams. Alongside the affluent live the urban poor, known around the world for their ramshackle shelters. In Brazil the *Lei Áurea* (The Golden Law) abolished slavery on 13 May 1888—it was implemented with immediate effect, leaving freed indigenous and African slaves to somehow try to find work and to make an independent life. The jump from one condition to another is always huge and very quick in Brazil. Passing from the desert to the rain forest, you can see all kinds and classes of people living side by side. It is tropical, it is lush vegetation, it is a mix, a mess, a sudden surprise—this is nature as reflected in the brothers' work.

From their relatively remote enclave, first Humberto and later Fernando arrived in the large city of São Paulo, which at the time constituted a strikingly modern, subtropical, urban framework and, especially for South America, one that was very advanced. Humberto studied to become a lawyer, though he never lost sight of his creative ambitions. The beautiful shelters conceived by Oscar Niemeyer, Lina Bo Bardi and Brazilian Modernism make up the baroque part of the city's old town. This urban environment not only opened the brothers' minds and senses, but along with their sensibility to nature, also became one of the main themes of their oeuvre. When Fernando, the younger Campana, arrived, a certain path had already been laid down, but with him he brought his boundless energy and intuitive sense for the glamorous.

Left: The Museo de Arte de São Paulo (São Paulo Museum of Art), 1968, designed by Lina Bo Bardi. Center: The Pavilhão Ciccillo Matarazzo (Ciccillo Matarazzo Pavilion), 1957, in Ibirapuera Park, São Paulo, designed by Oscar Niemeyer and Hélio Uchôa. Right: Edifício Copan (Copan Building), 1966, a vast residential and commercial block in São Paulo, designed by Oscar Niemeyer

Walking with them from the heart of São Paulo to their studio, one begins to understand their novel aesthetics. Here, life in its various facets interacts with layers of history; modern architecture combines with the downtown hut-shelters. At a certain point one comes across a vast, two-level bazaar, which sprawls across a long road as well as rises up above it. The main street, 25 de Marco, is the soul of São Paulo. There are stores offering precious stones, dolls, watering cans, plastic piping, samba costumes, glitter, feathers, and thousands of fabrics—a real labyrinth of trade and goods. It's easy to see how street life, shops, and market stalls offer an endless source of inspiration to the Campanas.

Brazil's *favelas* grow in much the same spontaneous way as its lush vegetation. These amazing constructions have given rise to a unique social context that has fostered among some of the world's poorest people an independent state of mind—not to mention a singular understanding of lawfulness. In the book *Shadow Cities: A Billion Squatters, A New Urban World,* journalist Robert Neuwirth describes what bidonvilles around the world today have in common, proposing that they form an elaborate sub-economy. Unauthorized builders are mixing more cement than official constructors; they are the biggest home investors in the world and are defining the cities of the future. Since 2007, for the first time in history, there have been more people living in cities than in rural areas. Victor Mallet, *Financial Times* correspondent for Asia, has commented that urban growth will become a synonym for slums.

By the end of the 1980s, when Humberto and Fernando were developing their oeuvre, the *favelas* were as yet a largely ignored social phenomenon. In Western societies, the problem was seen as marginal and remote. Some people used to say that they were not interested in India because it was poor, or in China because it was Communist; now such people are having to reconsider the world's fastest-growing economies. The Campanas anticipated the inevitable breakdown of this age-old imperialistic view, sublimating the explosion of shantytown poverty and distilling it into a new aesthetic that reflects the changing nature of such urban living conditions today.

The Western world is perhaps unfamiliar with the Brazilian phenomenon of "Favela Pop"— a form of soap opera devoted to misery, violence, and oppression. Films such as *City of God* and *City of Men* by Fernando Meirelles have also been a huge success on many social levels. There is clearly widespread concern about such stark inequality and a strong will toward social dignity and solidarity. As Jean Ziegler suggests in his book on the victory of the vanquished, the problem is greater for rich societies than for poor ones, and not just because the latter are

Papelão chair, 1995, corrugated cardboard and iron
(Produced by Edra as **Papel chair** in 2001)

better equipped to cope with hardship. The capacity to play with a piece of wood and to be happy is rare in a world of screens and virtual games. The ability to feel satisfied by simple pleasures or to make do with modest means is vanishing, but such romantic ideas are embodied by many of the Campanas' pieces, evoking an idealized notion of the past while raising issues about the complexities of production and consumption today. What makes the Campanas' approach particularly interesting is their ability to translate these social phenomena into an aesthetic code.

The inventiveness of Brazil's poor and their ability to adapt, modify, and reuse materials is a crucial element in the Campanas' approach to design. Take the Papelão chair (1995), conceived out of a desire to create a practical domestic item of furniture using found and low-cost materials. With their eye for quality, the brothers added something more to the original inspiration, so that from humble origins a luxury item was created. This dialectic between the lowly and the luxurious is often curiously self-evident in their works, raising questions about material value and the different kinds of value that culture and society place on objects. With such reflexivity, the pieces exude a forthright and engaging awareness of the current condition—its issues, problems, paradoxes, contrasts and, indeed, its beauty.

Walking through the streets with the brothers and exploring their context and heritage, one encounters an exotic, tropical panorama: myriad colors blend with intricate plants and bright plastic roofs punctuate the cityscape. Beneath the sun-drenched, colorful, and vibrant surface, violence looms. Perhaps for Westerners and tourists this sense of danger is different to the feelings experienced by inhabitants of the city, brought on by the culture shock of suddenly being immersed in the chaos and intensity of such bustling Brazilian cities, and with tales in the back of the mind of ruthless gangs and violent street crime. The brothers weave together the myth and the reality, the imagined and the experienced, revealing a seductive yet hard-edged poetry in the urban fabric that surrounds them. Of the two, it is perhaps Fernando who expresses more the dimension of social reality, while Humberto communicates a more individual consciousness. Needless to say, both predispositions contribute to the intensity that imbues their work with a distinct and precious quality, full of imagination and yet very much rooted in reality.

Plastic drain cover, found throughout Brazil

Mosaico collection bracelet
2001
Yellow gold and diamonds

Something vulgar can become extraordinary, as was witnessed by Arte Povera, the Italian art movement of the 1960s and '70s that often involved artists using inexpensive and everyday materials with which to make works of art. The most common drain gratings found in São Paulo are the source of inspiration for the Campanas' Mosaico ring and bracelet, as well as the Tattoo table (1999). Both pieces provoke a strong aesthetic response whilst quietly signaling that the environment is perilously out of balance: climate change and pollution demand urgent action. Water is one of the most precious resources we have, and its quality and availability is an especially pressing issue for Brazil. Since the early 1990s the World Bank has been working along with a variety of agencies to address the scarcity of clean water in Brazil and the country's inadequate sewage systems. Naturally, the poorer an area is, the less likely its inhabitants are to have access to good water facilities. And for a coastal city such as São Paulo, water contaminated by sewage is still a real problem. For the Campana brothers to have made a bracelet based on drain gratings is a clear reference to a national environmental issue with implications for many other parts of the world. For them to have made the bracelet from gold was a brilliant idea, and not just because of the irony of a cheap plastic drain grating being created from such a precious material. Wearers of this piece will proudly display the gold drain gratings—both a sign of elegance and a constant reminder of the need for us all to make better use of water. On seeing the bracelet, many Brazilians will instantly make the association: will there be enough pure water to flow through these gratings?

Along with the issue of clean water, the coexistence of the various racial groups in Brazil has also often been a headline issue, leading to concerted efforts by the Brazilian government to address problems of racism and equality since the early 1980s. The combination of whites, "Mestizos" and "Mulattos" (mixed-race), blacks, indigenous Amerindians, and "Quilombolas" (primarily Southern European, Jewish, and Arab minorities) has at times come to function as a kind of caste system with social and economic inequality at its core. Understanding, communicating, encouraging, and implementing better integration, equality, and diversity

Liana chair, 1989, iron

in Brazil is as vital for the older generations as it is for the younger generations.

An interesting example of both cultural diversity and the interface between older and younger generations in the work of the Campana brothers can be found in the Multidão chair (2002). In Esperança, a town in the province of Paraíba in the northeast of Brazil, a team of ladies of a variety of ages produces very special "hope" dolls, (which is also the translation of the name of their town). These small handmade cloth dolls, popular with children and cheap to make and to buy, reflect many of the different types of people living in Brazil, and are made from all manner of off-cuts and scraps of fabric. Working with this group of ladies, the Campana brothers designed a chair made up of dozens of these dolls. The Multidão chair is a symbol of the Brazilian mix—a mix that is not only racial, social, and religious, but also an incredibly complex cultural melting pot. It is a patchwork that some might describe as "tropical modernism" and which is in many ways epitomized by the Brazilian carnival. The dolls of the Multidão chair, pressed up one alongside the next in a mass of colors, patterns, and fabrics, capture something of the spirit of carnival, of the people lining the streets, walking, talking, and dancing in their famously ostentatious costumes. The Multidão chair, as with carnival, is a celebration —a celebration of diversity and of the Brazilian people. Individually, the dolls seem humble and there is even something quite melancholy about them, but the moment the Campanas put them together they become joyful—a statement of understatement that is at the same time a riot of color and life. The Multidão chair, which in some ways might be considered a political object, is equally a significant work of art: in it we find some hope of meaningful racial, social, cultural, and religious integration for the next generations in Brazil and beyond.

As well as the people of Brazil, the natural world is equally integral to the brothers' work. Indeed, the Liana chair (1989) is named after the long-stemmed vines that hang off trees in the Brazilian rain forests. They often attach themselves to trees such as the kapok, the giant roots of which are sinuous, gnarled, and knotted. The incredibly rich biodiversity of the Amazon

Multidão chair, 2002, stainless steel and rag dolls

Campanas in the Garden bamboo installation created for the John Madejski Garden at the V&A, London, 2007

and the wider landscape of Brazil offers an almost endless source of inspiration to the brothers, as it has to a variety of traditional craftsmen, both in terms of materials and ideas. Nature is often the best guide for design—plants and trees can grow like barriers and shelters, not unlike the bamboo installation created by the brothers for the gardens of the Victoria & Albert Museum in London in 2007. The vertical, leaning poles of bamboo combine to form a structure that could function as either a fence or an enclosure. The Vitória Régia (2002/2007) seats that accompanied the bamboo installation were themselves inspired by the large water lilies found in the Amazon rain forest and named after Queen Victoria.

The ideas of hybrids and crossovers are vital to the work of the Campana brothers and often represent a meeting of specifically Brazilian ideas, materials, and themes with universal ones. Pieces such as the Multidão chair demonstrate a conversation between traditional Brazilian handcrafts and contemporary design; the Shark chair (2000) combines Brazilian cane with plastic; and the Jabuticaba fruit bowl (1990) brings together branches of the Brazilian jabuticabeira tree with die-cast aluminum. Such combinations, mixes, and dialogues have been developed in the TransPlastic collection. The collection revolves around the combination of everyday plastic objects such as garden chairs with woven rattan to create beautiful and unusual items of new furniture. Plastic water containers, such as can be found outside any favela home, are transformed into unorthodox yet elegant lamps, single plastic garden chairs become integrated into a curiously organic rattan bookshelf, or embroiled in a staircase-like wicker configuration. With elements of the series ranging from ceiling-fitted, cloud-like light features to chairs for children, the TransPlastic collection is an exciting way of creating designed hybrids, meetings, and crossings. Indeed, the notion of "Trans" suggests the exchange and blending of values that is very much characteristic of the brothers' work, as well as perhaps being something inherently Brazilian—whether natural or synthetic materials, the handmade

or the industrially manufactured, traditional or contemporary, lowly or luxury, the reused or the newly made, the ostentatious or the understated, the passionate or the restrained, the modernist or the carnivalesque.

On a global scale, while in some ways cultural differences are as pronounced as ever, in others the world is becoming increasingly homogenized: there is no more East or West, left or right— only a series of interests to be safeguarded. However, the difference between North and South still very much exists. But the South is slowly catching up and Brazil is one of the foremost emerging countries. With economic growth comes a change in lifestyle, design, architecture, and aesthetics. What is fascinating here is that a new idea of domesticity is developing in this part of the world, and the furniture that is produced exists somewhere between art and design. In a land where social codes are still rudimentary, where rival gangs can block the course of daily living, and where prison riots can hold cities hostage, there is a strong energy from public opposition to such forces damaging society; there is resilience, a resistance and, beyond, a desire to survive, to improve the situation. Thus many new values must evolve in order to lighten the burden of survival and for Brazil to continue to address its social and economic issues. The work of the Campana brothers is a symbol of the spirit and ambition of Brazil and South America, capturing the social reality, reflecting its problems, and celebrating its achievements, taking it to the rest of the world with passion, imagination, and style.

27

Jabuticabeira tree at JWT garden, São Paulo, landscaped by the brothers   **Jabuticaba fruit bowl**, 1990, die-cast aluminum and jabuticabeira branch

Cathy Lang Ho

Something from Nothing: Materials and Process in the Work of the Campana Brothers

Form follows material. In upending the classic modernist dictum with their personal credo that material precedes function or form, Humberto and Fernando Campana have instigated a new school of thought that has revolutionized contemporary design. "We discovered that it wasn't the design or the function that would give us the key to a product, but rather the material and its production," Fernando explains.[1] Humberto elaborates, "We never begin with a set form. We learn from the materials; they tell us what forms they should take."[2] This approach was quite radical at the moment when the Campana brothers made their international debut in 1998 with the introduction of their Vermelha chair at the Salone Internazionale del Mobile in Milan and, later that same year, their exhibition at the Museum of Modern Art, New York (MoMA).

At the time, a kind of neo-modernism dominated the fields of contemporary furniture, industrial design, and architecture, exemplified by the pared-down, minimalist statements of Antonio Citterio, Piero Lissoni, John Pawson, Richard Meier, Tadao Ando, and even the high-tech modernism of Norman Foster. Fire-engine red and cartoonishly loopy, the Vermelha chair (which was actually conceived in 1993) stood out like a sore thumb at the Milan fair and became the most photographed object of the event. Meanwhile, their MoMA show proved to be a watershed for their career, giving credence to their idiosyncratic, material-led, craft-based approach. Their exuberant, emotionally charged work was a breath of fresh air, a welcome change from a landscape of objects that seemed to converge on the same image of reduction, so single-minded in their emphasis on function that they appeared ever more predictable, sterile, and devoid of personality.

This is not to say that the Campana brothers are working outside the modernist tradition, however. Quirks and all, their designs share the modernist predilection for transparency; intention and process are always evident. In fact, transparency is easy for the designers to achieve given their fondness for familiar materials—the stuff of everyday life, readily available and affordable—and the fact that these materials are left largely unadulterated in their final form as furniture or products. And this is the secret of the work's allure: the sight of ordinary materials, such as cardboard, rope, fabric and wood scraps, plastic tubes, and aluminum wire,

28

nudged a few degrees to become chairs, lamps, screens, and bowls is startling, amusing, fascinating. Akin to the surrealists who destabilized and delighted viewers by recontextualizing and juxtaposing common objects in surprising ways, the Campanas have pioneered a practice of breathing new life into the old, the discarded or the mundane. In a process they liken to alchemy, the brothers "ennoble what is common, or ignored," in Fernando's words, "finding ways of making something from nothing."[3] Their works always add up to much, much more than their parts.

The Campana brothers first gravitated to common or affordable materials out of necessity. "At the beginning of our careers, our fondness for low-cost materials as well as our peculiar handmade designs had to do mostly with our lack of resources," Humberto explained in an interview with Brazilian artist Vik Muniz.[4] "We simply did not have enough money to invest in machinery and expensive products." This might be the story of struggling artists and designers everywhere, but it is a fact of life for average Brazilians, who have perfected a unique brand of survivalist creativity: in a country with so many living below the poverty line (Brazil is 70th out of 177 ranked countries in terms of the United Nations' Development Program's Human Development Index) and with more than 28 percent of urban dwellers living in *favelas* (informal, mostly illegal, self-built shantytowns), very little is taken for granted. "If someone leaves something on the street, someone else picks it up and uses it," Fernando once observed.[5]

Describing São Paulo, where the brothers are based, as "the largest informal recycling center in the world," they marvel at the way a rattan seat has been fashioned into a window screen, an old sign reborn as an awning, or a jumbo-size olive oil can converted into a street vendor's peanut roaster. "You learn that smart, poetic solutions can be developed without technology, money, or skills," continues Fernando.[6] Brazilians even have a word to describe this homespun form of problem-solving: *gambiarra*. The term was once commonly applied to illegal or poorly executed services but is now popularly used to define an improvised or temporal solution to a

Photographs of *gambiarra* taken by the Campana brothers. In one, an outdoor bathroom has been created using wood, rope, and an improvised plastic tank; in the other, salvaged signage and tree branches have been used to make a table.

One of many improvised homeless shelters in the Zona Oeste (West Zone) of São Paulo

Papelão sofa 1993
Cardboard and stainless steel structure

problem. According to Humberto, "*Gambiarra* is a way of living for a certain part of the Brazilian population. It is spontaneous 'design,' produced with a lot of mental agility and adapted to fast changes due to the fragility of their lives."[7]

The Campanas' early cardboard seating, screens, and lighting (Papelão collection, 1993, later produced by Edra) share a kinship with the towering bundles of used, flattened cartons on wastepaper collectors' pushcarts and the ad hoc shelters that fill the space under the freeway ramp near their studio. The Anemona chair (2000, manufactured by Edra the following year as the Anemone chair) proposes a sublime use for plastic garden hoses, which are commonly discarded. With a mass of curling transparent tubes draped over a simple metal frame, the result resembles the product's namesake sea creature or an ethereal cloud. And the mound of flowering fabric they named the Sushi stool (part of the Sushi collection, started in 2002) is reminiscent of the common practice among Brazilians of sewing together scraps of cloth to create colorful throws or furniture covers. As is characteristic of all their work, the constructions are relatively straightforward while the materials take center stage.

A casual walk in the Santa Cecília neighborhood, where the Campanas' studio is located, invariably turns into a treasure hunt. Once a wealthy enclave for plantation owners and now a slightly run-down (though rapidly gentrifying) mixed commercial and residential quarter, the area is lined with convenience and supply shops proffering an array of utilitarian wares from picture frames to plastic bins, religious paraphernalia to hardware supplies. "You see how things are put together in a non-conscious way that can be very beautiful," says Humberto. Pointing to bunches of brooms, bushels of steel sponges, and piles of rubber mats, he enthuses, "In Brazil, you can find a lot of things cheap—there is such a great diversity all on one block, so

Vitória Régia stool, 2002, carpet, rubber, EVA, fabric

Anemona chair, 2000, stainless steel and PVC tubes

you don't have to go far to find everything you need."[8] His eyes twinkle when he talks about one of his favorite streets not far from the studio that's devoted to all things plastic.

Materially, ordinary life in Brazil is like an endless tour through the most discounted of discount stores. Only special excursions into wealthy shopping enclaves and select malls bring the average person into contact with what might be considered "quality," "luxury," or "designed" goods—concepts that are consistently perceived by Brazilians as equivalent to "European" or "imported." The mass availability of low-cost goods, whether basic household items, building materials, or clothing, is extraordinary, as is the fact that this is one of the few places in the world where one sees "Made in Brazil" more often than "Made in China." The needs of average consumers are remarkably well met as a result of stiff trade protectionism and the government's efforts to foster domestic industry rather than see its capital and resources flow out of the country, as they often have since colonial days.

Where most see kitsch, the Campana brothers see potential; when they reach for something banal or borderline ugly, it's with sincere interest and excitement, and with no trace of the irony that's palpable in many other contemporary designs based on the reappropriation of found objects. Through the brothers' eyes, ordinary life in Brazil is not crowded with junky, disposable goods but with intriguing patterns, surprising textures, and compelling elements that can be combined, inexpensively and directly, through low-tech means, into other useful—and more valuable—goods. Key to their approach is that they let the materials take the lead. With echoes of Louis Kahn's "what does a brick want to be" discourse, the Campanas "flirt" and "play" with materials, to use their words, "pushing them as far as we can" to divine what forms they should take.[9] Their process is adaptive, unpretentious, and spontaneous—like the brothers themselves. They have an assistant who is fully charged with investigating new materials and objects, though all of the Estudio Campana employees and the brothers themselves seem forever on the look-out for latent design components. The offices reflect their methodical madness: prototypes abound, including a bizarre bowl made of plastic doll limbs, a variety of leather patchwork vases, and platters of stitched screen mesh and wicker. By their own admission, the majority of what they attempt fails; if they weren't such optimists the world would probably never have heard about them—they struggled for a good ten years with their *gambiarra*-esque creations before Edra or MoMA came calling.

Just as they initially gravitated toward simple materials out of economic need, so did they adhere to simple production techniques: "We could not be more high-tech or industrialized

Prototype for **Leather Vessel**, 2008

Prototype for **Doll basket**, 2008

Humberto and a seamstress
working on the Banquete
chair in 2002

than we are," says Fernando. "It would be impossible for us to design something the way a German or Japanese designer would. We can only be Brazilian."[10] In other words, it would have been both out of reach and out of character for them to design products requiring complicated tooling or industrial processes like metal stamping or injection molding. In essence, their use of finished products such as hoses, ropes, rubber place mats, and bubble wrap as raw materials is a production shortcut: for example, the Tattoo table (1999, produced by FontanaArte the following year), made of plastic drain grills, is a clever demonstration of how to create a patterned, perforated tabletop without the need for costly custom tooling. Similarly, their Banquete, Alligator, Teddy Bear, and Multidão pieces, along with others in the series (begun in 2002) offer an inspired way of creating soft seating without going anywhere near springs, foam, or upholstery; instead, dozens of plush, inexpensive toys are sewn into an orgiastic mass to soften a basic metal frame. Beyond cost savings (and propitious affinities to Duchamp's readymades), the added advantage of using such existing objects is that it avoids contributing to the waste associated with creating and using new materials.

The Campana brothers were not the first in recent design history to rely on found objects and low-tech production techniques: in the 1950s and '60s, another brother team, Achille and Pier Giacomo Castiglioni, experimented with readymades, creating such iconic works as the tractor-seat and bicycle saddle stools (Mezzadro stool and Sella stool, respectively, both manufactured by Zanotta, 1957) and lighting made with car headlamps (Arco and Toio, both by Flos, 1962). In the 1980s Tom Dixon and Ron Arad turned to traditional practices like welding and weaving as well as found objects, embodying the punk do-it-yourself attitude of the time. And in the 1990s, concurrent with (though an ocean away from) the Campanas, the Dutch collective Droog was developing its wry body of work, which included chandeliers made of 85 naked light bulbs and a chest of old drawers, strapped haphazardly together (85 Lamps by Rody Graumans, 1992, and Chest of Drawers by Tejo Remy, 1991). What they all share is a sense of humor and certain delight in discovering beauty or solutions in unexpected places: these are designs that make you look twice and smile when you see humble objects assuming different identities. Unlike some others, however, the Campanas' approach evolved not as a critique of the state of design but as a natural expression of being Brazilian. The materials they choose, the methods they employ, and the dramatic, carnivalesque results are all highly personal commentary on the joy and chaos of living and working in Brazil.

Achille and
Pier Giacomo Castiglioni
Sella stool
1957 (manufactured
by Zanotta, 1983 edition)
Black saddle of racing
bicycle, pink lacquered
steel column with
cast-iron base

Rather than lament their own lack of resources or their country's underdeveloped industry,

Humberto Campana with a local shopkeeper

they tapped into the strong tradition Brazil does have: artisanal handcrafts. The tradition is an integral part of Brazil's material culture—in every Brazilian household one will see something made by hand, by a Brazilian, such as a woven cotton hammock, a ceramic vase, carved wooden toys, or papier-mâché masks. Handcrafts are also deeply ingrained in the Campanas' design mind-set. In fact, when the brothers started working together it was to make utilitarian objects such as handwoven baskets and picture frames embedded, mosaic-like, with tiny shells. Humberto began making things first, retreating to Bahia after finishing his law degree in the 1970s, feeling it was the only place in Brazil, then under military dictatorship, where one could enjoy relative freedom. When he returned to São Paulo in 1984, he continued to make baskets as well as sculptures, and engaged Fernando to collaborate. Fernando, who by then had completed his architectural degree, was the force who pushed the sculptural works to evolve into more functional objects. From there, furniture design was a short leap.

Their penchant for manual invention can be traced even further back. As boys growing up in Brotas, a small agrarian town not far from São Paulo where they still spend most weekends, they were constantly making toys such as animals and aircraft using twigs, wood scraps, and anything else they could find on their family farm. The wildness and variety of the natural terrain ignited their imaginations: a regular day for them would include leaping off the sticky, red clay banks into the white rapids of the river that cuts through the center of town, getting lost in the area's poplar farms or bamboo forests, or trying to connect to the center of the earth by swimming in a magical aquatic "oculus"—a placid, isolated blue-green pond that is the only aboveground aperture to one of the largest aquifers on the continent. To this day, the brothers take their energy from Brotas, with routine trips to a wondrous environment that feeds their souls.

Seeing them relax and play in the countryside gives the impression that, for them, the man-made world offers little compared with what mother nature has created. It's not surprising, then, that nature's logic is often mimicked in their work: in their bamboo pieces (begun in 1992) and the Taquaral chair (2000), bamboo rods are bunched in a manner that replicates the way they grow in thick stands, while swatches of cloth are furled petal-like in their Sushi series, and thin metal rods fall seemingly randomly, like twigs, in their Blow up tabletop accessories (produced by Alessi since 2004). They have a special fondness for natural or minimally processed materials, and they allow their found objects (no matter how synthetic) to behave as "naturally" as possible. As if to echo their own situation of having one foot planted firmly in Brotas and the other in São Paulo, many of their works play with the uncomfortable confrontation between

Rody Graumans
85 Lamps (for Droog)
1992
Light bulbs, cords, sockets

Tejo Remy
Chest of drawers (for Droog)
1991
Wooden drawers, cord

The young Fernando (right) out on the family farm in Brotas

Mirror (detail)
1982
Mirror and shells

33

the natural and the man-made, with high-contrast combinations such as a glass tabletop suspended among three beautiful, sanded tree stumps, or natural cane married to cold, engineered materials such as polycarbonate and plastic.

Their childhood, which also includes the strong influence of their agronomist/naturalist father, is surely what has made them so down-to-earth, so tactile, and so instinct-driven—traits that are clearly reflected in their designs. The Campanas can't help putting their hands (or feet, or bodies) into everything. Those who know them and their working process can vouch for how it would be impossible for the brothers to be anything but physically involved in every piece. And in Brazil, where skilled manual labor is plentiful and affordable, their hands-on method is viable. The ground floor of their studio is given over to a workshop, which serves as both a testing ground for new ideas and a mini factory that makes and sells works that are not licensed to longtime partner Edra or other clients.

Under the rubric of Estudio Campana, half a dozen artisans—including one man who has been working with the brothers for 20 years—produce goods that are made to order, for exhibition or distribution by their representatives in New York (Moss) and London (Albion), or for one of their many specially commissioned installations. A group of seamstresses spends the day sewing handmade folkloric dolls or industrially produced Mickey Mouses into colorful chaises. Inspired by apuí, a parasitic jungle vine that must be manually extracted to prevent it from choking its host tree, another worker weaves vine through and around cheap plastic café chairs, creating marketable versions of the successful TransPlastic collection exhibited at Albion in 2007. In the studio's open-air courtyard, one worker might be assembling blossoms of mix-matched textiles into Sushi chairs, while another pieces together mirror fragments into a chandelier. Even the products that are licensed to Edra for production require a substantial amount of manual labor, which is achievable in Italy because the furniture industry remains supported by mid-size factories employing artisan workers. At Edra, for example, one craftsman is in charge of making the Vermelha chair, basically following the exact method of the brothers, weaving, knotting, and looping 450 meters of cloth rope through a metal frame.

On a spectrum that runs from gallery-priced art and design objects at one end to industrially produced furniture for the masses on the other, it's true that the Campanas' output veers closer to the former. This perhaps seems ironic given that their work springs from humble materials and is inspired by the "poor" processes of making in Brazil. In fact, their practice straddles the craft workshop and the factory, defining a category of production that might be described

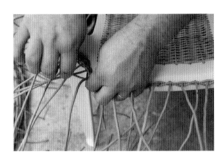
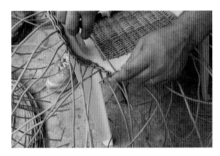

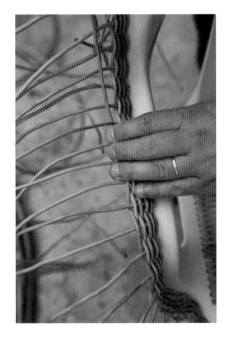

The process of making a Café chair

Giuseppe Altieri assembling the Vermelha chair at Edra, Italy

as "limited serialization." It's not dissimilar to the practice of small design ateliers throughout Brazil and beyond, from Helsinki to San Francisco, Amsterdam to Barcelona, producing their own goods in-house, in small batches, relying in some measure on manual talent. In terms of annual production per year, few of the Campanas' designs surpass the 50-unit mark, and many remain one-of-a-kind. Each product has industrial aspects, such as the presence of mass-produced readymades or the outsourcing of components, such as the frames for Sushi and stuffed animal chairs, to metal fabricators. But the bulk of the production work, whether preparing materials or assembling parts or final detailing, is left to artisans. Each Vermelha chair takes an astonishing 84 hours to make. A Multidão chair requires three full days of sewing, not counting the labor involved in the making of the dolls, which are purchased from an artisanal collective in the rural village of Esperança in Paraíba. The Café chair also takes between two and three days, starting with a worker drilling holes along the edges of a store-bought plastic chair, followed by days of wicker-braiding, and finishing with the chair being lightly torched to remove loose fibers. Harking back to the ideals of the nineteenth-century Arts & Crafts movement, their process humanizes the product—the hand and spirit of the worker are embodied in each work—setting them apart from the "pasteurized" offerings (to use Fernando's term) of the mainstream design industry.

The Campanas' reliance on artisanal work dovetails with a resurgence of interest worldwide in handcrafts. Today, you see countless countries attempting to preserve traditional crafts as a way to safeguard their cultural identities. For example, in 1994 France established the Conseil des Métiers d'Art, which awards the title of Master Craftsman to valued artisans working in diverse (and often waning) fields such as decorative silversmithing, haute couture, tapestry weaving, and bookbinding. UNESCO recently founded a mission to preserve what it calls Intangible Cultural Heritage (ICH), recognizing that traditional crafts and other unique know-how are "the mainspring of cultural diversity" yet are endangered by globalization's rationalizing and homogenizing effects. Brazil, too, has considerable official and grassroots activities geared toward preserving traditional crafts, from festivals devoted to its varied artisanal arts to attempts to broaden their market by NGOs such as fair-trade advocate Artesanato Solidário, (which supports the Esperança doll-making collective). It makes sense, given the substantial dependence of Brazil's economy, both officially and unofficially, on the sale of artisanal goods.

A huge undeclared economy sustains countless entrepreneurs, seen hawking purses made from aluminum can lids on the beach, for example, or jewelry made from used telephone cards sold at tourist-frequented street fairs. According to the Instituto Brasileiro Geografia e Estatística, the nation's informal economy generates an income of nearly $18 billion. In Brazil today, some of the most active NGOs are those that see the revival of crafts as a way for certain populations to generate income under non-exploitative circumstances, such as setting up fair-wage worker collectives in *favelas* or working directly with marginalized communities to preserve handed-down practices, as Rio-based fashion company AmazonLife is doing, collaborating with indigenous Amazonian tribes to preserve traditional rubber-tapping—a sustainable forest use that has declined due to the rise of plantation and synthetic rubber.

The Campanas don't overplay the sustainability aspect of their practice—it's just a natural constituent of what they do—but it's certainly a large part of the reason why they have been so inspirational to a whole generation of designers. Whether reducing their carbon footprint by using existing materials or working with hard-up communities such as the women of Esperança to help preserve a craft that's been passed down for generations, their work is consistently eco- and society-minded. In some instances, their environmentalism is overt: for example, the concept for the TransPlastic collection emerged from their vision of a future where ugly plastic outdoor chairs have overtaken every bit of public space. But they imagine nature overrunning them, morphing them into more naturalistic, less offensive forms. It's the Campanas at their best: they've taken the world's most banal chair and transformed it into something charming and desirable, simultaneously embedding a sharp critique of the dreary ubiquity of our postindustrial surroundings while reviving the fading technique of manual wicker-braiding.

It wouldn't be an overstatement to suggest that the Campanas have launched a movement of sorts, proving that designs can fetch collectors' prices no matter what they are made of, provided they are rich in concept, wit, and elegance. The concept that even garbage has value has captivated the imagination and conscience of wealthy industrialized nations, lending momentum to the Campanas' ascent and legitimizing a practice of inventive reappropriation that's forever been a reflex of the world's poor. One telltale sign of their success is the abundance of contemporary designs, unavoidable at every international design fair, that are unmistakably Campana-esque. Fortunately for the post-Campana generation of designers, who seem to be primarily concerned with conserving resources, the growing awareness of the Earth's predicament has also created a larger market for sustainability-driven designs. The only shortcoming of such approaches is that they can sometimes have a discernibly earnest, if not ungainly,

Woman attaching Esperança
dolls to the Multidão chair
at the Estudio Campana

eco-sheen; and as we all know, good intentions are rarely sufficient to qualify something as good design. The Campanas' work stands apart in the sense that it never has a hint of recycling or down-cycling: their designs are executed as flawlessly as the best the design world has to offer, and their material choices always seem utterly logical, as if the hose, drain grill, rope, and so on, always aspired to be something more.

The brothers do admit to having some activist or subversive impulses: they'll accede to trying to find beauty amidst ugliness, and that they are reacting to the chaos of a world that's allowed its natural beauty to be superseded by infinite junk. Interestingly, in this regard they are disconnected from the estimable lineage of Brazilian modern furniture, epitomized by the mid-century work of Sergio Rodrigues and Joaquim Tenreiro, among others, which, despite sharing the Campanas' love of sensuous forms and craft techniques, was quite careless about precious resources. "When I began designing, I saw how wasteful it was to use wood," notes Humberto, referring to this legacy. "I didn't want to follow this path."[11] (Admittedly, this had to do with the epoch during which the modernists were practicing; these days, for example, Rodrigues, still active at 81, is working with renewable hardwoods.) Moreover, whereas their predecessors' work was highly formal and stylized, the Campanas' output is unruly, expressing a kind of controlled disorder that reflects the brothers' perceptions about their own lives and their beloved country today.

The Campanas have put Brazil back on the global design map and have written the latest chapter of the design history books. Who could have expected that a strategy as personal and idiosyncratic as theirs, and as entrenched in a country as far away and multifarious as Brazil, could produce a model for design practice in the twenty-first century? Certainly not the unassuming brothers, who always speak from the heart and act with their hands.

1
Cátia Fernandes, "Campana: Cada móvel é um documento," *House Traders* 16 (June/July 2007): 38–44.

2
Cathy Lang Ho, "Brothers of Invention," *I.D. Magazine* (June 2003): 68–75.

3
Interview, March 2003.

4
Vik Muniz, "Interview: Campana Brothers," *BOMB* 102 (Winter 2008): 22–29.

5
Cathy Lang Ho, "Brothers of Invention," *I.D. Magazine* (June 2003): 68–75.

6
Ibid.

7
Interview, October 2008.

8
Interview, April 2008.

9
Cathy Lang Ho, "Brothers of Invention," *I.D. Magazine* (June 2003): 68–75.

10
Interview, April 2008.

11
Vik Muniz, "Interview: Campana Brothers," *BOMB* 102 (Winter 2008): 22–29.

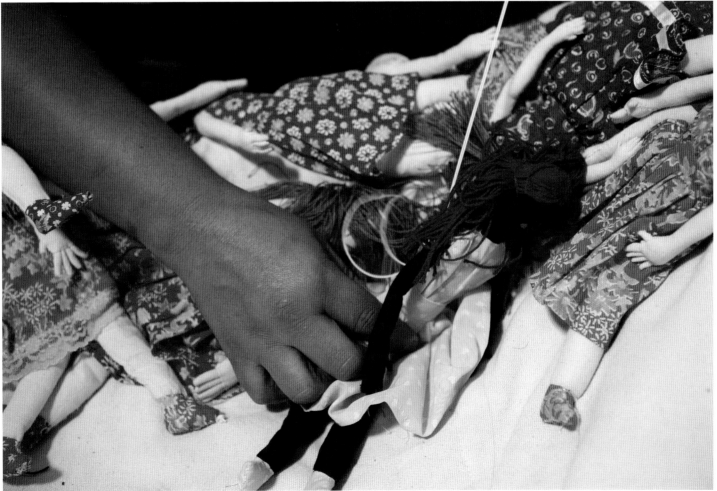

Top: The ground floor workshop at the Estudio Campana   Bottom: Woman attaching Esperança dolls to the Multidão chair at the Estudio Campana

Deyan Sudjic

Meaning Beyond Utility:
The Campana Brothers and Postindustrial Design

In its first modern incarnation, design was a form of practice that became necessary, or even possible, only when mass production had made craftsmanship redundant. This development wasn't exclusively the reflection of the impact of the Industrial Revolution at the turn of the nineteenth century, as might often be assumed, although it could not have happened without it. Coinage, medals, and amphorae had all been "designed," rather than crafted, for millennia. And all of them were mass-produced, the result of production drawings, new tools, and industrial processes that created multiple versions of the same object. In a way this multiplicity changes the status of the object: chairs, lights, and TV sets become more like categories than things.

Ironically this is much the same as the way that art operates in our own times. It has become dependent on a similar range of skills. The artist's studio has become a production office. For Jeff Koons or Damien Hirst, teams of assistants labor on drawings. Factories produce their works, the quality of which is measured in much the same way that a car would be—how smooth a surface is, how well a junction is finished. Perhaps what the Campana brothers have reinterpreted in their oeuvre are the qualities that make an object unique.

It was the Steam Age that created the most decisive shift in the relationship between people and things. From the mid nineteenth century, objects were not made to measure for specific commissions or users, but rather were produced in huge quantities and with standardized dimensions that could meet the needs of everyman. Objects were made differently and as a result the consumer had to be seduced into wanting to purchase them, and in this way the language of design was transformed. Desire was being manufactured for the first time. Branding became increasingly important. You can see the process most clearly with the impact on the chair of the Thonet factories, scattered around the fringes of the Austro-Hungarian Empire so as to take advantage of cheap labor and abundant supplies of raw materials.

Left:
One of the basement workshops at the Estudio Campana, São Paulo

Right:
Thonet factory at Bistritz, Moravia, c. 1900

Thanks to Michael Thonet's patent techniques for bending wood, furniture making was de-skilled from the middle of the nineteenth century and turned into a process of assembling prefabricated components. You would not have to be a Luddite to understand this as doing to chairs what fast food was one day to do to lunch. But the essential qualities of Thonet's chairs come not from the skill of craftsmen but from the intelligence with which designers made the most out of the potential of the material and the techniques at their disposal. In the process, they changed our relationship with our possessions. Thonet made identical chairs by the million. It would undoubtedly have horrified William Morris, who wanted to restore the direct relationship between maker and user, but it gave a lot of people beautiful, simple objects at an affordable price, something that Morris never achieved despite his socialist agenda. And it was done with an unselfconscious aesthetic based on a "first principles" approach rather than reference, evocation, or memory.

Even to rehearse this idea of design now has a quaintly old-fashioned tinge. Design has become about a lot of things beyond utility and affordability. Indeed, utility has come to be seen in some circles as a burden. The useless is valued above the useful as design has aspired to occupy the territory once associated with the ultimately most useless, and therefore the most valuable form of all, which is to say art. This did not happen all at once. Ettore Sottsass's generation of designers wanted to emphasize the emotional aspects of everyday possessions. Sottsass looked for ways to give industrially made objects, even the first generation of computers, some of the qualities and rituals that mankind has traditionally invested in its possessions. But at the same time, he was also ready to pursue design as a fundamentally rationalist process. While he was making ceramics inspired by his quasi-mystical experiences travelling in India, he was still exploring the properties of plastic and polycarbonate, of extrusions and moldings.

Ettore Sottsass (with Penny King)
Valentine Typewriter
1969
Produced by Olivetti & Co., Italy

Ettore Sottsass
Totem
1962–67
Handmade ceramic elements
c. 200 x base Ø 60 cm
c. 78.7 x Ø 23.6 inches
Produced by Bitossi, 1996
Edition of 10

Eileen Gray
Prototype of E1027
Adjustable table
1926–29
Chrome, steel, and aluminum
61.8 x 50.5 cm / 24.3 x 19.9 inches

Now the balance has tipped toward understanding design almost entirely as a form of self-expression without much of the ballast that comes from industrial production. But the question that we still have to deal with in coming to terms with the relatively new phenomenon of a form of design that is not primarily interested in mass production, or in the alibi of utility or function as is clearly the case with the work of the Campana brothers, is how to assess its success or failure. It may still be design, but we need new tools to understand it, since by the old criteria, it is clearly failing: made in small numbers rather than large, costly rather than affordable. There was a slyly intelligent exhibition at the Crafts Council in London a decade ago called "Industry of One," which sketched out a landscape in which, because they had little other choice, industrial designers without industrial clients survived by making objects in small quantities—in the way that Ron Arad used to salvage car seats from the Rover 2000 and team them with scaffolding frames.

It was a kind of surrogate for the real thing, a holding pattern for a more industrial future that might one day be open to designers, if they had the patience and the survival skills. The ecology of this world has shifted since then. It is now possible to build a career entirely in what was once marginal territory for design, without ever aspiring to move into the mainstream of industrial production. And so what is called design is no longer measured by the ingenuity or skill with which designers manipulate production techniques, or give shape and form to new technologies. There is another design conversation now that concentrates on the emotional resonances that objects can communicate, rather than what they can do, the way that they reflect on their owners, and the way in which they are acquired and collected. In one sense

43

Ron Arad
Rover Chair
1981
Rover car seat and steel framework
69 x 90 x 90 cm
27.2 x 35.4 x 35.4 inches
Produced by One Off

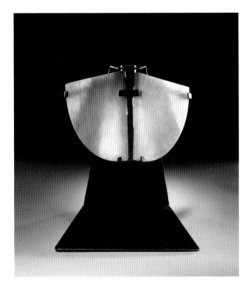

Pierre Chareau
Masque
Table lamp (LP 180 model)
c. 1922
Metal and alabaster
29.5 x 25.5 x 21.4 cm / 11.6 x 10 x 8.4 inches

this is what decorative art has always been. It's the quality that sixteenth-century nobility looked for in the decorative flourishes of the suits of armor that they purchased from Milanese workshops without ever intending to use them to fight in. And despite their interest in mechanisms and the aesthetics of the machine, Pierre Chareau and Eileen Gray were content to use their imagery but not their substance.

That is certainly the way that the Campana brothers have been presented. Their work has been described as political commentary, as a kind of cultural assertion of the Brazilian national identity. But perhaps it doesn't have to be either of those somewhat weighty things to be successful. By looking to find ways to give everyday objects a layer of meaning beyond utility, the Campanas have played a significant part in recalibrating the objectives of contemporary design. There have been other designers who have used their observational skills to take the unselfconscious inventiveness demanded by the pressures of everyday survival and transformed them into consumer objects that could be understood as celebratory. Ingo Maurer, for example, built a family of lights on the flash of inspiration that he got late one night in a Caribbean ghetto from the sight of a bar lit from electricity stolen from overhead power lines with the aid of clips and dangling cables. But that does not mean that their work is to be understood as a form of social commentary as is sometimes assumed by those who take a blinkered view of the nature of contemporary Brazil.

São Paulo, Humberto and Fernando Campana's hometown, is South America's largest city. Approaching 20 million people, it is the single most important driving force behind the emergence of Brazil, alongside Russia, India, and China in that recently identified economic phenomenon to be reckoned with, BRIC. It is São Paulo's factories that produce the avionics for the country's

Ingo Maurer
Ya Ya Ho
1984
Low-voltage halogen system
Dimensions variable
Produced by Ingo Maurer GmbH, Munich

burgeoning aircraft industry and make it possible for Brazil to launch satellites, and which give Brazil its enviable GDP.

And it is São Paulo's television studios that churn out the *telenovelas* that have a grip on the popular imagination of half the world. It has the largest Japanese community outside Japan. It has the largest fleet of privately owned helicopters in the world. It has skyscrapers and minimalism, sushi and high fashion, and an art biennial to be reckoned with. It has a mayor who attracted attention around the world when he made the decision to beautify his city by banning outdoor advertising, leaving the traces of redundant hoardings across the skyline.

Of course it is also true that Brazil has a prison system permanently on the brink of insurrection, street children, police death squads, and a problem with the future of its rain forest. But let us challenge the idea that the Campana brothers are in the business of creating work for the impoverished traditional craft workers of the *favelas*, or like some latter-day William Morris, reinvigorating a craft agenda. They are part of a confident and entirely contemporary culture. Nor are they manipulating any kind of traditional vernacular, as is sometimes claimed, in pursuit of a political agenda. One idea that gained currency after their work was first shown in Europe was that they were offering a political critique. By using what were considered poor materials and industrial waste, it was claimed that they were putting forward a radical point of view. "Handmade products represent the possibility of social redemption in a poor country. Their intention is, however, to find a way for Brazilian design, avoiding European colonisation."

I don't see it this way. It is not folklore or the Third World that interests the Campana brothers. Their work is as knowing and sophisticated a manipulation of the language of contemporary design as anything produced by Damien Hirst or Marc Newson. They design jewelery for H. Stern, a company which may be Brazilian but sells gold bracelets everywhere. They may be interested in the handmade, but they work with mass production to make cheap shoes. It is true that their first appearance was regarded as some kind of exotic eruption from the left field, although that was more to do with myopia elsewhere than anything to do with the specifically Brazilian condition. They are part of a Brazil that, with good reason, sees itself as part of the First World, not the Third.

Design has previously been regarded as an entirely European and North American pursuit, with room made since the 1980s to accommodate the Japanese. In fact Brazil has a long tradition of working at the leading edge of contemporary design even before Le Corbusier got off the liner on his way to lead the team that went on to design the Ministry of Education building. In the 1950s and early 1960s, as well as the obvious work of Oscar Niemeyer, there was the even more exotic work of Lina Bo Bardi. The harder question to answer is to explain the lack of a new generation of architects and designers in Brazil to live up to these precedents.

In an entirely angst-free way, the Campana brothers have developed a working method that makes their work instantly recognizable and yet free of the mark of their own authorship. They appropriate what are usually quite humble workshop or manufacturing techniques, and ready-made artifacts, and put them to work to make highly decorative objects. They can be aimed at mass production or at the art market, and as such they can have different targets. When they choose to upholster an armchair in soft toys, they ask us to consider the uncomfortable territory on the edge of surrealism and kitsch. Then they do the same trick with Disney characters and leave us at risk of drowning in sugar. They work with fragments of timber, assembled with painstaking care and attention to detail, as well as clear extruded plastic. They confront banal plastic chairs manufactured to evoke the texture of cane basket weaving with the handmade real thing. And of course to do it, they place considerable demands on the artisans who are responsible for the craftsmanship—after all, basket weaving is not easy on the hands.

46

In the end these projects are all inviting us to think in a fresh way about the things that we use every day and how they are made. These are big questions, and the Campanas do not flinch from asking them. To make them more palatable, the objects that they create have an unfailing lightness and a benign tone. They may refer to the miseries of life in the *favela*, but they are rendered with the lightest of touches to look nothing but seductive in their aestheticism. And of course, like William Morris, the objects that they have made are aimed at those who are wealthy enough to be able to afford them.

Ministry of Education (MEC) Rio de Janeiro
(Formerly the Ministry of Education and Health (MES))
Designed by Le Corbusier, Lucio Costa, Oscar Niemeyer, and team
1937–42

This is not the work of a dispossessed slum dweller, an outsider at the window of the West looking hungrily in on an opulent feast that they can only dream of joining. Instead it is the quietly confident changing of the subject of design. And the questions that they ask of design are no different from those that face the gallery system as it has emerged in Europe and America, rather than the specifics of the Brazilian condition. The Estudio Campana explores the potential of working with the tradesmen who can weave baskets or the skilled craftsmen who can work with wood to evoke the apparent randomness of a *favela* shack in an exquisitely crafted piece of furniture.

In the end, what the Campana brothers represent is a new version of a long-running dialogue about the nature of design—one that can be traced back to the tension between the views of design represented by William Morris and that of his contemporary, Christopher Dresser. Morris questioned the nature of the industrial system while Dresser worked on creating a vocabulary that embodied it.

What makes the Campanas so significant is the contemporary flavor that they have given this debate and its translation to an entirely new context. As things stand, Brazil is an emerging industrial giant. In its next incarnation it is likely to have a more commanding presence on the world's economic landscape and when that happens, the Campanas' work will reflect not just on the cultural aspects of design and the way in which it can shape a national identity. The next step is for them to help shape a new kind of industrial economy too. Brazil is already past the stage of China. It makes things that have a distinctive personality of their own, rather than copies. In the meantime, the Campanas have been co-opted into the landscape of post-industrial design.

Lina Bo Bardi
Glass House
São Paulo
1950

HOTEL JARAGUÁ

"São Paulo is a city full of chaos and with no fixed architectural standards. The patchwork and layering of the city is a fascinating observation field. São Paulo often presents itself as a hostile place, but what is captivating is to find humanity in its urban dynamics."

"In São Paulo there is a wild juxtaposition of spaces in which No man's lands infiltrate bubbles of richness. It is stimulating to go through highly cosmopolitan areas and end up in an alley that could be from *Blade Runner*."

"In spite of the self-satisfaction of being the wealthiest city in Brazil, São Paulo still has pockets that have stopped in time, where a small community feel prevails. This is the grocery store next to the studio. We love to see the brooms arranged outside!"

"In the hustle and bustle of downtown São Paulo you can see how multicultural this city is. Here you can find all sorts of cheap knick-knacks, in between delis and restaurants that exhale all kinds of scents. The agglomeration of stores, materials, and colors make this area look like a samba school! Around here people walk on the street, not on the pavement."

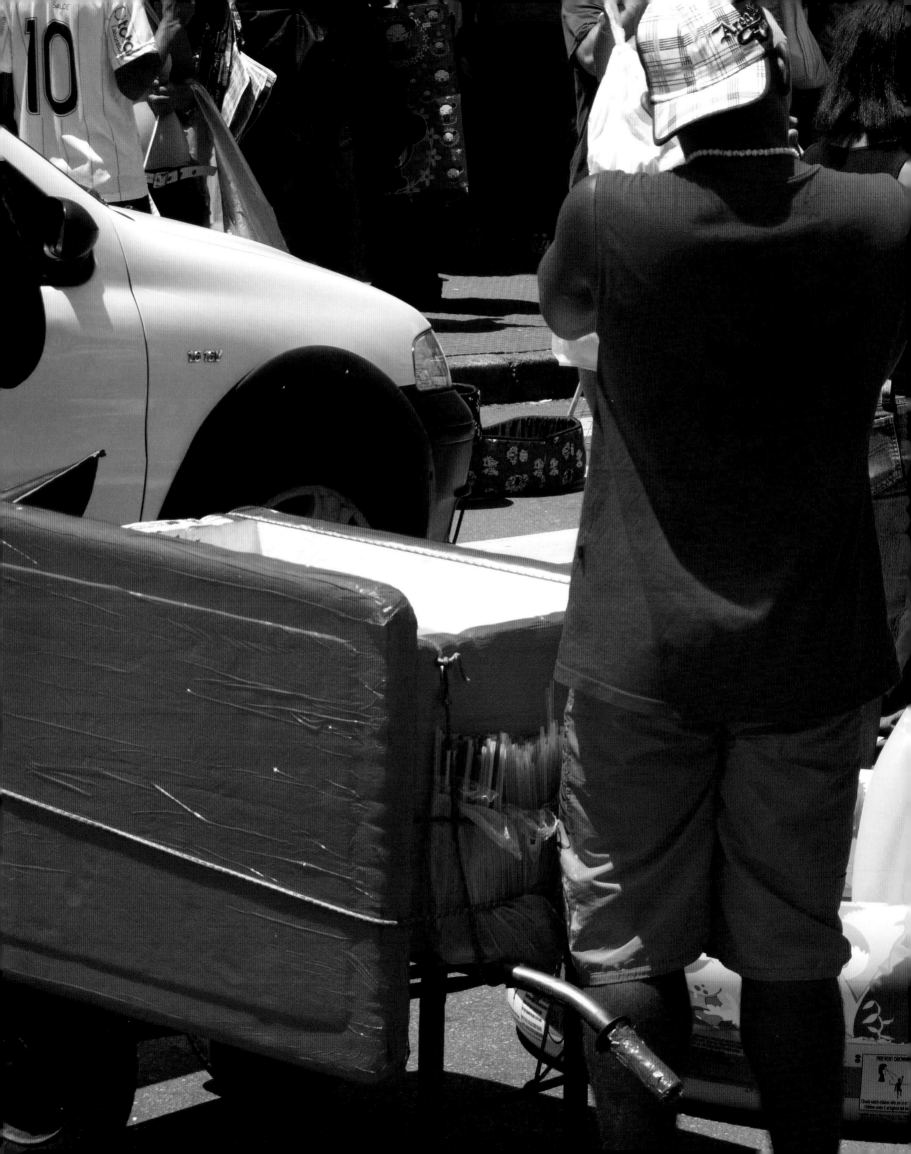

"Carnival is like an open-air opera. It shows 'the richness of the poor,' as Stephan Hamel might say. With very limited means the samba schools create maximum opulence and luxury. The waste of society becomes the 'gold' of poverty."

"When we were children, we liked to rearrange the saints and figures of these roadside shrines. Even though there is a level of profanity in this action, we imagined the saints as warriors protecting us."

"This picture is really inspiring. It moves us to be optimists. It provokes a reaction of catharsis and a desire for change. Most of our recent workshops have been affected by these kinds of ideas. Recuperating gold from trash is our tool to help change the world."

"This is a tree house we built in Brotas."

Humberto: "For me, Brotas is my garden."
Fernando: "Brotas is the place where I don't have to talk about design!"

"This is our studio. It's far from being the glamorous place that people often expect, but that's how we like it—down to earth."

SECTION 2

Darrin Alfred

Early Experiments

Fernando and Humberto Campana have been creating furniture together since the early 1980s. Their early studio period encompassed a variety of "expressive" designs, such as the notable Desconfortáveis collection (also sometimes referred to in English as "the Uncomfortables collection"). Within these early handcrafted experiments the Campana brothers focused on creating an expressive aesthetic in which design was thought of more as sculpture or a work of art. **"We didn't try to be something that we weren't. We even had a sense of not really being designers, but much more like sculptors,"** comments Humberto.[1] To this end, the forms contained within the works took precedence over function and, as such, the creative process was highly intuitive. These initial objects were coarsely textured, a characteristic obtained from the inherent qualities of the materials used—mostly iron—or from the method of construction. It is an emotional body of work that tended to be very gutsy, crude, and rough, for the designers were in some sense rebelling against the modernist resurgence of the mid-1980s whilst simultaneously engaging with the social and cultural climate of Brazil.

During a two-week journey along the Colorado River in 1989, a near fatal boating accident became a significant turning point for Humberto. **"My boat flipped over and I was trapped inside the rear. I thought I was going to die. Surviving was like having a new life. Today, it's something that's very symbolic for me, something that I have lived. The next day I started drawing spirals. Soon after, I came to Brazil and made the Positivo chair. At that time I was making sculptures out of iron, so with pliers and my welding equipment I designed a spiral. It was heavy, made from a very thick blade of iron."** This expressive response by Humberto marked an incipient transition in his work from sculpture to furniture. Fernando replied with the Negativo chair, which repeated the same spiral motif but reinterpreted it. **"Out of the Positivo chair Fernando made another chair, much lighter. Both had the typology of a chair. It was not that they were particularly new chairs—the thing that spoke louder was the material, being rusty, heavy, and not finished, uncoated."**

Fernando and Humberto's Desconfortáveis collection perhaps best illustrates the sheer variety of forms employed during this early expressive period. The collection of around 20 pieces made of unfinished, coarse iron was unveiled during June 1989 in an exhibition at São Paulo's Nucleon 8 Gallery. The resulting sculptural tour de force included a sofa with a back shaped like an armadillo; chairs, such as Newman chair (1989), in which the silhouette of a man's head is carved out of the backplate; or the Yanomami chair (1989), with its indigenous-inspired cutouts made with a blowtorch. One witty work in the series, the Samambaia chair (1989)[2], consisted of a single sheet of curved iron sculpted into a vertebral form. The object calls to mind a similar chaise longue by the Brazilian architect Oscar Niemeyer, but with a sinister edge. The works were one-off pieces fashioned in the Estudio Campana, in which the raw material and basic construction were left exposed. The visible welds clearly illustrate how the objects were made. The Campanas chose iron because of its instability—the material's surface

Costela chair
1989
Iron

Samambaia chair
1989
Iron

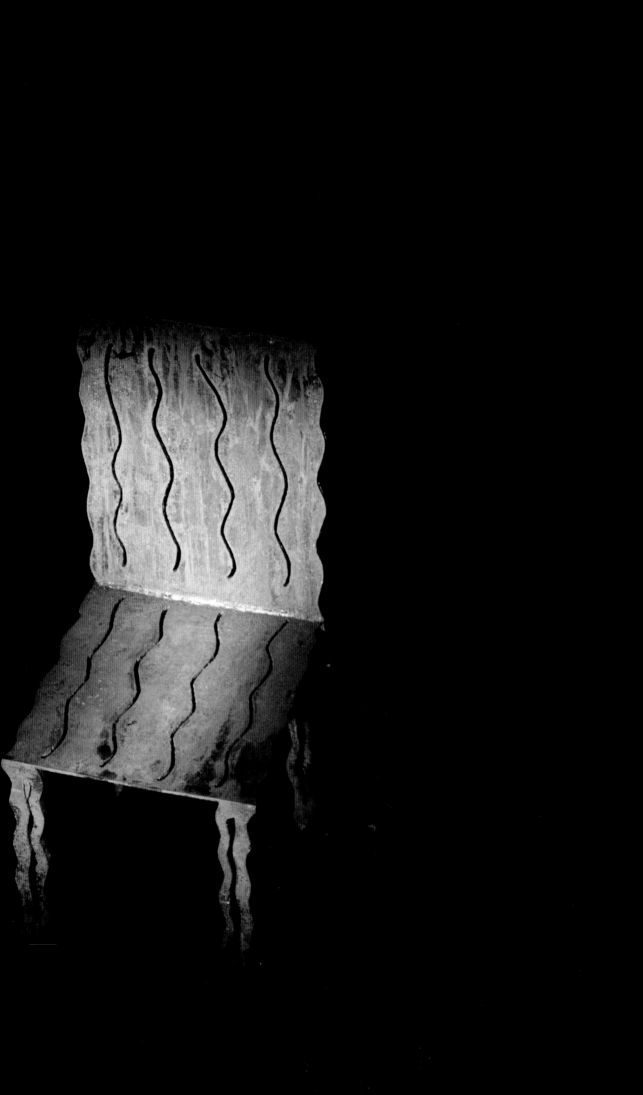

Peixe chair
1989
Iron and copper

Yanomami chair
1989
Iron

Flintstones chair
1989
Iron

Trono chair
1989
Iron and copper

Jean Genet chair, 1989, iron and copper

Hate 1 chair, 1989, iron   **Hate 2 chair**, 1989, iron

changes over time, taking on a painterly appearance. In this case, the lack of finish became the finish itself. The quasi-primitive forms lent themselves to a scale and irregularity that was consciously non-modernist. Fernando and Humberto attempted to salvage the symbolic quality of design that they felt had been obscured by modernism's reductiveness and obsession with functionalism. Humberto asserts: **"This collection developed out of the Positivo chair, but within it there was also a kind of unconscious focus on the roots of Brazil and the question as to what Brazil is today. Since the 1980s there has been a period here in Brazil during which people have been very influenced by Italian and Scandinavian design. We refused to go in that direction. We were adamant that we didn't want to work with wood, noble wood, from the Amazon, so we chose iron with which to make a collection of forms, typologies. That was the seed for our future projects."**

As the collection progressed, Fernando and Humberto found support in the work of Danny Lane who, along with Ron Arad and Tom Dixon, was a key figure of the avant-garde furniture movement that shook up the United Kingdom in the 1980s. As Fernando recalls, **"We saw a lecture by Danny Lane, the British designer,**

talking about his furniture at Nucleon 8. It took the form of piled glass, which was also heavy. It was our language. We had found someone who could give affirmation to our early works. So we said, 'Let's try to present our work to this gallery— maybe they will want to make a show with us.' And they loved it." Lane's provocative designs brought broken glass to the highly polished design world of the 1980s. His bold and innovative designs, such as the Etruscan chair (1986) and Stacking chair (1986), dramatically opened up the parameters of how designers might look at furniture conceptually. Lane demonstrated to the Campanas that it was possible to do something without having to consider whether it was ergonomic or if it would be a commercial success.

"At the time, we weren't embarrassed about saying that our work is uncomfortable," explains Fernando, **"We wanted to provoke people into thinking about the issues and about the materials that Brazil has. Copying is too comfortable; we were looking for another kind of design inside our community. There were many things in our minds that we wanted to push with this collection."** The collection was composed of objects of great expressive force, eliciting strong

Flama chair, 1989, iron

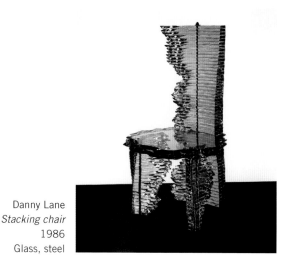

Danny Lane
Stacking chair
1986
Glass, steel

Danny Lane
Etruscan chair
1986
Glass, stainless steel

emotional responses, and often apprehension, in their ostensible coldness. The Desconfortáveis series was aggressive and strange-looking. Indeed, these early designs were often quite uncomfortable in a very literal sense.

A year later, in 1990, the Campanas had another exhibition at Nucleon 8 Gallery, this time presenting the Orgânicos collection, which was conceived by Fernando and Humberto as a series of hybrid objects that combined both industry and craft along with a flair for the unexpected. **"Our work is a kind of hybrid, between two molecular fields: the natural and the synthetic; the warm, the cold,"** explains Humberto. Characterized by a remarkable sense of vitality and imagination, the works this time were geared more specifically toward the design market. He continues: **"We didn't want to stay in the same easy form, welding iron, so we set about looking for new materials."** The Campanas began to blend these organic and synthetic materials in unusual ways. The base of the Costela fruit bowl (1990)[3], for example, was fashioned from the jabuticabeira, a small fruit tree native to Brazil. Cast aluminum ribs were inserted into the sides of the woody limb to create a cradle for the fruit. The brothers saw the flaws that were a result of the casting process as valuable, ultimately adding character to the pieces. In fact, they even provoked some imperfections. The skeletal shape of the bowl was influenced by the Campanas' interest in fossils and dinosaur skeletons. The strangely anthropomorphic object with its man-made prostheses looked as if it had escaped from a surrealistic jungle. For another piece, when the

brothers noticed some graffiti in a São Paulo square that depicted a ball encased by wire, they decided to create a three dimensional version. The result was the Casulo cabinet (1989)[4], an iron mesh cabinet with three aluminum shelves. The cabinet's door handle was made from the limb of a tree. With their ingenious use of contrasting elements, the works that make up the Orgânicos collection are balanced delicately between art and craft, oscillating between the real and the imagined.

[1]
Unless otherwise stated, all quotes are from interviews conducted by the author in São Paulo, August 2008.

[2]
Samambaia translates as "Fern."

[3]
Costela translates as "Rib."

[4]
Casulo translates as "Cocoon."

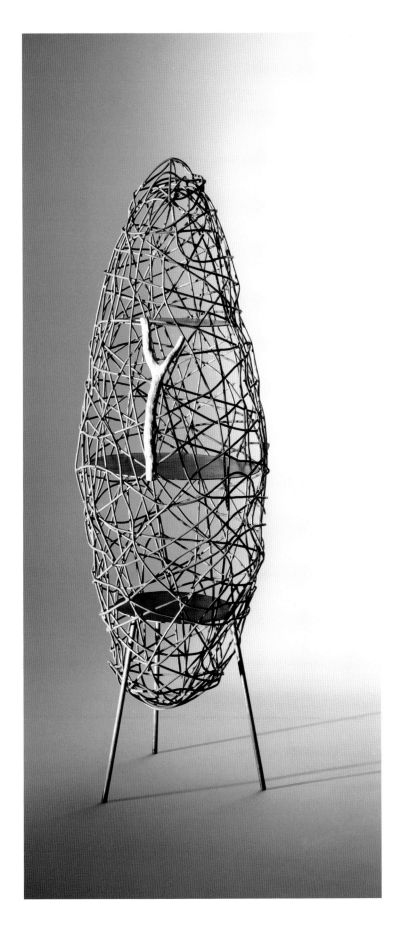
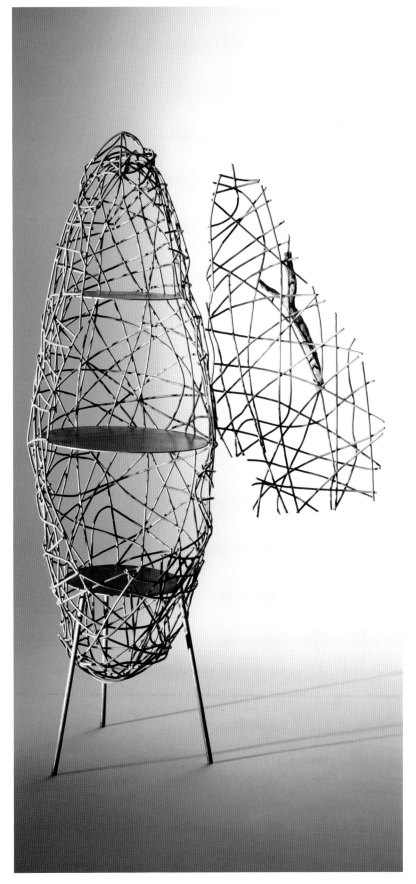

Casulo cabinet
1989
Iron and jabuticabeira branch

Costela fruit bowl, 1990, die-cast aluminum and jabuticabeira branch

Favela chair
1991
Wood

Darrin Alfred

Accumulation

View of a *favela*, São Paulo

In Brazil, the Portuguese word *gambiarra*[1] is applied to the cheap and inventive approach to problem-solving that is ubiquitous throughout São Paulo. The results are so crude and apparent they often demonstrate, rather than conceal, the problems at hand. Many of Fernando and Humberto Campana's designs represent, on many levels, the quick-fix practices developed out of necessity by the inhabitants of one of the most populous cities in the world. Lashing things together and crudely joining components are very simple methods of making furniture. In the case of the Campana brothers, cardboard, bamboo, rattan, scraps of wood, and a variety of other materials are gathered together, creating an aesthetic of improvisation and imperfection. Spontaneous and relatively immediate, objects such as the Favela chair heralded a new concept in the Campanas' work: accumulation.

In 1991 the Campanas applied their fascination with the haphazard and erratic architectural expansion of São Paulo to assemble the Favela chair. The original armchair was constructed solely of small wood slats gathered from discarded fruit crates, glued and nailed together by hand. The result was an intuitively assembled chair, carefully built up piece by piece using hundreds of similar components. The most ingenious aspect of the design was the way it visually captured the *favela*'s chaotic architectural coalescence. As Fernando explains, **"The Favela chair was made with slats of wood from supermarket fruit boxes, but the idea came from observing the *favelas*. The people who live in *favelas* construct their own homes, so I thought to myself, 'Why not construct a chair myself?' We** started gathering and buying discount wood, just as the materials for *favela* houses are assembled. People in the *favelas* fill up the space around them with wood and plastic without any obvious rational thinking—their building method is very intuitive. I tried to emulate their behavior in order to make the chair." Perhaps more than any other object, the Favela chair expresses a core impulse in the Campanas' oeuvre to grapple with social history and wrestle it into the present on their own terms. Humberto explains, **"It's a kind of portrait of our environment, of our society. There really is a huge gap between rich and poor, and this is reflected in the country's architecture and design in interesting ways. The mix of races is also fascinating. Globalization started here five hundred years ago with the Indians and Africans, the Europeans, then the Koreans, Bolivians, and others too. Brazil is a large melting pot of races."**

In 1993 the Campanas' Papelão, or Cardboard, collection began as a series of one-off lamps, a side table, a cabinet,

Papelão lamp, 1993, corrugated cardboard and aluminum

Papel collection
2001
Stainless steel structure and corrugated cardboard

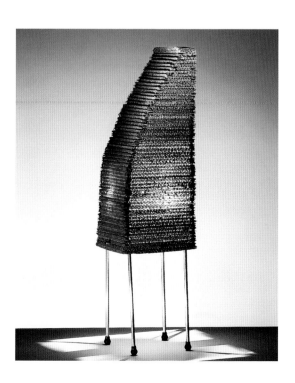

Papelão lamp, 1993, corrugated cardboard and aluminum   **Papelão table**, 1993, corrugated cardboard and aluminum   **Papelão cabinet**, 1993, corrugated cardboard and aluminum

Papelão screen
1995
Corrugated cardboard and iron
(Produced by Edra as Papel screen in 2001)

and a sofa. To create the objects, Fernando and Humberto combined corrugated cardboard, an extremely durable, versatile, and lightweight material frequently employed for industrial uses, with cast aluminum. The brothers, who favor the simplicity of the paper product, were fascinated by the diffusion of light through the cardboard's corrugations. Exploring the material's translucency, they began stacking it sheet upon sheet. The undulating lines and slight ripples of the intentionally misaligned layers came together as an assortment of oddly whimsical objects. The resulting shapes are not typically associated with furniture and each work, due to its craftsmanship by hand, was unique. The Campanas were inspired by the heaps of discarded cardboard collected by the poor of São Paulo for recycling. Folded into striking patterns, the material is pulled through the city streets on handcarts. Fernando describes how **"In the afternoon you can see many people collecting boxes in order to clean the city and make a little money. They pick up all the discarded cardboard from stores and from bars, gather everything and take it to recycling companies."** A recurrent theme in the Campanas' work is to treat such cheap everyday materials with reverence typically reserved for the expensive and scarce. He continues, **"And the great challenge is to transform those materials, to give them nobility, a second skin. The hope is to bring an elegance to those materials."** The Campanas were not the first, nor the last, to experiment with cardboard when applied to furniture design. After discovering that single sheets gained exponential strength when layered, architect Frank Gehry manipulated the simple material into graceful, curvilinear chairs and tables to create his celebrated Easy Edges and Experimental Edges furniture (1969–73 and 1979–82).

Cart for collecting paper and cardboard, São Paulo

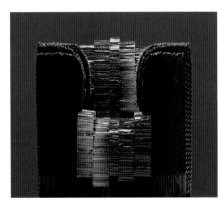

Frank Gehry
Grandpa Beaver armchair
1986
Corrugated cardboard

Frank Gehry
Wiggle Side Chair Design
1972/2005
Corrugated cardboard, edges made of hardboard, natural or lacquered

Papelão chair, 1995, corrugated cardboard and iron (Produced by Edra as **Papel chair** in 2001)

Papelão table
1993
Corrugated cardboard, aluminum, and aluminum wires

Papel sofa, 2001, corrugated cardboard and iron

Cactus lamp
2004
Bamboo, iron,
and lamp

The Campanas' Papel collection[2], put into production by the Italian furniture maker Edra in 2001, continued their exploration of cardboard. The muted, straight-lined furniture comprising seating, coffee tables, and screens with iron frames, fused multiple layers of the corrugated material and added metal mesh to give strength to the pieces. With cleanly finished edges and a more polished look, the objects took advantage of the internal ridges and troughs of the cardboard to create a fluted pattern and retained some of the imprecision of the Papelão collection. The shapes were more universal and practical, as in Cardboard side chair and screen, and reached out to a broader audience.

Fernando and Humberto's inspirations are not always drawn from the chaos and disorder of the streets of São Paulo. The Campanas have expressed the concept of

accumulation with materials not typically associated with the city, as demonstrated by the Mixed series. The undulating form of the Pilha screen (1994)[3] was constructed of bundles of wicker rods held together by bands of iron. It's an apt example of the Campanas' interest in manipulating basic materials in unconventional ways to produce objects that are functional yet also visually striking. The back of the Taquaral chair (2000)[4] was made of a cluster of freestanding upright stems that flexed independently when they were leant on. The bamboo was neatly cropped at shoulder height. Humberto comments, **"Bamboo also comes from our childhood—there were plantations of bamboos where we grew up. Many people would dry the bamboo in front of their houses. Our ideas for how to use the material stem from seeing all those piles of bamboo. Also, it's a material you can bend, it's not heavy, so we**

Cerca screen, 1994, stainless steel and wicker rods

Taquaral chair
2000
Bamboo and iron with electrostatic painting

Pilha screen
1994
Wicker rods, iron, and metal
wheels

Bamboo chair
2000
Curved bamboo and acrylic

Leatherworks chair, 2007, metal and leather

were keen to explore applications of the lightness of the material." Whereas bamboo was once the poor man's wood in Brazil, this renewable grass resource is now recognized as a vital component of sustainable development within the country.

Made from panels of compressed wood and colored paper, the Célia chair (2004) for Habitart was named after Fernando and Humberto's mother. It is one of the first chairs that the brothers developed to be manufactured for the Brazilian mass market. **"The Célia collection came by invitation from Masisa, a multinational company,"** explains Humberto. **"The director of the company invited us to create a new pattern of OSB."** OSB, or Oriented Strand Board (known as Sterling board in the United Kingdom), is an engineered wood product formed by layering strands of wood that are bonded under heat and pressure. It usually has a rough surface with the individual strips lying unevenly across each other. Fernando describes the genesis of the collection: **"We went to the south of Brazil, where the factory is located, and brought lots of materials along with us—teddy bears, dolls, and pieces of bamboo. We saw that the manufacturer produced melaminic**

paper, with Formica to cover the tables. In the backyard of the factory there was a plant full of melaminic paper. We asked if it was possible to throw the paper in during the process of making the OSB. The Célia collection was born from this investigation. Whenever someone invites us to go to a factory, we love to see the garbage! Also we like to see if the materials that they have in large quantities can be tried out in different ways."

Drawing upon materials and methods indigenous to Brazil, the Campanas have blurred the boundaries between art and design—often treating functional objects more as metaphors much like the surrealists of the early 1930s. The Leatherworks (2007) collection of chairs for Edra stemmed from Fernando and Humberto's investigation into the intricacies of leather and hide preparation. The brothers first came across the material during a conference in the south of Brazil, where a long-standing tradition of working with leather exists. Humberto recollects, **"We went to the factory that makes the leather and they gave us a gift of many pieces of leather. It was material that stayed in our studio for ten years without us making any use of it. For a long time we**

Leatherworks small armchair, 2007, metal and leather

Furworks armchair, 2007, metal, leather, and synthetic fur

Celia dinner table
2004
OSB wood

Celia chair
2004
OSB wood

OSB experiment
2002
OSB wood

stared at the leather wondering what to do with it. Finally, we started to make a kind of puzzle."

The Campana brothers experimented with the fragments in the studio to understand the material's possibilities as well as its limitations. Once those characteristics were understood, they eventually transformed the fragments into something concrete, by making a fabric and experimenting with applying it to a chair with their own hands, creating two prototypes. Humberto grew fond of the material. **"You can bend it easily, pile it up or create a rigid structure out of it. We had the idea of 'growing' the leather over the chair, little by little, piece by piece, like a parasite, an organism growing over its host."** The results were seemingly random ensembles created out of the scraps of leather. The chairs were loosely clad in an irregularly overlapping patchwork of bits of stamped leather in multiple browns, white, or black. The clever method of accumulation that worked so well in the brothers' earlier body of work went one step further to both shock and amuse. The peeling upholstery resembles animals in the process of shedding their skins. Imperfect and ragged, the manufactured objects conceal the outstanding craftsmanship involved in their assembly, stitching, and trimming. The industrialized system developed by Edra masterfully retains the essentially random composition of the studio's prototypes.

Fernando and Humberto's Nazareth centerpiece (2008) for Bernardaud displays the Brazilian characteristics of spontaneity and creative improvisation, combined with the Campanas' command of transformation. In part an homage to Brazilian artist Nazareth Pacheco and her body-related objects, the project was built out of an assortment of dismembered and fragmented plastic doll arms. **"We have started to shape things from these loose members, heating and deforming them. When Bernardaud showed interest in doing a collaboration, the first thing that came to our mind was these doll arms and how to transform them into something different, until they were no longer parts of a doll, but something else."**[5] The results are gut-wrenching. The body was a common thread within surrealism that was explored in a variety of approaches—from eroticization and desecration, to dismemberment. The prototype of merged plastic parts was then translated into cast Limoges porcelain executed by Bernardaud craftsmen and glazed by hand.

In 2009, the Campanas designed an exclusive range of polo shirts for Lacoste featuring a variety of erratic yet coordinated accumulations of the French apparel company's iconic green crocodile logo. An edition of 20,000 pieces, the Holiday Collector's Series embodies many of the same qualities as the designers' Alligator chair (2002), such as luxury, curiosity, and humor.

Celia buffet
2004
OSB wood

These characteristics are replicated for Lacoste by embroidering a cluster of eight crocodile logos onto classic men's and women's white polo shirts. The mass of reptiles is a representation of how the reptiles accumulate in the mud beds of their natural environs during the dry season.

Crafted from various sizes of the same logo, the Campanas + Lacoste series consisted of a limited edition of 125 pieces for men inspired by the Anavilhanas—an immense archipelago encompassing over four hundred islands in the Brazilian Amazon. The liana, long-stemmed woody vines that grow in the tropical rain forests of Brazil, served as the inspiration for the 125 pieces designed for women. In the latter, the crocodiles appear as if they are forging a random path, like roaming ants along the forest floor.

A super limited made-to-order edition of up to 12 men's and 12 women's polo shirts is handcrafted completely from the logos. At first glance, it looks as though a swarm of miniature crocodiles has descended upon a polo shirt with tremendous force, devouring every piece of fabric and leaving nothing behind that may have previously existed. It's alluring and chaotic. A see-through lace when worn directly, the handcrafted shirts evoke the traditional lacework of Northern Brazil. The entire Campanas + Lacoste series is produced in cooperation with COOPA-ROCA, a socially responsible cooperative that provides work for the craftswomen and seamstresses who live in the Rocinha *favela* of Rio de Janeiro.

1
In Brazil, the dominant meaning would be "improvisation."

2
Papel translates as "paper"; *Papelão* as "cardboard."

3
Pilha translates as "Stack."

4
Taquaral is a municipality in São Paulo.

5
Fernando and Humberto Campana, Nazareth brochure, Bernardaud, France, 2008.

Wood floor lamp
2008
Wood and iron

Favela bookshelf
2008
Wood

Nazareth centerpiece
2008
Porcelain

Campanas + Lacoste
Lacoste polo super limited edition (male)
2008
Fabric / Lacoste logos

Darrin Alfred

Suspended Lines

A thread of investigation that has woven its way throughout the Campana brothers' career has been a preoccupation with opposing or defying gravity. Growing up, Fernando was captivated by the Apollo space missions. The body in space is both a primal yearning—many of us dream about floating and flying—and a contemporary reality. The brothers bring that desire to a facet of their work. Like many of their designs, works such as the Corallo armchair or the Escultura screen express a polarity between the dream and the actuality, between fantasy and gravity. The objects embody a penchant for expressing an effortlessness and weightlessness. More recently, Fernando and Humberto have fantasized about taking this string of experimentation even further.

After giving up law very early in his career, Humberto began taking sculpture courses in clay and metal. The Bob chair (1990) was conceived during his metalworking course taken at São Paulo's Fundação Armando Álvares Penteado. Humberto's objective was to create a chair that would convey a feeling of suspension. **"We were working with lines in space, floating. We were searching for something very immaterial, trying to get an immaterial materiality."** Not unlike the Campanas' early experiments, neither the technology nor the material of the chair was particularly advanced, but the depth of imagination displayed in the concept was undeniable. The Bob chair was formed by an accumulation of bent then welded linear iron rods. Its shape suggests an internal explosion frozen in time, with fragments spinning out in all directions from the center. The chair appears to have materialized entirely on its

109

Bob chair
1990
Iron

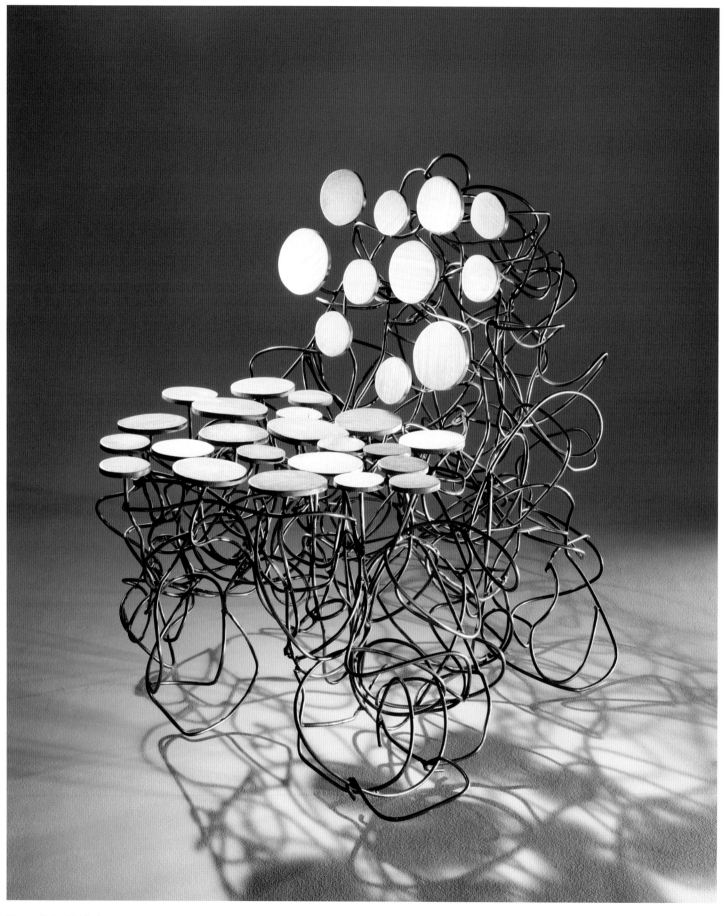

Discos chair, 1992, iron and wood

own and maintains a sense of fluctuation. Despite being made of iron, it expresses a movement toward weight-lessness and transparency that had scarcely been seen in the Campanas' body of work up to that time.

Two years later, Fernando and Humberto drew upon the same reference for their Discos chair (1992)[1]. It suspended the sitter on an unruly tangle of metal supporting wooden disks of varying diameters that formed both the chair's seat and back. Experimenting with a variety of techniques to achieve this effect, the Campanas would later refine the idea in the Vermelha chair (1993)[2]. **"When we have an idea, we go straight ahead to the prototype. What is important is that we materialize the idea. We live with that proto-type for a while, and this enables us to see other alternatives. The prototypes also provide inspiration for other products, as was the case with the Bob chair."**

A spontaneous 1989 drawing by Humberto for an iron sculpture was transformed fourteen years later into the Corallo chair (2004)[3]. The wiry seat was formed by irregularly woven hand-bent steel wire and finished with coral pink epoxy paint, and resembled the sprawling coral reefs found off the coast of Brazil. The Campanas, encouraged by Massimo Morozzi, the artistic director of Italian furniture manufacturer Edra, had developed a series of full-scale models, transposing the two-dimensional sketch into a three-dimensional structure. **"I started the concept for the Corallo but it was too heavy. When Fernando saw it he took off all the heavy elements and made it lighter. Our creations are half and half in terms of the collaboration between us. I'm much more involved with the phys-ical part, working with my hands, because that's the way I learned. Fernando comes along once I've got the initial prototype and starts to work with it."**[4] Unlike the Bob chair, there appears to be no friction

111

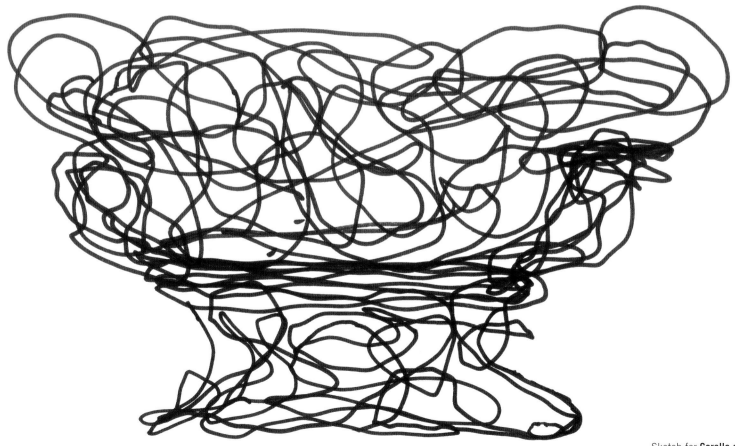

Sketch for **Corallo chair**
1989
Ink on paper

Corallo chair
2004
Steel wire with epoxy paint finish

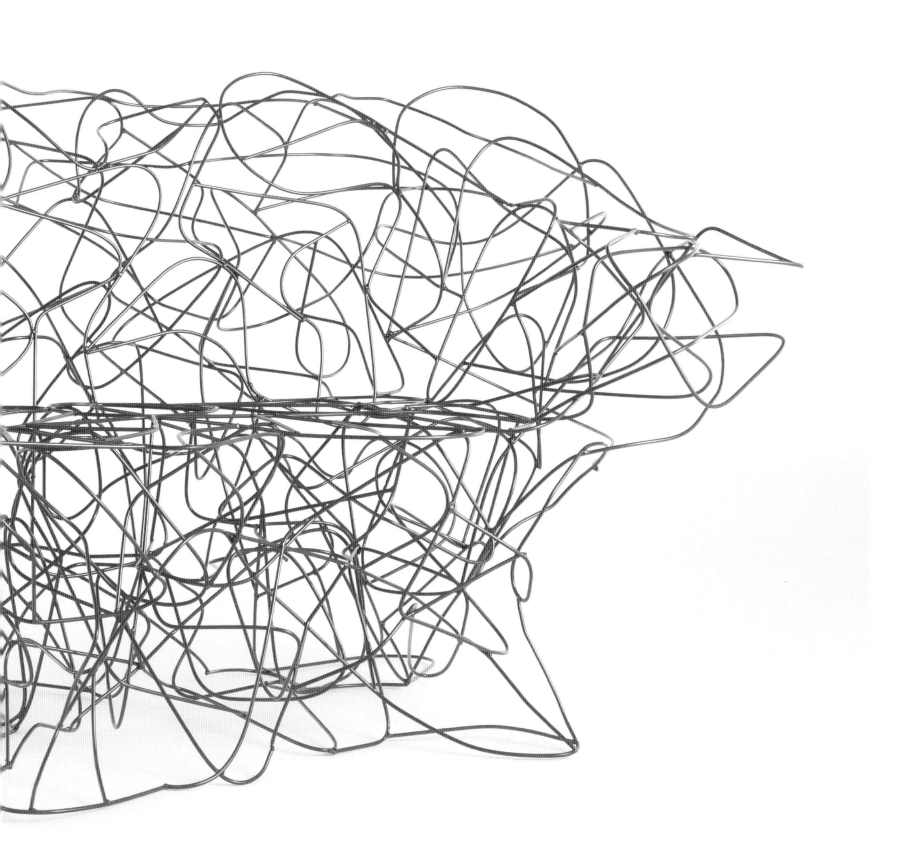

between the Corallo and the area around it—the chair and the space it encircles are equal, sitting side by side in such a way that they are intertwined. Morozzi had previously commissioned a number of designs from the Campanas before recognizing in 2003 that the coral drawing could be made into an armchair. The handcrafted chair, mass-produced since 2004, remains distinctive from one to the next, as the integrity of the original prototype demanded. The Corallo, often described by the Campanas as a three-dimensional scribble, dynamically captures the fluidity of the steel wire. Photographs of the armchair are often mistaken for a drawing. Its curves are sensuous and in this way the chair embodies the antithesis of the hard right angles that typified the minimalist furniture of the time. Coupled with its brightly colored painted surface, the chair was more fun and less severe than previous examples of the Campanas' furniture.

In contrast to the entangled Corallo, the elliptical body of the one-off Novelo sofa (2003) incorporates a continuous structural shell to support the load. A slight indentation provides the seat. The Novelo sofa translates the Casulo cabinet's irregular, coarse metal mesh into sensuous and self-supporting lacquered steel wire. Fernando and Humberto's Iron series (2004) pushed the experimentation with stainless steel wire further. Formed by hand in unusual shapes, the series had a familial likeness to its earlier counterparts by creating the effect of frozen lines floating in air. However, these more recent works, such as Blue Iron chair, Black Iron chair, and the Pedra bench[5] were a development away from the explosive linear or jumbled forms toward more serene, geological structures. While still expressing a feeling of suspension, these more recent works appear grounded. It's as if the objects' molecules are slowly moving together to form solid matter.

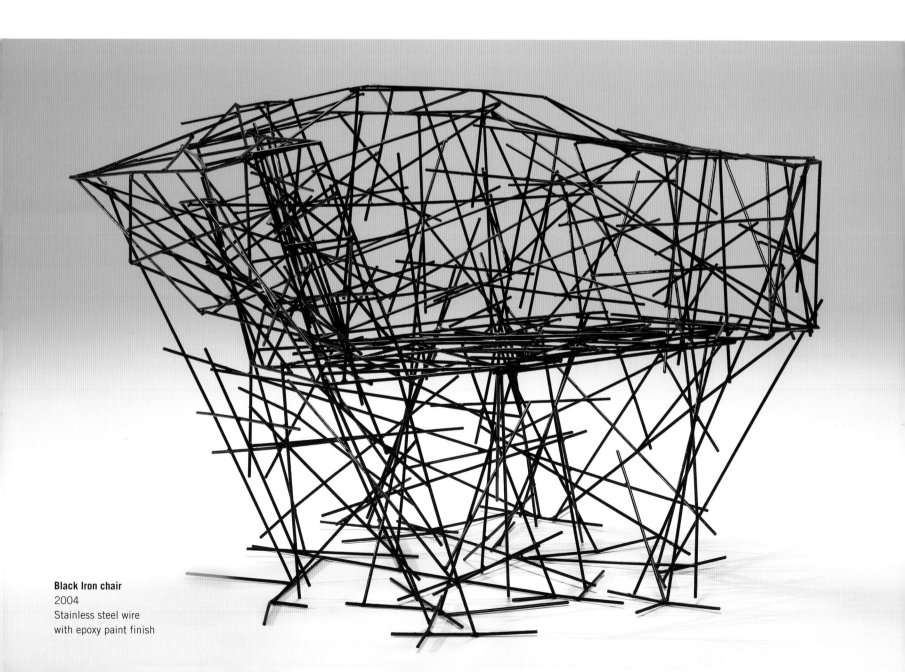

Black Iron chair
2004
Stainless steel wire
with epoxy paint finish

Blue Iron chair, 2004, stainless steel wire with epoxy paint finish

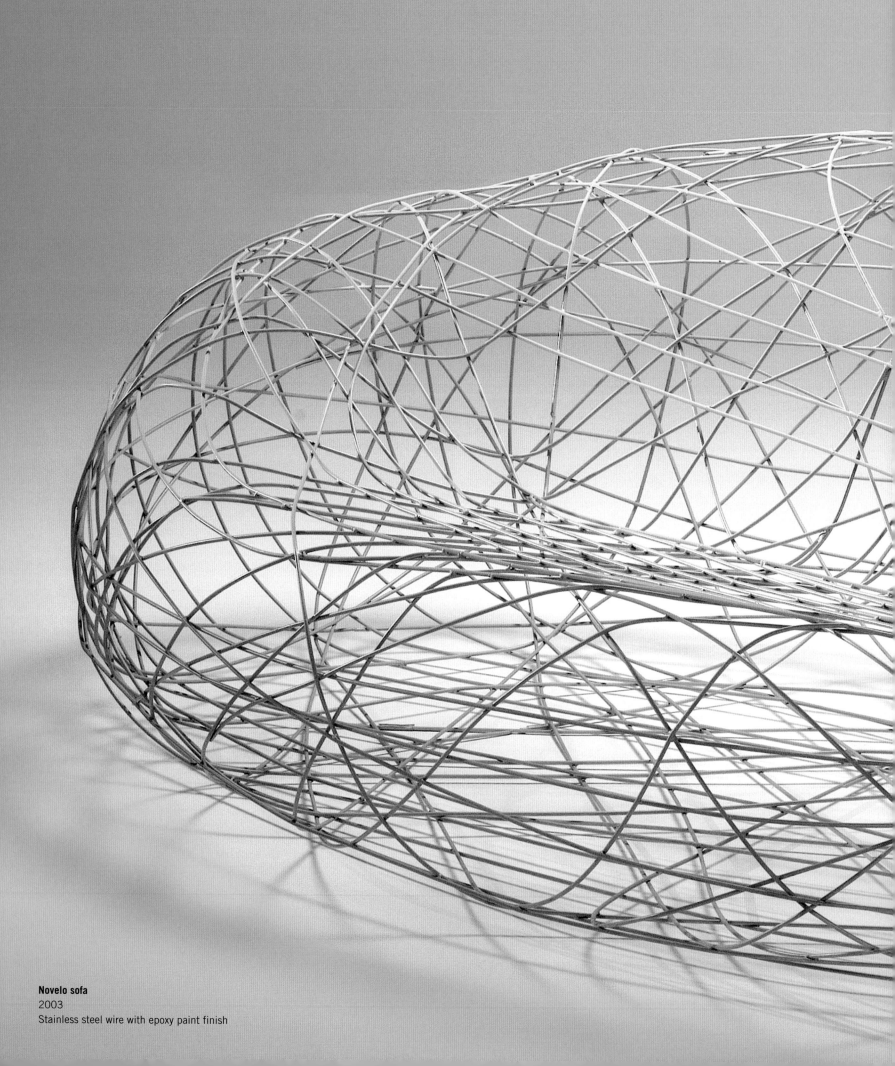

Novelo sofa
2003
Stainless steel wire with epoxy paint finish

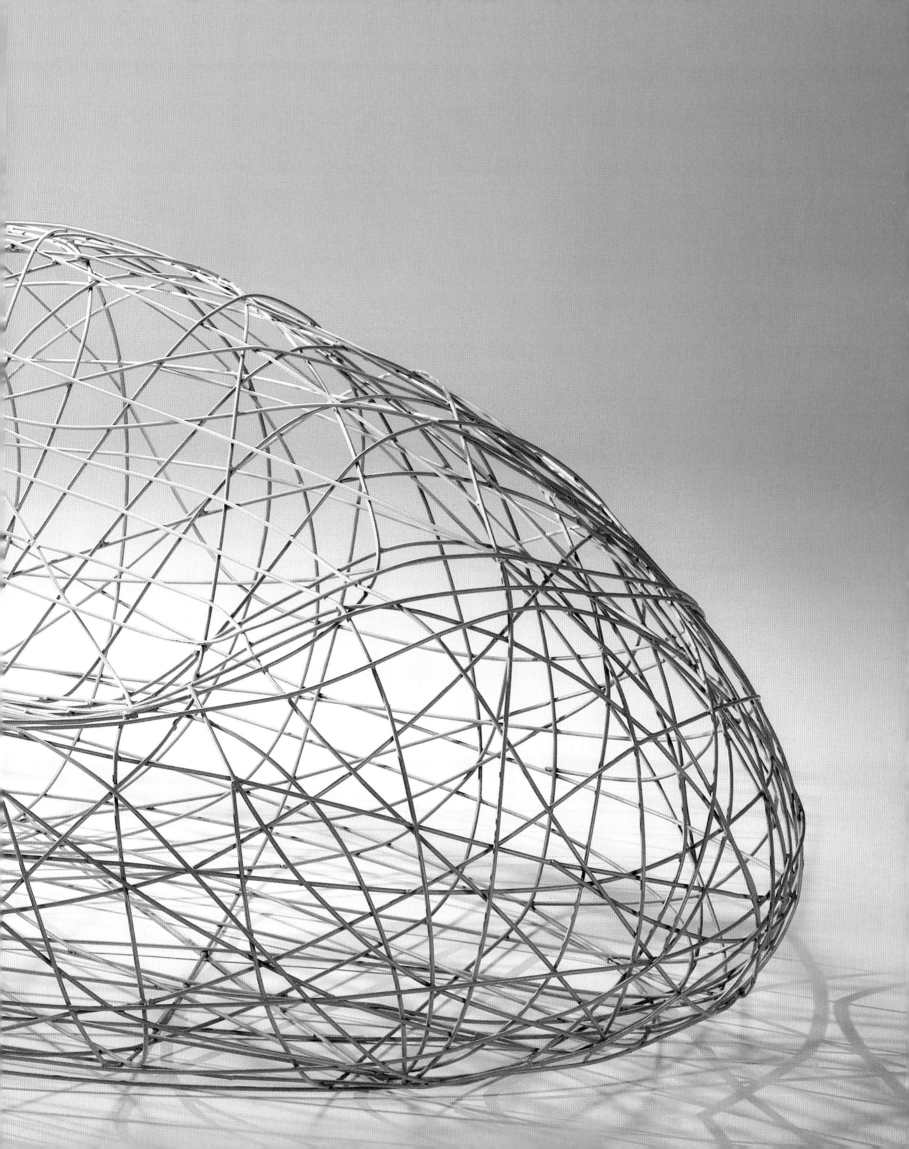

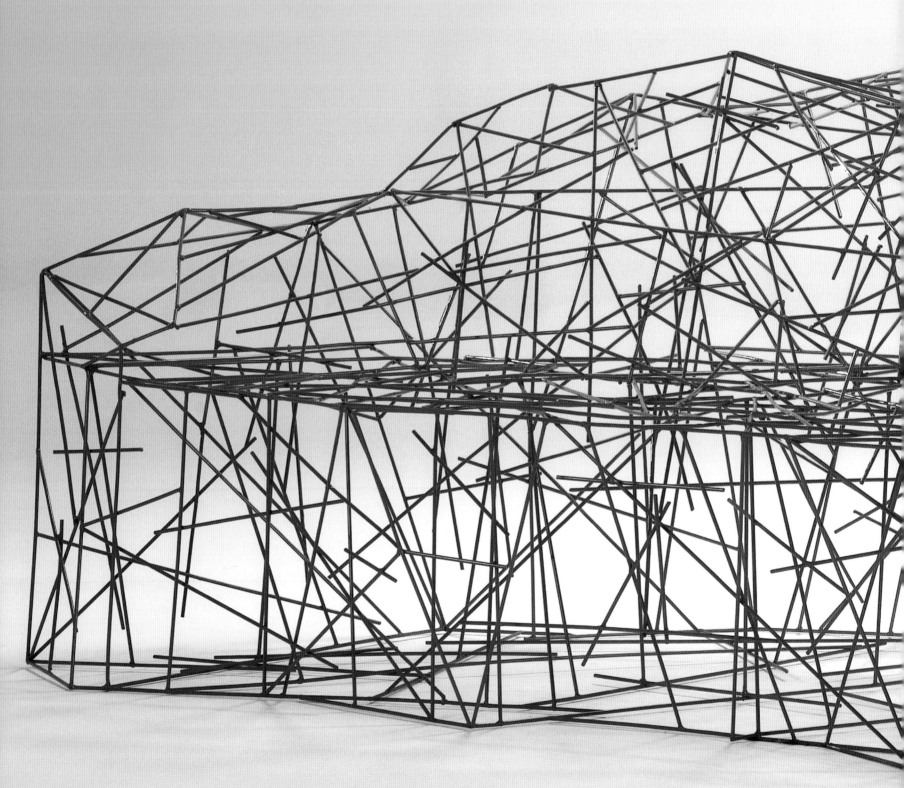

Pedra bench
2003
Stainless steel wire with epoxy paint finish

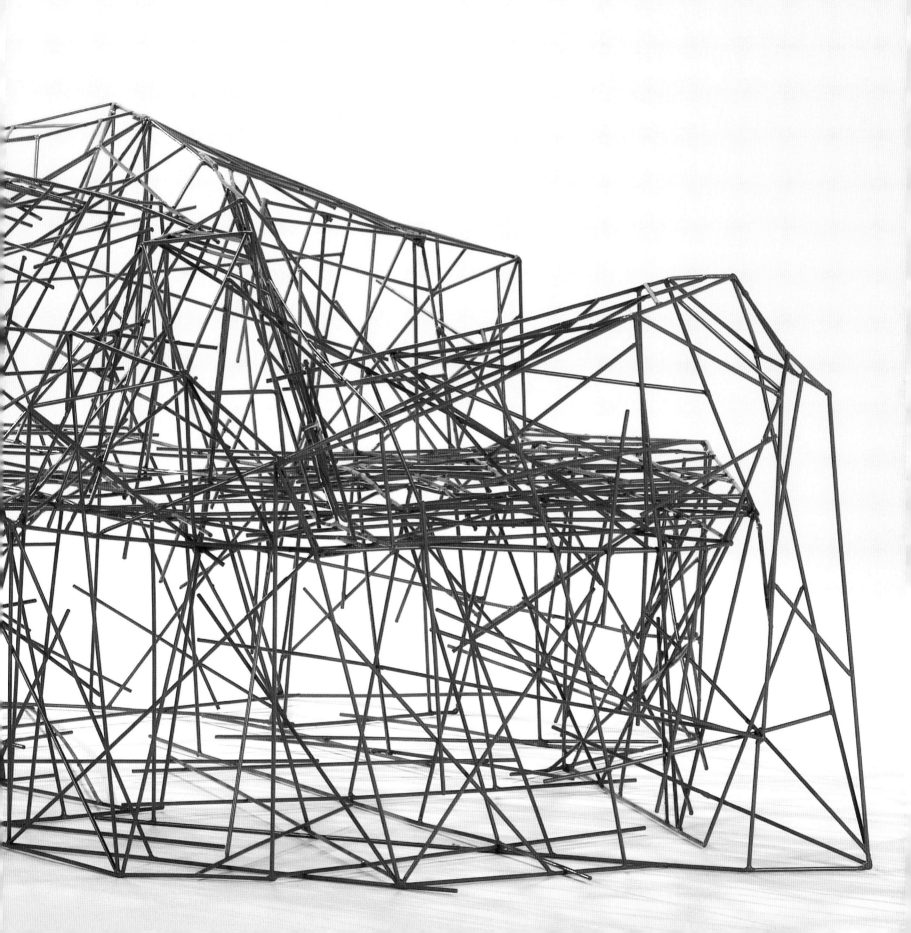

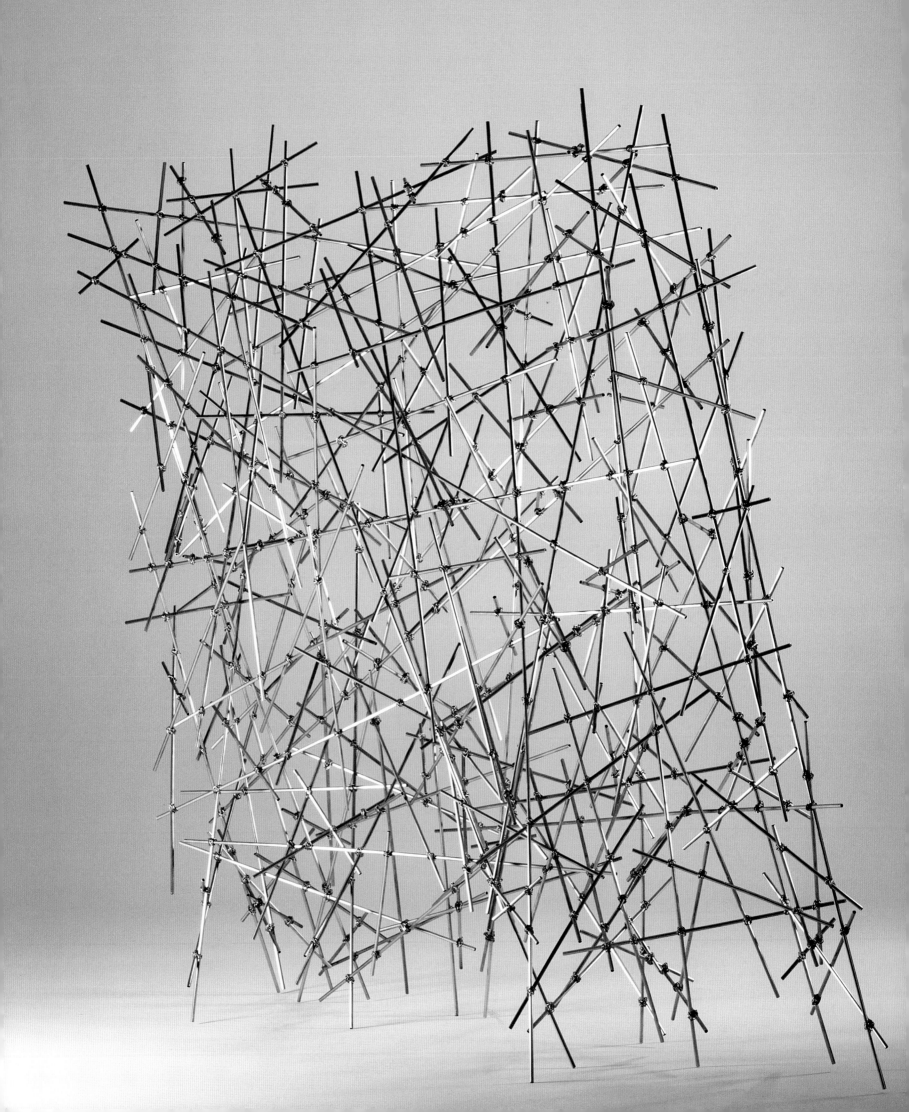

The Campana brothers' Escultura screen (1993) fuses an exquisite blend of artisan techniques and industrialized materials by treating television antennae like poles of bamboo. The recycled linear aluminum rods are secured to one another with aluminum wire filament, forming an organic and intricate scaffold that reflects the light while casting unique shadows. Made from antennae and manufactured in a small series by Estudio Campana, the screen illustrates Fernando and Humberto's interest in using appropriated objects and materials in a handcrafted manner. The work also mimics the antenna-covered rooftops of São Paulo in the 1990s. Humberto remarks, **"Until recently, in the suburbs of São Paulo, everyone had TV antennae in their living rooms and on their roofs. Now they are all supplied by cable. We made the antenna screen in the '90s when São Paulo was covered by such antennae."** The object is just one way that the Campanas recognize São Paulo's evolving identity and reflect the social fabric around them:

context again becomes content. As Fernando comments, **"We try to reinvent existing materials and make a portrait of what we see in our environment."**

Exploring their interest in fusing industrial process with the traditional techniques of Brazilian craftsmanship, Fernando and Humberto collaborated with Alessi to produce the Blow up (begun 2004) and Nuvem[6] (begun 2006) collections of housewares. The Blow up family of objects, inspired by the Escultura screen, was constructed by assembling offcuts of aluminum, randomly fused together to form various types of three-dimensional containers. **"Alessi asked us to visit their factory to see if we wanted to present them with something new, or from existing work,"** says Fernando. **"We saw some leftover metal lying around and we thought about creating sculptures made from antennae. They took the idea and loved it, so the Blow up collection was born."**[7] The Campanas'

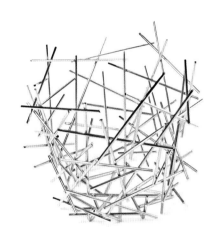

Blow up citrus basket
2004
Stainless steel

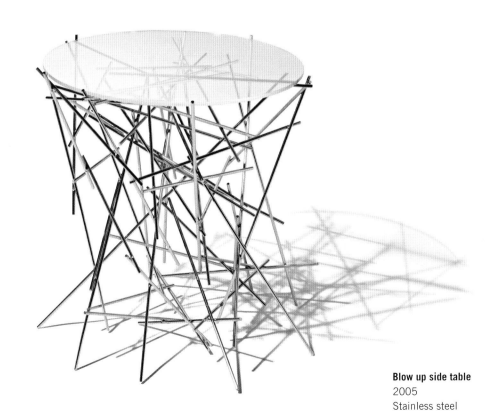

Blow up side table
2005
Stainless steel

Escultura screen
1993
Anodized aluminum

response was a fruit bowl made by spontaneously arranging the varying lengths of steel to form a light and airy object—a chaotic snapshot of metal fragments emanating from a central explosion. The original prototypes, created in the Estudio Campana and constructed out of bamboo, were just as successful. **"Because we didn't have a welder at that time and it was difficult to find one, we started cutting bamboo and gluing it ourselves, attaching one piece to another to make the prototype in real scale,"** explains Humberto. **"Then we sent those prototypes to Alessi and they constructed the Blow up collection."**

In 2007 the Campanas' Nuvem line of home accessories was a sinuous response to their successful Blow up series of products and followed on from their much earlier Ninho collection of 1991. Nuvem, or "cloud" in Portuguese, alludes to the irregularly woven aluminum wire skin that was tangled, flattened, then molded and spun to achieve a range of products such as citrus baskets and flower vases. Nuvem resulted from an investigation into the movement of people's hands, creating meaningful objects that capture the freedom of human gestures. *Weave*, *redesign*, and *disarrange* are all words that belong to the lexicon of this collection. The design puts together and takes apart these gestures in a poetic way, as if the lines are floating in air. Developing a manufacturing method proved difficult for Alessi, though they were eventually able to ensure a production method that would retain the purely artisanal, handcrafted, and arbitrary aspects of the Campanas' concept while keeping production costs viable.

122

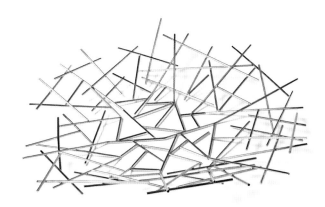

Blow up centerpiece
2004
Stainless steel

Discos translates as "disks."

2
Vermelha translates as "red."

3
Corallo translates as "coral."

4
Humberto's remarks were quoted in "Estudio Campana: Absolute Charm," *Three Layer Cake* (online) Monday, 31 July 2006, accessed August 2008. [Adapted by author.]

5
Pedra translates as "rock."

6
Nuvem translates as "cloud."

7
Mark C O'Flaherty, "Brothers of Invention," *The Financial Times* (1 January 2008).

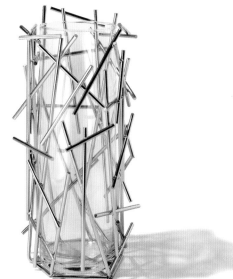

Blow up vase
2005
Stainless steel

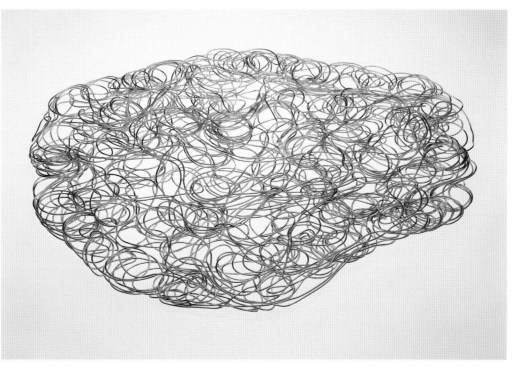

Nuvem – wire mat, 2007, aluminum

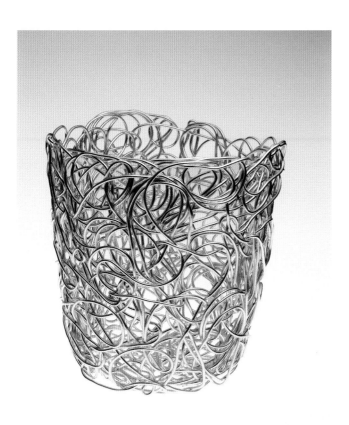

Nuvem – citrus basket, 2007, aluminum

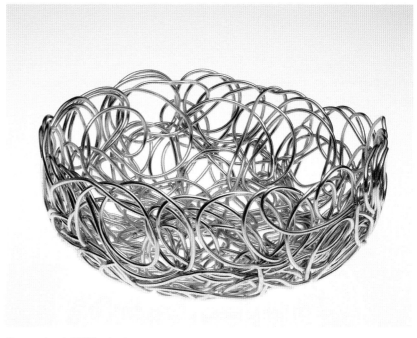

Nuvem – bowl, 2007, aluminum

Ninho collection,
1991
aluminum

Darrin Alfred

Displaced Materials

For many years Fernando and Humberto Campana have scoured the streets of São Paulo in search of unusual materials. They began experimenting with metals, moved on to natural materials such as wicker, wood, and bamboo, then—drawing on a visual language we all share—the ubiquitous materials found about our own homes, such as rope and broom bristles, and even garden hoses and outdoor drain covers. These materials, banalized by daily use, are all but invisible in contemporary culture—a culture that is so often obsessed with newness and novelty. **"Our intention is to investigate materials that are already industrialized for a specific function and incorporate them into our projects. In this way, they start having another kind of visual code."**[1] In various ways the Campanas explore the inherent properties and latent potential of these mass-produced everyday products to create functional furniture and objects. They are modest essays in the investigation of new production processes and the reinvention of existing materials. **"We have great respect for materials, especially those that are not noticed by ordinary people's eyes. The very banal ones, our great challenge is to transform them into something that looks precious."**[2]

The Vermelha, Azul, and Verde chairs,[3] all constructed from rope, formed a collection of seating that the Campanas first designed in 1993. Born from a tangle of thick rope purchased at a São Paulo street market, their most famous project, the Vermelha chair, was **"not so much a concept"** as it was **"an exercise in construction and deconstruction,"** according to

Humberto. Uniting this common household object with techniques borrowed from Brazil's long-standing tradition of craftsmanship, five hundred meters of pliable red cotton cord were knotted and loosely woven by hand in and out of a simple steel frame, then plaited by repeated overlapping. Loose-fitting loops were then formed with the surplus material to shape the seemingly chaotic design. A glimpse of the finished work reveals no discernible beginning or end.

The Campanas first handwove the Vermelha chair, originally intended as a one-off, in small numbers in their studio. There was an honesty and simplicity about the way in which they constructed the work. A large ball of rope sat in the studio for weeks before Humberto began to play with it. Without preliminary studies or drawings he relied solely on the spontaneous discoveries that happened in the making process. **"The material came first—before the form or the function,"** asserts Humberto. Inexpensive, manageable, and obtainable in abundant quantities, rope was an ideal material for the kind of expression and experimentation the brothers wished to explore at the time. Like many emerging designers, it was also a time in their career when factory resources were not available to them. Humberto recalls, **"We didn't have the money to invest in new tools so we started looking around us, to suppliers, what they had. We wanted to work with much cheaper materials that we could buy a lot of to construct with."** According to Fernando, their basic objective was **"to construct something by repeating the same material until you get a whole object."** The

128

Vermelha chair
1993
Cotton ropes and stainless steel structure

mass-produced everyday materials appear to have been a means of doing something more directly and quickly, or at least circumvented the division between craftmaking and designing for industry.

The Vermelha chair demanded great manual dexterity—the weaving, apparently random yet created with practiced art, was built up over a week to form both the chair's unusual padding and cover. This, however, did not deter the Italian furniture manufacturer Edra from acquiring its rights five years later in 1998. Trained by the Campanas, one of Edra's highly skilled factory workers, Giuseppe Altieri, applied the same handweaving techniques. **"Massimo Morozzi wanted a drawing or model, which was impossible. So we decided to transmit all this highly unscientific knowledge in a video that showed us going through thc whole manufacturing process. We edited a shorter version with the most explanatory bits. That, together with a few sketches and telephone calls, allowed the product to come into being."**[4] Working time on the Vermelha chair was

eventually reduced to a day and a half as Edra developed a new technique for braiding the ropes in an effort to streamline the manufacturing process. **"Despite the fact that we did not supervise manufacturing on site, we were really surprised when we saw the Vermelha at the Milan Furniture Fair [Salone Internazionale del Mobile]. It was an improvement on the version we had made in our own studio."**[5] The chair received a great deal of coverage and became a commercially successful product, eventually projecting Fernando and Humberto onto the international stage. **"Even Edra wagered that it would only be an image product. Today, it is our visiting card."**[6] The partnership marked the beginning of the industrial production of the Campanas' furniture and a thriving relationship with Edra.

The Campanas employed a similar technique and the same material to construct Azul and Verde. As in Vermelha, two standard simple metal frames are transformed by patiently winding either blue- or green-colored cotton cord around and through the bare metal framework. Square

130

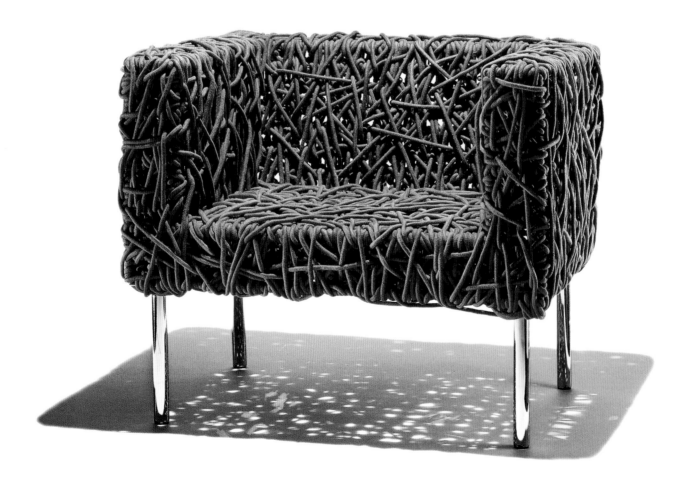

Azul chair, 1993, cotton ropes and stainless steel structure

Verde chair, 1993, cotton ropes and stainless steel structure

Bubble wrap chair, 1995, plastic bubble sheet and chrome-plated iron

Xingu fruit bowl
1999
Acrylic and recycled PET threads

in shape, Azul's allusion to upholstery was handmade by skillfully weaving 650 meters of rope, while the comparably pared-down Verde was completed with a mere 220. The loose-fitting loops that heavily characterize the Vermelha chair, however, have been significantly reduced or eliminated entirely when creating both Azul and Verde, where the rope appears to have been more tightly woven.

At times the designers' hands are very slight, as the Campanas illustrated in two chairs. Bubble wrap chair (1995)[7] naively exploits the unique material characteristics of the flexible transparent plastic after which it is named. In the guise of upholstery, Fernando and Humberto layered thirty sheets of the cheap protective material commonly used for packing fragile items, including furniture, to create a distinctive and comfortable seat—a design with startling appeal. Six bolts secure the material and are in turn welded to steel metal squares fused into the corners of yet another simple steel frame. Plástico Bolha is the antithesis of a mass-produced industrial design and represents a gauntlet to the modernist furniture designs of the 1990s. Rolls of bubble-wrap were

effortlessly obtainable in the hardware stores near Fernando and Humberto's studio in São Paulo's Santa Cecília neighborhood. **"Sometimes displays in stores give us ideas,"** says Humberto. **"For instance, we might see a pile of ropes or rows of garden hoses. If we see an interesting structure, we can sometimes make a drawing in there, just focusing on that area of the store."** Utilizing a material never intended for upholstery, the Campanas opened up a new direction for fabric development—padding and upholstery as one and the same material. **"We were interested in investigating this material as an attempt to give much more comfort to our work,"** asserts Humberto. The bubble-wrap's regularly spaced, protruding, air-filled hemispheres provided a unique cushion and, without diminishing its comfort, its surface bestows an unexpected texture. In a similar fashion, a second chair was constructed with layers of the Mylar sun shield material usually placed in car windows for heat and UV reflection or used as insulation. The material's aluminized coating provides an out-of-the-ordinary surface treatment, while the middle foam layer adds rigidity and padding to the seat.

The sides of the Campanas' Xingu fruit bowl (1999), originally for Zona D, were made of several small clusters of freestanding upright broom bristles arranged in a circular pattern. The playful and unconventional fruit bowl was born from observing the colorful brooms arranged in a nearby shop. As Humberto comments, **"These kinds of street boutiques always catch our eye. São Paulo is like a big market full of people selling everything. It's impossible to miss them."** The same economy of means characterized the Campanas' use of plastic drain covers, which acquired a new attribute in the brothers' Tattoo table (1999). The objects, which ordinarily prevent debris from entering a drain opening, initially drew the Campanas' attention with their decorative pattern. When several covers were placed side by side and attached to a stainless steel structure, they created a permeable mosaic tabletop that filtered light, essentially "tattooing" a ghostly carpet on the floor. Nothing about these works was disguised, or superfluous to their function. By 2000, however, the Tattoo table had a new incarnation at FontanaArte. When licensed to the Italian manufacturer, a rectangular version was created in addition to the initial square table, in five length x width x height combinations. A tabletop with white silk-screened float glass was manufactured, in addition to the polycarbonate opal tiles of the original, perhaps losing some of the impact in translation. The results of these designs were intentionally naïve and curiously literal.

Tattoo table, 2000, stainless steel and float glass. Produced by FontanaArte

Tattoo table, 1999, stainless steel and PVC strains. Produced by Estudio Campana

Jardim chair
1995
Plastic hose and chrome-plated iron

Jardim easy chair, 1995, plastic hose and stainless steel

After rope and bubble-wrap, the Campanas repurposed an equally unlikely material—plastic (PVC) garden hose. In 1995, they designed two variations on the modernist chair with the readily available material. The first garden-hose chair, the Jardim chair,[8] utilized clear hoses cut into strips and placed on the seat and back in vertical alignment. The second chair layered bands of blue hose in a horizontal configuration that were heavily stacked on top of one another to form a considerably more substantial "cushion" than the first chair. More significant lengths of the transparent garden hose were later wrapped around a steel frame to make the Anemona chair (2000). The designers were seduced by the superimposed transparency the clear tubing could provide. **"We developed the Anemona chair when we didn't have the capital to invest in injection molding for plastic,"** recalls Fernando. **"Since our aesthetics are complicated and elaborate, to make a chair like Anemona with plastic, to weld and to extrude, would be very expensive, especially with all the holes and transparency. So we looked around at things that were already on the market, in plastic, that we could utilize to make the chair."** However, while this provided a background conducive to creativity, what led to the work being so well received was undoubtedly the sensitivity with which the materials were used and the resulting intellectual alacrity of the design. Crisscrossed lengths of the hosing are methodically handwoven and screw-attached to the metal frame, forming an elastic seat. The long ends are left dangling over the edge like the tendrils of the sea creature it resembles. Along with the use of raw materials and the ostensibly basic construction, the translucency of the hose makes a piece such as the Anemona chair particularly vivid. **"Design is about cleaning,"** says Humberto, curiously. **"We accumulate when we make something. Then we start cleaning it, stripping it back in order to let the materials speak for themselves, or so that we can create a sense of shock between different materials."**

Anemona chair, 2000, stainless steel and PVC tubes (Produced by Edra as **Anemone chair** in 2002)

Zig Zag stool, 2001, stainless steel structure and PVC tubes

As the name suggests, the Zig Zag collection of stools and screens was made of deliberately irregular garden hose tubing handspun and knotted over an O-shaped steel frame, as if it were wicker. Forming a permeable skin that could span the open area, the candy-colored extruded plastic tubing served as a comfortable seat or separated space. The collection, put into production by Edra in 2001, was made available as a screen and as a stool in three sizes. **"We couldn't have just approached an injection molding company in Brazil—they wouldn't have trusted us! Instead, we attempted to translate processes of industrializing raw materials into using things that are already industrialized—like the garden hose, weaving it to make a plastic stool or screen. We didn't need more than a simple metal structure and a garden hose to make it."**[9]

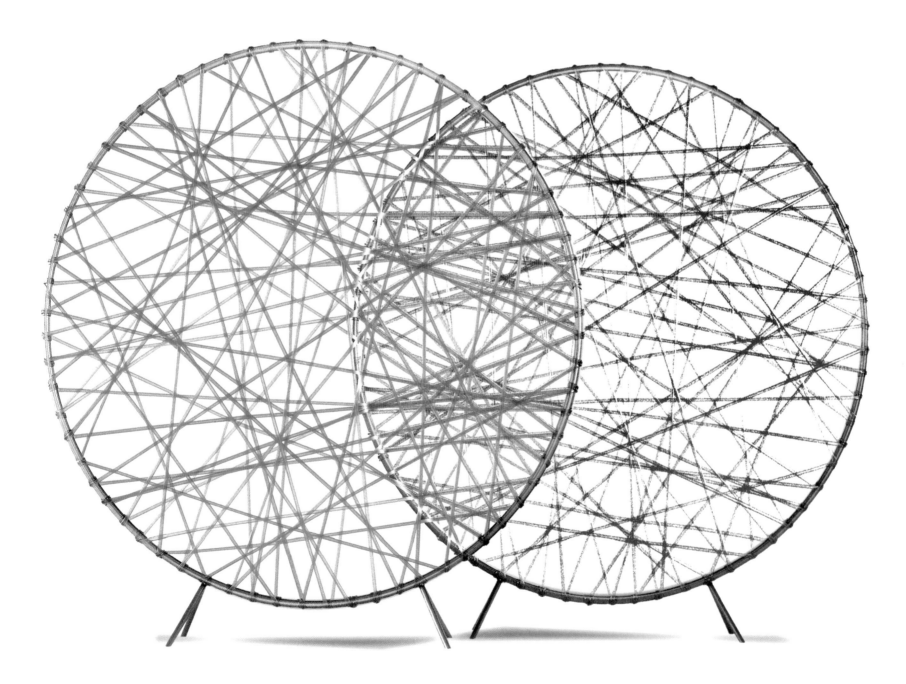

Zig Zag screen, 2001, stainless steel and PVC tubes

Melissa Zig Zag – bag and sandals, 2005, PVC

The Campanas are not opposed to industrialization, although their inspiration does not usually begin with technology, as Humberto explains: **"We believe that what makes us investigate these materials and create objects is quite the opposite: working with very little technology and turning it into a high tech-like object."** More recently, in 2004, Grendene, one of Brazil's largest shoemakers, approached the designers to reposition their Melissa product line as a (once again) fashionable and desirable accessory. Founded in 1971, Grendene is one of the world's largest footwear manufacturers and the holder of an exclusive technology for injected thermoplastic. Melissa utilizes sustainability concepts from the inception of an idea to the production of the final product. Fernando elaborates, **"It's fun because we often promote wicker and natural fibers... because of this we should be against using plastic, but with this project we are trying to do more and more in terms of recycling, in terms of the percentage of recycled plastic being used. In 2008 we achieved up to 30 percent recycled PVC."** The brothers drew inspiration from their Zig Zag collection in order to reimagine the company's beloved jelly, a shoe invented in Brazil in the '80s and the manufacturer's most popular footwear. The result is the Melissa + Campana line of vinyl random-mesh jellies including shoes in two styles (high and low) and a matching handbag. From a cheap material seen as common, plastic acquired a new glamour in these creations. **"You know, there are no boundaries between fashion and design,"** muses Fernando. **"In a way, furniture also accommodates the body, just on a different scale."**

142

1
Siobhan O'Brien, "Treasure Hunt," *The Sydney Morning Herald* (8 May 2003).

2
Ibid.

3
Azul translates as "blue" and *Verde* as "green."

4
Morozzi, Cristina (Ed.), *True Stories with Edra*, Edra, 2007.

5
Ibid.

6
Ibid.

7
Bubble Wrap chair is often referred to by its Portuguese name of Plastico Bolha.

8
Jardim translates as "garden."

9
Fernando's remarks were quoted in Marcus Fairs, "The Campana Brothers," *Icon Eye: Icon Magazine Online*, July/August 2004, accessed August 2008. [Adapted by this author.]

Melissa Zig Zag – tennis shoe, 2005, PVC

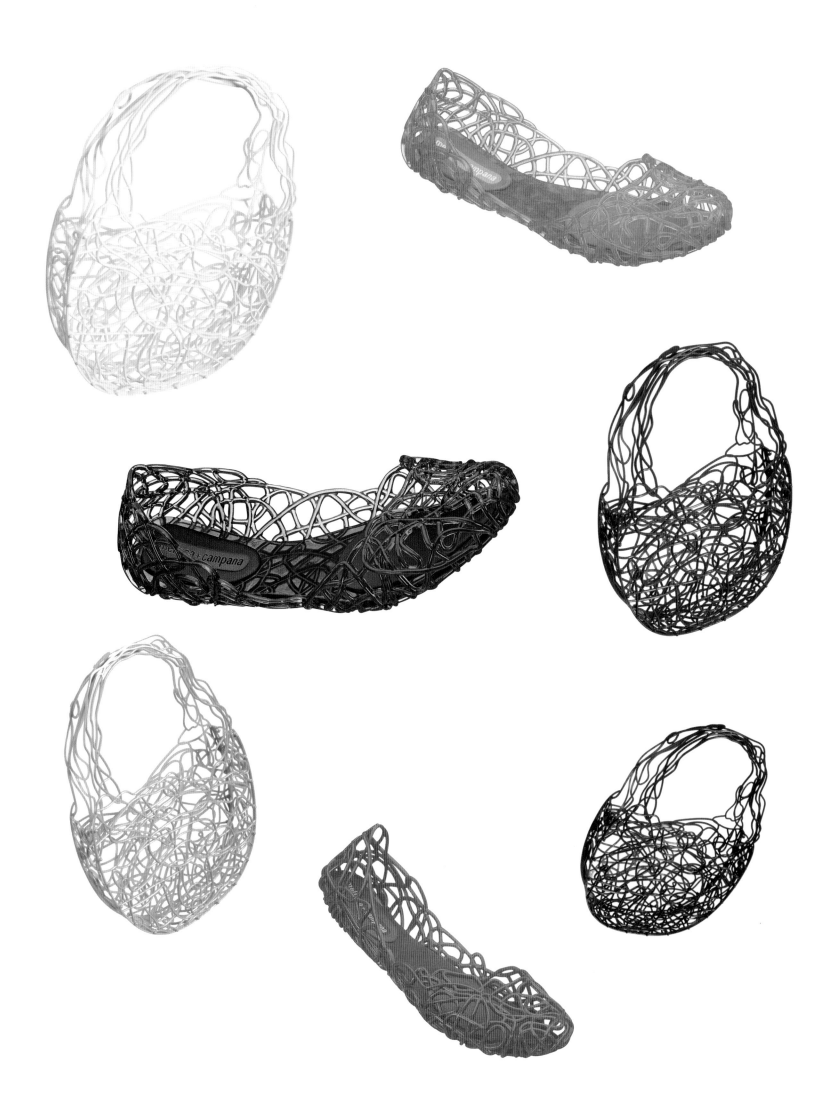

144

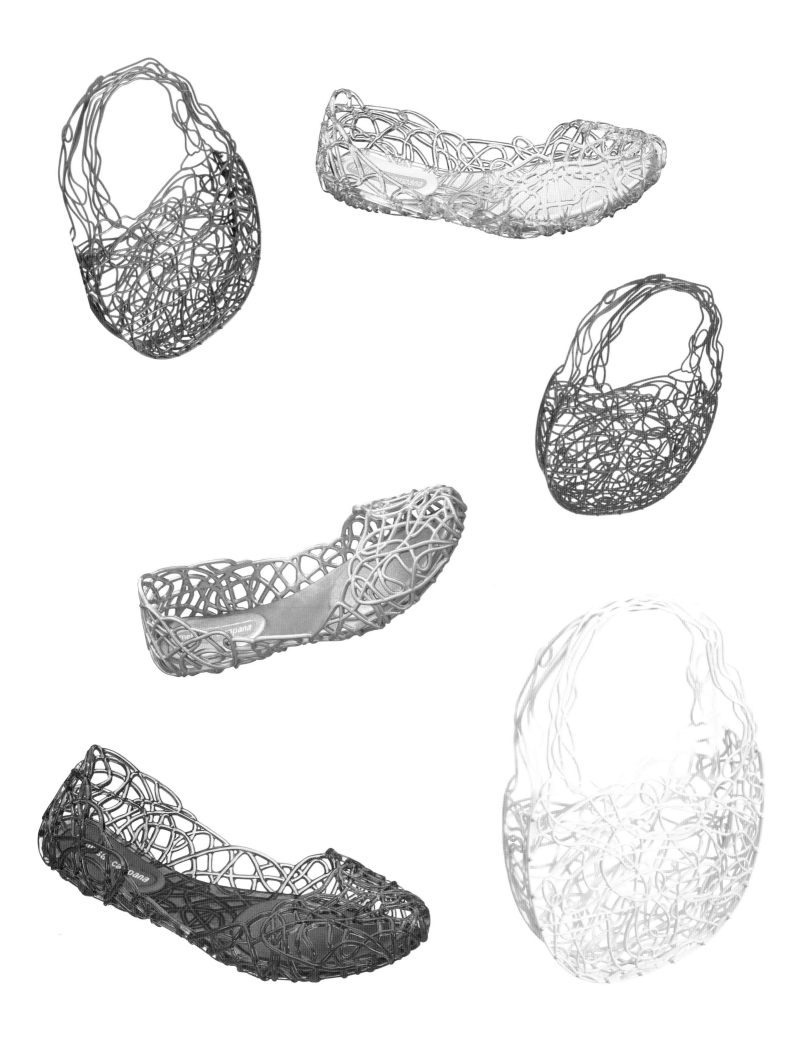

Melissa Pump – handbag and slippers, 2008, PVC

Cone chair
1997 (Edra edition of 1999)
Stainless steel and polycarbonate sheet

Darrin Alfred

Translucency

Fernando and Humberto Campana have created a variety of inflatable, sculptural, and illuminated objects out of numerous plastics, such as polycarbonate, acrylic, and polypropylene. Visually and physically light, they embody the modernist goal of weightlessness and transparency. Once considered a cheap substitute for other materials, plastics have become an attractive alternative for high-end consumer goods. The modern materials can be flexible and exceedingly strong. Their translucency and malleability have provided the Campanas an opportunity to experiment with the effect. This body of work embodies the Campanas' penchant for exploring various plastics through bending, folding, and inflating. When realized, the objects take on a sense of the ethereal.

By the mid-1990s, plastic furniture, chairs in particular, had become associated with poor quality. Inexpensive garden chairs, for example, the offspring of 1960s experiments in plastic injection molding, are now often seen as cheap and disposable. This trend was reversed in the 1990s due to a legion of designers, such as Philippe Starck, Jasper Morrison, and the Campana brothers, who elevated the status of the humble plastic chair to the luxurious. Fernando and Humberto's strikingly shaped Cone chair (1997) is a deceptively simple shell made of a single sheet of clear polycarbonate (a tough, non-deteriorating plastic). Gently folded like origami, the seat was not achieved by applying groundbreaking applications of new technologies, but rather by exploiting the resilient and flexible material in an innovative way. The Campanas began by bending and cutting single sheets of clear plastic in an effort to create a small fruit bowl and eventually

realized they could make a "bowl" big enough to sit in. Humberto elaborates: **"The Cone chair was also born from the material. I was making a fruit bowl at the time. It was a small piece, you know. And then, looking at the bowl, Fernando saw the possibility of a chair. So we made the bowl bigger and took it from there."** The development displays how the Campanas' design process is a truly creative hands-on experience. The technique for constructing the shape of the seat was the result of careful thought coupled with the Campanas' innate artistic sense. The straight lines of the polycarbonate were transformed into soft curves by partially splitting the clear sheet and reuniting it to form the cone-like shape. The material appears to have generated its own structure. **"We make some changes and**

Philippe Starck
Lord Yo
1994
Stackable armchair with polypropylene
seat shell, aluminum frame and legs

Jasper Morrison
Air chair
1999
One-piece, gas-injected polypropylene chair

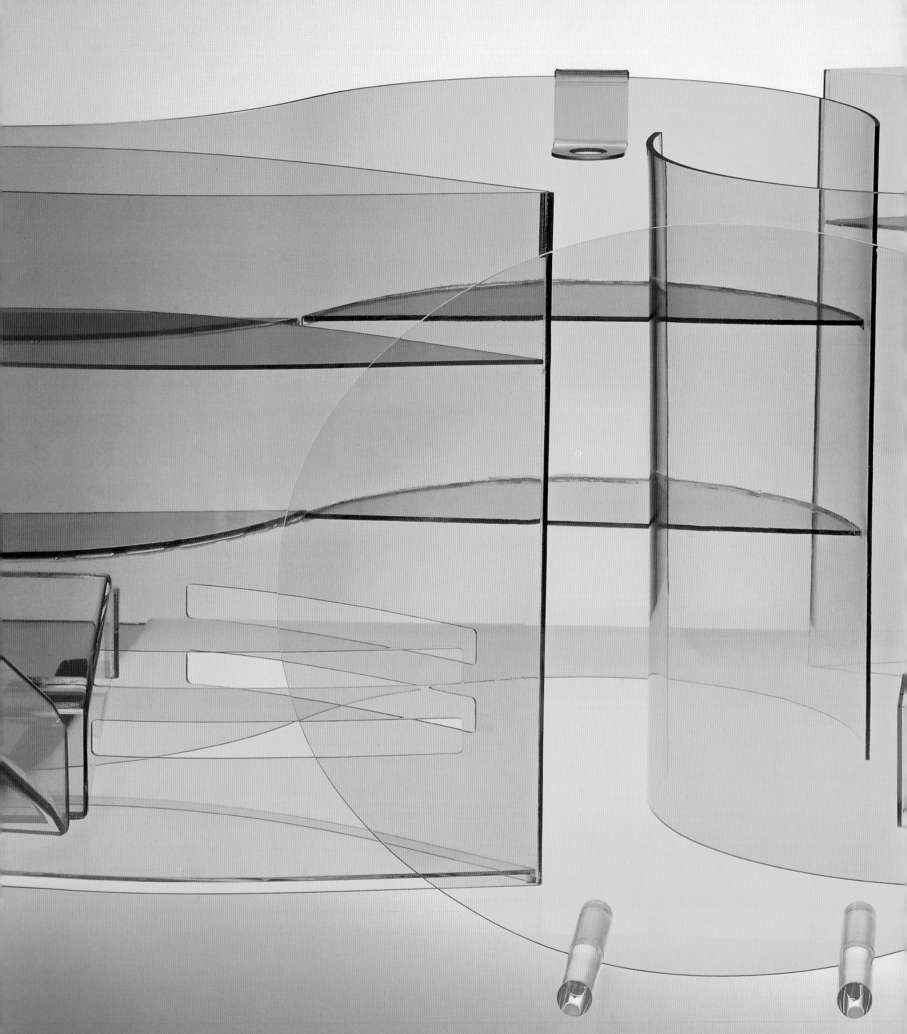

Split partition, 2001, acrylic

then we amplify them to see what other possibilities there might be," explains Fernando. The seat was placed point-down then anchored by pins to a cross-shaped metal base finished in metalized grey. The legs and frame, which are exposed by the polycarbonate's transparency, seemingly disappear. And despite its strictly geometric form, the chair is unexpectedly comfortable. The tooling of the Cone chair required little investment and was put into production by Edra in 1999.

In 2001, Fernando and Humberto designed a diverse array of desk accessories made entirely or partially from colored acrylic. A fluid synthesis of material and design, the objects conveyed a futuristic, streamlined aesthetic. In sheets that could be bent, cut, and folded, transparent plastics such as acrylic were a favorite plaything of designers in the 1960s because of their space-age look. The ethereal prototypes the Campanas designed for the Split Partitions collection, commissioned by Forma, Brazil, were created with colored acrylic. The collection, which never went into production, included seven models. From curved partitions, tiered organizers, and pencil cups, the Campana brothers made maximum use of the limited desk space by employing the transparent material. Constructed without the use of bolts or screws, the clean-lined and pristine accessories reveal the contents of all their compartments at a glance. In a similar vein, the

Elétrico collection (2000), produced and sold by Estudio Campana was made up of a wall mirror, tall vase, bowl, fruit bowl, and picture frame. Produced on a small scale, the unembellished and straightforward objects seize the eye. They display the same economy of construction, modesty, and improvisation demonstrated in the Campanas' earlier Cone chair.

The brothers continued their quest to eliminate gravity through the use of inflatable PVC, which can be cut, glued, heat-formed, used to cover a surface, or, as was famously discovered in the 1960s, filled with air. **"We chose this material to make a visually and physically light object,"** asserts Fernando. It is this task that they have found to be the most demanding facet of their design process. The Campanas first adopted the material in the playful and practical Inflatable table (1995), origi-nally produced by Estudio Campana in a small edition of fifty before being modified and put into production by MoMA in 1998. It is both a low circular side table and its own packaging. A cylinder of skin-like translucent PVC, the inflatable body of the object is formed by heat-sealing and expands when filled with air. Two large pizza pan-like lids held the flexible opaque film of the original prototype (designed in yellow PVC, it was molded from an existing promotional beer barrel) between them. The production series employed makeshift aluminum parts.

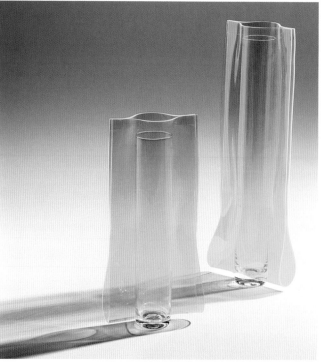

Elétrico mirror, 2000, acrylic and mirror

Elétrico vase, 2000, acrylic and glass

The aluminum components are attached to the top and bottom of the inflated bladder with contact glue. Three aluminum rod legs are screwed into the bottom dish. Simply by removing the legs and deflating the body of the table, the furniture is transformed into its own packaging —the table's aluminum top and bottom serve as the object's container. Secured by two wide elastic bands, the flat, compact package can be stored and transported effortlessly. When MoMA took over the production, they had it produced in China as a whole. The Inflatable table is an innovative design that is practical, not merely novel, and captures the ease and mobility for which the Campanas often aim.

Soon after, Fernando and Humberto designed their Inflatable vase (1997). Visually luminous and lightweight, the container was molded after a promotional object for a battery. An array of machinery was employed to achieve what appears to be an effortless object, while the industrial plant workers cut and fused the vase. The translucency of the PVC body imbues the vase with a fragile quality that is almost counter to reality. Once available exclusively at Zona D, a contemporary design shop found throughout Brazil, the collection was later discontinued. A flexible inner tube serves as the canal that holds the flower stem. An external sealable valve provides a means of inflation. The spontaneously

playful structure gains solidity when filled with water for the flower.

The limitations of the production facilities, materials, and technologies available to designers within their geographical context at a given moment in time can often play a significant role in determining the kind of product produced. In many ways, Split Partitions or the Inflatable table and vase, for example, reveal the reluctance or difficulty of many Brazilian manufacturers to embrace such new designs, particularly in the Campanas' early career. As daring as they were restricted, the Campanas grasped the sources and resources available to them at the time, often altering the function of available manufacturing methods. While sophisticated furniture and products poured from the assembly lines of Italian companies such as Edra, Alessi, and Oluce, who took great pride in discovering and building the careers of emerging talent, their Brazilian counterparts had a tremendous disadvantage. This difficulty of production may explain why some of the aforementioned collections were less successful or well-known and why the Campanas have not extensively pursued the use of these materials to date.

153

Delicate, fragile, and poetic, the Campanas' experiments with glass have offered the pair new directions for

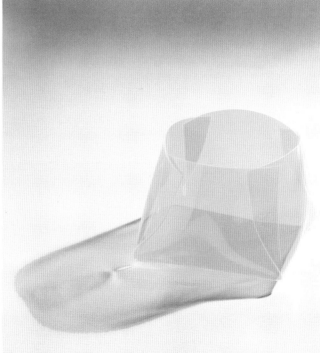

Elétrico photo frame, 2000, acrylic and glass

Elétrico bowl, 2000, acrylic

exploring translucency and transparency. Constructed from a seemingly random collection of test tubes, the Batuque vase (2000) alters its form and appearance depending on the position in which it is placed. The work is open to multiple readings. The Italian manufacturer Cappellini produced a small series of the vase in 2001. The Galho vase (2004) was a continuation of the dialogue between artificial and organic that has accompanied Fernando and Humberto since the beginning of their careers. Realized in glass, the vase (a manmade container for storing water) integrates the natural configuration of a tree branch (a natural water storage medium) through the fluid transparency of the material.

The Campanas' most notable experiments into the potential of glass have developed through their collaborations with Venini, the legendary manufacturer of fine Italian art glass. Founded in 1921, Venini is famous for its classic and modern glass design, having worked with respected designers and artists such as Vittorio Zecchin, Gio Ponti, and Ettore Sottsass, among many others. Campane di Campana (2005) was a joint venture between Fernando and Humberto and Venini for Moss Gallery. **"The project began with an invitation from Murray Moss. He wanted us to make a show in his gallery in New York. We came up with the bells because our name is Campana, and in Italian 'campana' means 'bells.' We said to ourselves, 'so why don't we make bells?'"**[1] With no end result in mind, the project was improvised over a five-day period. The factory became a kind of laboratory for the Campanas as they worked quickly and directly in the furnace with Venini's maestro. **"We told them please be imperfect... we don't want perfection."**[2] The results were a collection of 175 clear crystal bells of diverse size, composition, and sound, each hand blown by glassmaker Luciano Sanavelli over an eight-week period.

On view at Moss from November through December 2005, the bells were hung from coarse hemp rope similar to the twine used to wrap the packages and crates at Venini. The final installation formed a modern-day horizontal campanile. Humberto comments: **"It was very challenging to make something with a noble material such as crystal, you know. We tried to create shocks between the appearance of the crystal and the other elements, and we used cords to hang them all, as if to make a curtain of bells."**[3]

"We also had this idea of making a kind of spiritual design. Bells are used in churches and monasteries to announce things—to alert people, to bring people together, to celebrate, to signal happiness and the joy of life,"[4] Fernando adds.

More recently, Fernando and Humberto have entered the early stages of a chandelier project with Venini. This is not the Campanas' first foray into designing a chandelier. As part of the Crystal Palace project for the Austrian crystal company Swarovski, Fernando and Humberto

Inflatable vase, 1997, PVC film and PVC tube

Inflatable table, 1995, PVC film and anodized aluminum (MoMA edition of 1998)

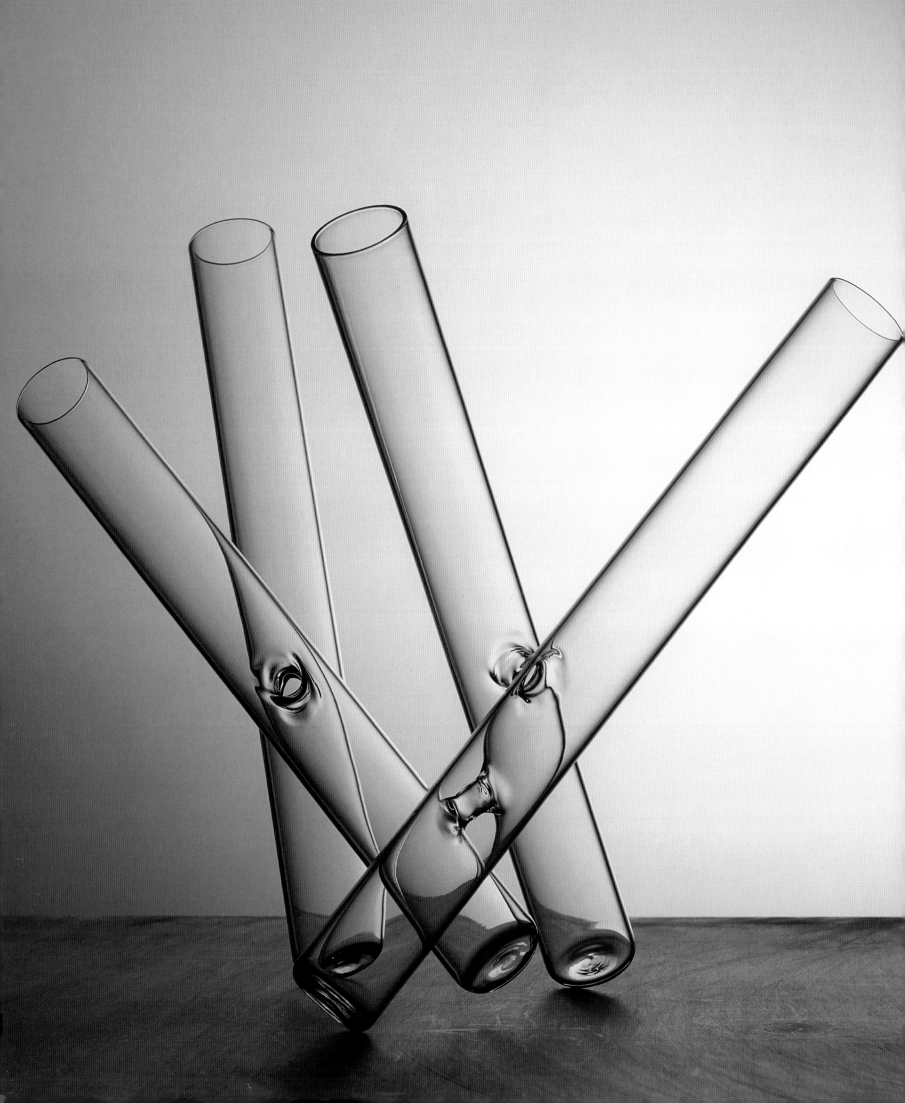

created Prived Oca in 2003. The results were a tangle of wild raffia combined with the luxury and precision of Swarovski crystals. A departure from Campane di Campana, the preliminary collages for this latest collaboration with Venini appear to combine previous elements from works within the Murano-based glassmaker's archives. One study, in particular, proposes the creation of one-of-a-kind "cocoons" made of remnants of glass gathered from Venini's factory and melted to one another to form a single shell that dresses the structural and electrical components of the chandeliers. The odds and ends are combined to form a kaleidoscopic shock of color.

1
Humberto's remarks were quoted in *Campana di Campanas*, a film directed by Thais Stoklos, 2005. [Adapted by the Campana brothers.]

2
Ibid.

3
Ibid.

4
Fernando's remarks were quoted in *Campana di Campanas*, a film directed by Thais Stoklos, 2005. [Adapted by the Campana brothers.]

Galho vases
2004/7
Glass

Batuque vase
2000
Glass

Campane di Campana (Campana Bells)
Bell 1968 – Whales, Ladybugs, Cartoon Characters, Frogs, Scorpions
2005
Mouth-blown glass

Prived Oca
2003
Natural fiber,
Swarovski crystals,
and optic fiber

Darrin Alfred

Upholstery

Fernando and Humberto Campana have shaped a unique and surprising way of representing the world around them. Their combined curiosity for reusing mundane or discarded materials and an increasing attention to unusual methods of upholstery—the stuffing, cushions, fabric, and other materials used to upholster furniture— eventually led the designers to experiment with masses of discarded cloth, including rubber and carpeting, the plush toys from their childhood, and the traditional fabric dolls made in Esperança—a small town in Northeastern Brazil. **"It was a deeper investigation into upholstery,"** explains Humberto. **"We were interested in how to make upholstery without using traditional processes."** These techniques grew out of a concept articulated early in the Campana brothers' career: a notion in which materials banalized by daily use, such as rope, garden hose, and bubble-wrap, provided their designs with more padding and comfort. **"We were attempting to create much more comfortable pieces. We do not want to be like artists, otherwise we would have carried on making work like the Uncomfortables series."** Humberto continues: **"Our interest is in being designers and in having a connection with the people who use it."** These whimsical objects, while meeting people's desire for physical comfort and relaxation, also dramatically opened up the parameters of how designers might look at upholstery.

The Campanas' striking Sushi series exemplifies the visual vigor that characterizes Brazil. As Fernando points out, **"We are a country with a lot of life, textures, and color."** This vibrant collection of chairs, sofas, and other

Sushi chair
2002
Carpet, fabric, foam, and PVC

Sushi chair
2002
Carpet, fabric, foam, and PVC

Sushi II chair
2002
Electrostatic painted iron,
carpet, EVA, and fabrics

objects—made with tightly rolled bundles of carpet remnants and underlays, fabric offcuts and scraps of rubber—is among the most versatile examples of the Campanas' experiments with found materials, illustrating the range of forms the studio employs. The series is also a continually evolving assortment of investigations that are alive with color, heavy with striation, and animated by an imaginative approach toward traditional notions of upholstery.

The concept behind the Sushi chair (2002), for Edra, was to create upholstery while avoiding standard methods of construction often associated with furniture production: the wooden or metal frame and various spring support systems. **"We wanted to construct upholstery with less traditional materials,"** says Fernando. The final result is achieved by compressing and then rolling different types and thicknesses of fabrics and textiles in a concentric ring. The circle of remnants is then secured in place by a large elasticized polyurethane and fabric

tube. The free ends left uncovered or unsecured by the tubing naturally turn back onto themselves like the petals of a flower to collectively form the multicolored seat. When placed onto its side, the flat base of the frameless chair appears similar to an oversized version of the popular California roll, a kind of sushi. **"Sushi is very popular here in São Paulo,"** comments Fernando. **"You can eat it every day."** Though mass-produced in Italy, the work retains its intended handcrafted nature: the variety of the remnants and their random placement makes for an infinite number of patterns.

The Sushi chair was inspired by the *favelas* of São Paulo, where the residents of these shantytowns are known for making patchwork floor coverings and quilts using whatever random fragments of fabric they can find. **"People in the *favelas* make really beautiful patterns with cloth—mats and bedspreads and all sorts—by overlapping fabric remainders,"** explains Fernando. When invited by Massimo Morozzi to propose a new design

Sushi III chair, 2002, electrostatic painted iron, carpet, rubber, EVA, and fabrics

Harumaki chair, 2004, electrostatic painted iron, carpet, EVA, and fabric

Harumaki bench
2007
Stainless steel, EVA, fabric, and rubber

relating to the *favelas*, Humberto set about researching the piece: **"I started gathering textiles of different types, natural and artificial, felts, wools, carpets, and rubber, from which I made a kind of rug. Fernando took it, rolled it up, and transformed it into the Sushi chair."** By weaving the everyday materials used in the *favelas* of São Paulo into this work, the Campanas presented a fresh and liberating approach to upholstery that promotes the reuse of materials while revealing facets of Brazil's **"design of scarcity,"** as Fernando describes it, in stimulating ways. He adds: **"Where we can, we try to make the necessities of everyday life in São Paulo more beautiful and elegant."**

Following the initial armchair for Edra the Campanas continued this line of experimentation, developing a series of handcrafted one-of-a-kind chairs, tables, sofas, and other objects manufactured in their São Paulo studio. Sushi II (2002) was Fernando and Humberto's first attempt at using thin 1.5 cm-wide ribbons of carpet,

felt, rubber netting, and EVA to create "flat" sushi rolls. The narrow bands of the assorted materials, which come in varying lengths, are combined together in a random circular pattern and secured with adhesive to form the decorative discs. **"We got all these strips of leather, EVA, rubber, synthetic grass, carpet, and felt to construct with,"** explains Fernando. Formed in varying diameters, the circular objects are densely combined in a random pattern to cover the entire seat and back of a traditional L-shaped steel chair frame. Sushi III (2002) took the sushi-style upholstery to a three-dimensional level. Felt, textiles, and other synthetic materials were again rolled into concentric rings, but fixed into place within a welded iron frame. The individual components, or rolls, appear as if miniature versions of the Sushi chair for Edra. The bowl-like shape of Sushi IV (2003) was a variation on this design. **"Each piece is completely different from the next,"** says Humberto. **"And the many component parts reveal all the time that has gone into constructing each object."**

Sushi IV armchair, 2003, electrostatic painted iron, carpet, rubber, EVA, and fabric

Sushi sofa, 2002, carpet, rubber, EVA, fabric, wood, and stainless steel

Sonia Diniz chair
2003
Electrostatic painted iron, carpet, rubber, EVA, fabric, and wood

The Sushi sofa (2002) and Sonia Diniz chair (2003) fall in line with more traditional methods of furniture construction. A wood framework, not seen in the finished product, provides the surface on top of which the flat discs of upholstery are applied. Within the entire series, each individual object is unique. The changing surfaces of these objects delight the eye as it experiences constant oscillation—something that Fernando associates with the city in which they live and work. **"São Paulo is a very textural city. It is this texture that makes it such a big mess with so many different volumes, shapes and colors. We are always interested in investigating these aspects of our town. Some things you can find everywhere in the world, but there are also things that seem very particular to São Paulo. We try to bring these characteristics out in our work, and often in a very literal way."**

The three-legged Vitória Régia stools (2002) were an adaptation of the Sushi series. Made of unwanted remnants of tablecloths, carpet underlay, and brightly colored plastic, the highly decorative stools are hand-crafted into one giant sushi roll and fitted into a circular brushed stainless steel structure. Each piece is unique and has been made available in various sizes by Estudio Campana. Inspired by the Campanas' long-standing curiosity in botanical forms, the works recreate the allure of the Vitória Régia, a giant water lily commonly found in the Brazilian Amazon. **"Our father was an agronomic engineer,"** explains Humberto. **"Whenever he took us to Rio de Janeiro we would go to see the beautiful botanical gardens there, which are around two hundred years old—the King of Portugal had them built when he fled from Napoleon. Our time spent in the gardens then and since has been a considerable influence on our approach to design."**

The Campanas' Multidão chair (2002) is built out of dozens of traditional cotton dolls handcrafted in the town of Esperança. Meaning "crowd" in Portuguese, Multidão reflects the social complexities of life in São Paulo, the largest city in Brazil and the most populous in the entire Southern hemisphere. This city, the most ethnically

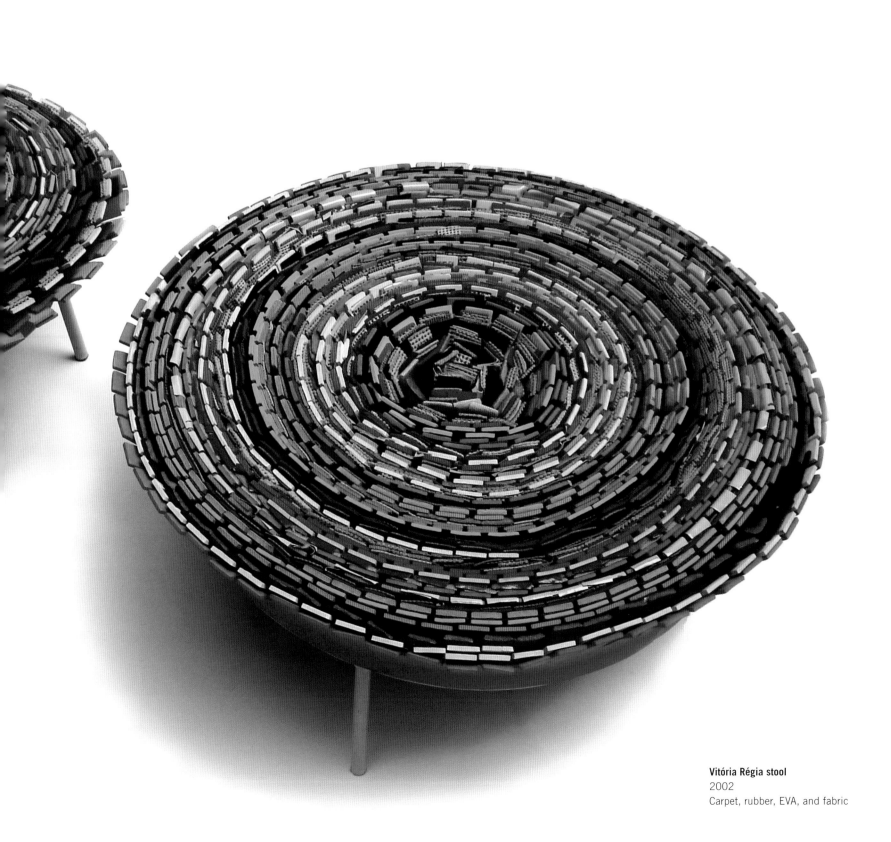

diverse in Brazil, is a crowded mishmash of urbanity, a tangle of people, and their place of refuge. The notion of a crowd can suggest an uneasy balance between democracy and mob violence, but for the brothers the idea of large groups of people conjure up more positive connotations. **"Brazil has a very chaotic side, but it's not chaos in a negative sense,"** asserts Humberto. **"It's chaos that's happiness, like the carnival. You see a parade and it's for everybody. At the same time it's very flamboyant, organic, and baroque— Brazil is a baroque country."**

Among the Campana brothers' more recent and much-admired approaches to upholstery is the Banquete range of chairs. Constructed from scores of children's stuffed animals combined in a seemingly frantic manner, the designers have composed miniature worlds out of the everyday objects. Handcrafted and offered in limited editions, the works broaden the Campanas' approach to upholstery by transforming the inherent properties of the plush toys. The chairs flaunt a wonderful sense of luxury, curiosity, humor, and, at times, an eerie or unsettling quality. **"Seeing materials presented in different ways gives us ideas,"** says Humberto. **"Imagine going into a tent filled with these plush toy animals—the tent might seem like a house, like an architectural structure made up of toys. This might lead us to imagine a house made of belts or sunglasses and so on. In our minds we would start redesigning the tent to see it as a chair. It's easy to imagine**

180

Multidão armchair, 2002, stainless steel, and stuffed dolls

Alligator chair, 2002, stuffed toys, canvas, and stainless steel

Dolphins and Sharks chair, 2002, stuffed toys, canvas, and stainless steel

Panda Banquete chair
2005
Stuffed toys, canvas, and stainless steel

things—everyone does it all the time—but to execute the idea without being kitsch, provincial, or folkloric is another matter. It's something else to transform that idea into design."

The initial Banquete chair (2002) combined a variety of plush toys in a similar fashion to form an assorted and exotic collection of animals: a modern-day menagerie. Subsequent examples were less diverse than the original, though equally, if not more, striking: Alligator chair (2002) as well as Dolphins and Sharks chair (2002); Teddy Bear Banquete chair (2004); Panda Banquete chair (2005); and Cartoon chair (2007). Currently, alternative versions of the technique are being worked on in the Campanas' studio, some of which mix soft toy seats with leather-covered legs, such as the Carvalho Leatherworks stool and the Multidão Leatherworks stool (both from 2008). The entire series represents some of the Campanas' most humorous work. **"People have a good sense of humor, even in São Paulo, which is a working city,"** observes Humberto. **"All the objects in our collections have some relationship with humor. When people see the banquetes, their first reaction is to laugh."** On the other hand, examples like Dolphins and Sharks or Alligator chair can be seductive but mildly menacing at the same time. As the brothers note: **"The Banquete does have a dark side… it's like the food chain in nature whereby one creature eats the next. At first it seems to be a chair for children or something very lighthearted. But there is also something quite perverse about this chair…"**

Fernando and Humberto's newest design for Edra, Cipria sofa (2009), displays yet another lighthearted approach to upholstery where color and material are the principal aesthetic components. The settee might be seen as a playful reinterpretation of George Nelson's iconic Marshmallow sofa (1956) for Herman Miller. Where Nelson might have used vinyl or wool, the Campanas have employed new materials, such as an eco-friendly faux fur. Nine comfortable cushions of various shapes emphasize their organic forms for visual impact and the design also features an invisible metal tube frame upon which the Gellyfoam® and Dacron wadding stuffed cushions are affixed. The synthetic upholstery comes in different lengths to produce variations on the theme.

Banquete chair
2002
Stuffed toys, canvas, and stainless steel

Cartoon chair, 2007, stuffed Disney toys, fabric, and stainless steel

Carvalho stool, 2008, stuffed toys, leather, canvas, and stainless steel

Multidão stool, 2008, stuffed toys, leather, canvas, and stainless steel

Cipria sofa, 2009, ecological fur, foam stuffing, wadding, and aluminum

Cipria sofa, 2009, metal tube frame, Gelly foam®, Dacron, and ecological fur

Darrin Alfred

Unstructured

Having been influenced by the wider Brazilian context all
their lives, the Campana brothers have regularly taken
inspiration from the sensuous shapes of the natural world.
Brazil's ecosystems—the Amazon Rain forest, Pantanal,
and Atlantic Forest to name just a few—represent the
greatest biodiversity of any country on the planet. These
biomes and their wide-ranging collection of flora and
fauna have provided the Campanas with limitless ideas.
One of the most striking results is a series of softly
sculpted objects that have their own kind of life—a new
breed of unstructured furniture whose flexible materials
and robust, organic shapes seem to modify and mutate
as their users interact with them. Without detracting
from their intended function, the overriding experience
lies in the thoughts and emotions these objects stir.

This collection of unconventional objects found their
initial expression in 1991 when the Campanas accepted
an invitation by Brazilian artist and sculptor Nazareth
Pacheco to participate in a joint exhibition called Projeto
ABC (Arte Brasileira Contemporânea), São Paulo. On
view from December 1991 through March 1992, the
sculptural objects were a departure from the products
that characterized the Campanas' design practice.
**"ABC made us break from our usual activities to do
art, to make sculpture,"** says Humberto. Given no
constraints by the then director, Maria Alice Millet, the
three of them were free to create whatever they wished
within two rooms of São Paulo's Pinacoteca do Estado:
one for Pacheco and the other for the Campanas.
Fernando and Humberto presented four sculptural
artworks covered in blue or purple velvet: an oversized

Projeto ABC
1991
Original invitation to the exhibition at the Pinacoteca do Estado, featuring
a mock-up of pieces by the Campana brothers and Nazareth Pacheco

bone that leaned upright against one gallery wall; a large ball of tubing wrapped around and suspended by four door-height wooden poles; a hollow cone positioned on its side and filled with roughly a half-dozen purple velvet rods that spilled out and onto the floor like a cornucopia; and lastly, a bulky anthropomorphic sack that could be mistaken for an oversized beanbag. **"That project was fun because it was kind of a deviation from our role as designers,"** Humberto recalls. **"We made a show with our friend, a sculptor, and as a team we decided to investigate velvet, creating sculptures using the material. It was one of these sculptures that gave birth to the Boa sofa."** Pacheco and the Campanas chose velvet because it is a material directly linked with Ramos de Azevedo, the architect of the Pinacoteca do Estado. Azevedo designed São Paulo's Teatro Municipal, a classic theater built in 1911 with an intimate gilt and moss-green velvet interior.

Fernando and Humberto's exotic Boa sofa (2002), manufactured by Edra, is a twenty-first-century reinterpretation of the casual living concept made popular in the 1960s. The three-meter-long writhing mass is made of ninety meters of velvet tubing that loops into itself in a seemingly endless fashion. The sofa's polyurethane-filled interior accommodates varying users in a reclined position without the need for a conventional internal frame. The structureless and sensuous velvet coils can be readjusted into head- and armrests. Wide enough to cover a substantial portion of the user so as to serve as a blanket or cover, the loops emphasize the sofa's texture, softness, and warmth. **"The Boa was an attempt to construct a sofa without a metal structure,"** explains Fernando. However, the brothers were not interested in creating

just another sofa. It is an unexpected contemporary reinterpretation of classic furniture. **"Other designers had done beautiful, comfortable sofas,"** says Fernando. **"We admire them, you know, but we always like to investigate other sides of design. That's why it took us so long to design a sofa. There was a need for the Boa to work as a product as much as sculpture. It hurt our heads thinking about it!"** The design displays the Campanas' signature talent for twisting, threading, and braiding unlikely materials to create unusual furniture. Indeed, the designers often take a form developed earlier on and adapt it for another use; the Boa, for example, can be traced back to the objects presented in Projeto ABC in 1991. **"Looking at the first velvet object, it's like we were coming back to it years later,"** comments Humberto. **"Some ideas can evolve quite unconsciously."** Additionally, the lounger has formal connections to their iconic Vermelha chair, as if offering a microscopic view into its loose-fitting loops. While curvaceous and organic in composition, the boa sofa is also slightly unsettling. The object bears a striking resemblance to its more threatening namesake, the boa constrictor, found throughout the Brazilian Amazon basin. In 2006, the Italian manufacturer even went as far as presenting the seating unit in snakeskin-printed upholstery, replicating the reptile's ruddy brown color and contrasting saddles.

Fernando and Humberto's limited edition Drosera wall pocket (2007) for Vitra and the Vitra Edition, is a soft architectural alternative to mainstream wall organizers. Framed like a picture and hung on a wall, the object is constructed from unique fabric—a sturdy yet flexible copper mesh holds the shape of the gathers and folds

Projeto ABC
1991
Velvet and mixed media
Four artworks created for São Paulo's Pinacoteca do Estado

Drosera wall pocket, 2007, copper, fabric, and aluminum

Boa sofa, 2002, stuffed foam and velvet

that reveal and conceal the pockets' contents. More than a malleable container for the clutter one might want to keep out of sight, Drosera is also an alluring invitation to our curious side: the user is meant to slide their hand into the inviting folds of the velvet fabric. The aura of the Drosera wall pocket marches in tandem with its functionality. Additional individual pockets can be added to form a verdant vertical garden within the home or office. The Campanas' design is both practical and decorative. The organizer is named after a carnivorous plant (more commonly known as the sundew) that lures, captures,

and digests insects using tentacles with adhesive "dew." Numerous species, which vary greatly in size and form, can be found growing natively on nearly every continent, including South America. **"I guess most of our furniture resembles animals, plants, or trees in some way,"** muses Fernando. **"The landscape has always been part of our fantasies. This is because we spent our childhood and teens living with the Brasilia project, from going to Rio de Janeiro with our father, and to the Aterro do Flamengo, a big area between the Central and the Copacabana area, landscaped**

Kaiman Jacaré, 2006, foam and leather

by Roberto Burle Marx." **"Before him, people were looking to the gardens of Europe,"** adds Humberto. **"Burle Marx introduced Brazilian flora, which is very rich, to the gardens. He has influenced a lot of people."**

Comprising Edra's Historia Naturalis collection, the Campanas' Kaiman Jacaré (2006) and Aster Papposus (2006) seating units, like the Boa sofa, are flexible, natural forms inspired by Brazil's species-rich environment. Named after the Brazilian crocodile that lives along the

rivers and lakes in the seasonally flooded Pantanal region, Kaiman Jacaré appears at first glance to be a twisting mass of the carnivorous reptiles engaged in a feeding frenzy. Describing the collection, Cristina Morozzi asserts that "the humid, tropical feel pervading the work […] hints at violent sensations lying just below the surface."[1] The irregularly shaped and softly sculpted individual elements have been designed to be assembled and disassembled at will. Reconfigurable for a variety of spaces and functions, the seating units are sensuous and accommodating. But then the innocent object can

Kaiman Jacaré, 2006, foam and leather

become disconcerting when upholstered in crocodile-print leather. As with most of their designs, the Campanas closely guided the entire design process, conducting the initial studies and developing multiple iterations of prototypes to progressively refine the work. On many occasions, the designers try out these full-size models in their own homes to verify the performance or suitability of the proposed design, endlessly reassessing it.

With the same concept as Kaiman Jacaré in mind, the Campanas' Aster Papposus (2006) applied a new form to the modular lounge. Recalling the beanbag seats of the 1960s, the luxurious and playful system is composed of two asterisk-shaped sections, one stacked on top of the other. Like the Common Sunstar, or Crossaster papposus (the marine animal its name is derived from), Aster Papposus resembles a gigantic

starfish. Extending outward, eight inviting arms radiate from the center of the two identical components. The lower arms are reinforced with expanded polyurethane foam and Dacron to create a sturdy seat. The upper tentacles are stuffed with polyurethane and feathers for a soft backrest. Launched at the 2006 Salone Internazionale del Mobile, Milan, the piece stands testament to the designers' humorous experimentation with form and material. Fittingly, Aster Papposus is upholstered in a scaly iridescent fabric. Like many of the creatures in the Amazon, these Campana creations emanate a predatory sensuality that envelops and embraces their users.

1
Morozzi, Cristina, Edra catalogue, 2008. p. 274.

211

Aster Papposus, 2006, synthetic fabric and foam

Darrin Alfred

TransPlastic

Fernando and Humberto's TransPlastic collection has, in a variety of ways, brought the pair full circle. These hybridizations—cheap plastics combined with natural fibers—demonstrate the Campanas' assertion to understand, negotiate, and challenge differences. An amalgamation of forms, the objects effortlessly cross the boundaries of design, sculpture, and art to create new sustainable structures.

214

Developed as part of Artecnica's "Design with Conscience" campaign, Fernando and Humberto's TransNeomatic container collection (2007) is a clever combination of repurposed scooter tires interwoven with slim strips of natural wicker. A small-scale experiment alongside their TransPlastic series, the bowls underline the Campanas' long-standing conceptual, craft-oriented approach to design. **"This project gave birth to the TransPlastic collection first shown at Albion's galleries in 2007. I have always loved tires, especially when you see them abandoned in the street. I wondered whether we could make a fruit bowl out of one and weave it with wicker."**[1] By perverting the original function of the object, in this case, a tire, and applying handcrafted techniques, the designers have once again reinvented function and aesthetic. The works exemplify Fernando and Humberto's experimental collisions of materials and textures as natural wicker meets manufactured rubber.

"The project is also interesting because it is made in Vietnam by a local community. They go out and collect old tires—in Vietnam there are quite a lot of motorcycles."[2] Artecnica, a California-based

TransNeomatic
2007
Rubber and natural fiber

homeware company that has developed competitive products that encourage the survival of indigenous craft, chose to produce the fruit bowls in Vietnam due to the country's huge numbers of discarded tires. In Saigon alone, the ubiquitous motorcycles and scooters number in the millions. They are often the most practical form of transport in a city that lacks sufficient public transit or major roads. Before weaving can begin each tire must go through a steam-cleaning process to remove all dirt and grime. Afterward, the tires are finished with a biodegradable sealant to help protect the rubber from everyday use. The project has successfully empowered rural Vietnam's highly evolved community of skilled artisans. In fashioning the bowls collaboratively, Artecnica has also provided an opportunity for collaboration with Hmong women and Hai Tai rattan weavers working alongside Craft Link, a leading nonprofit organization that employs artisans and poor and marginalized Vietnamese people. In developing these products, the Campanas have employed eco-friendly materials and production methods while promoting manufacturing processes that are environmentally, socially, and economically

216

Meteor, 2007, steel, natural fiber, plastic, lighting system

sustainable. **"This is an example of globalization in favor of the environment, not in the destruction of it."** [3]

Fernando and Humberto's TransPlastic collection also utilizes a tradition of weaving to spin a surrealist tale in which a world filled with synthetic material, in due course, reverts back to its natural state. The collection, presented at London's Albion Gallery in 2007, articulates many of the polarities expressed throughout the Campanas' trajectory. The series of thirty-one individually handcrafted and varied prototypes explores a new vocabulary for the designers. It is an expressive and impressive investigation that combines traditional woven natural fibers with cheap plastic chairs and water containers, makeshift timber constructions, and steel structures. Fernando explains: **"We wanted to create a kind of fantasy. We imagined the world being attacked by nature. There would be so many plants that they would gradually engulf all man-made objects, becoming inseparable from them. You could call it a science fiction story."**

Island, 2007, steel, natural fiber, plastic, lighting system

217

Café chair, 2006, plastic, iron, natural fiber

Inspired by the native Brazilian trailing plant apuí, the collection of hybrid objects—regular chairs, multiple-seating units, large multifunctional pieces, and sculptural works referred to as "meteors" and "islands"—emulates the natural fiber's elasticity by means of junco, another type of liana. **"I feel passionate about the possibilities of different kinds of natural fiber. It has a special meaning for me because when I left law school, I used to make wicker baskets. It has taken me twenty years to develop this idea and to return to** **this material that appealed to me in my first steps as a designer."**[4] A parasitic vine that thrives in the Amazon, apuí is harvested commercially by hand in an effort to help preserve the forest's biodiversity. Fernando elaborates, **"In order to relieve the trees, to enable them to keep on growing, they cut down the vines. This is a sustainable method to help keep the forest alive, and provided the idea for this woven process."**

220

Library with table
2007
Plastic, steel, and natural fiber

Double chair, 2006, plastic and natural fiber

The rattan-like fiber is woven around plastic garden chairs forming a cocoon. Like the rain forest trees, the ever-present chairs are almost entirely contained and concealed by their organic prostheses. The "host" chairs subsequently take on a geographic dimension through organic shapes, adding value and comfort to the original material. These works are meant as an ironic comment on the invasion of plastic in everyday Brazilian life, the disappearance of traditional outdoor furniture—replaced first by woven plastic and then solid polypropylene—

and the unrelenting rise of the insidious modern plastic equivalent. **"Humberto and I were trying to make both a kind of joke and a criticism by attacking plastic chairs with wicker,"** says Fernando. **"We were attempting to bring some nobility to such banal chairs, even though wicker is also very cheap."** The majority of the prototypes were made by artisans whom the brothers hired from a Brazilian wicker furniture company. Humberto recollects: **"It was interesting because they were used to making very normal**

222

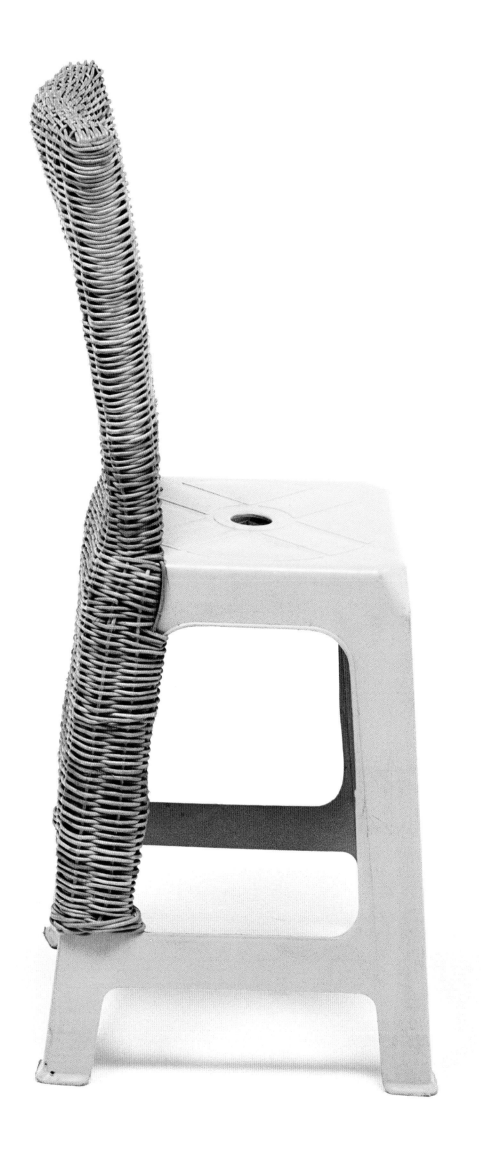

Children's chairs
2006
Plastic and natural fiber

chairs out of wicker. It took us six months to understand what we wanted to develop. We got hold of lots of these chairs but we didn't know what kinds of shapes to make or how to mix the two materials—we couldn't decide whether to hide the chairs or to reveal them. So it took a while for us to work out what we could achieve and how we could achieve it."

Large, uniquely sculptural works, such as the Una Famiglia chair (2006)[5] and massive TransRock chair (2006), integrate numerous plastic garden chairs into seating "islands." An unusually shaped wicker pod, Library with chair (2007) offers an opportunity to lose yourself within the confines of its embrace while providing an intimate reading space for one. Other man-made objects incorporated into these organic wicker forms include plastic water containers that Humberto collected over a three-year period. Woven together with the natural fiber, the canisters were combined to create numerous floor, wall, and table lamps like no others. Some wicker extensions appear to grow from or attach themselves to reclaimed leather stools, such as the Coast to Coast chair (2007) or the step-like Siwa chair (2007), while immense sculptural pieces called "meteors" are supported by an unseen system of welded metal and dotted with globular lights. Small, medium, and large versions of meteor-like works are gathered together to form the impressive lighting installation named TransCloud (2007). Humberto comments, **"For the artisans to understand the design process—to recuperate some traditional handcrafts, to adapt them and to make a dialogue with design—is a stimulating process. When a piece takes a long time to evolve, to explain and to make, we are relaxed about it and enjoy making a connection with everyone involved in its production."**

The Campanas' subsequent Trans… chair (2007) was designed especially for the Cooper-Hewitt, National Design Museum, New York. Unlike the previous objects, the Trans… chair is woven entirely in wicker, suggesting that nature has virtually completed its domination of synthetic materials. Reinforcing this battle lost (or won), the chair expels iconic plastic matter, like toys, dolls, flip-flops, and tires, from its wicker structure. **"It's like a detox for the chair,"** exclaims Fernando.

Una Famiglia chair, 2006, plastic, iron, and natural fiber

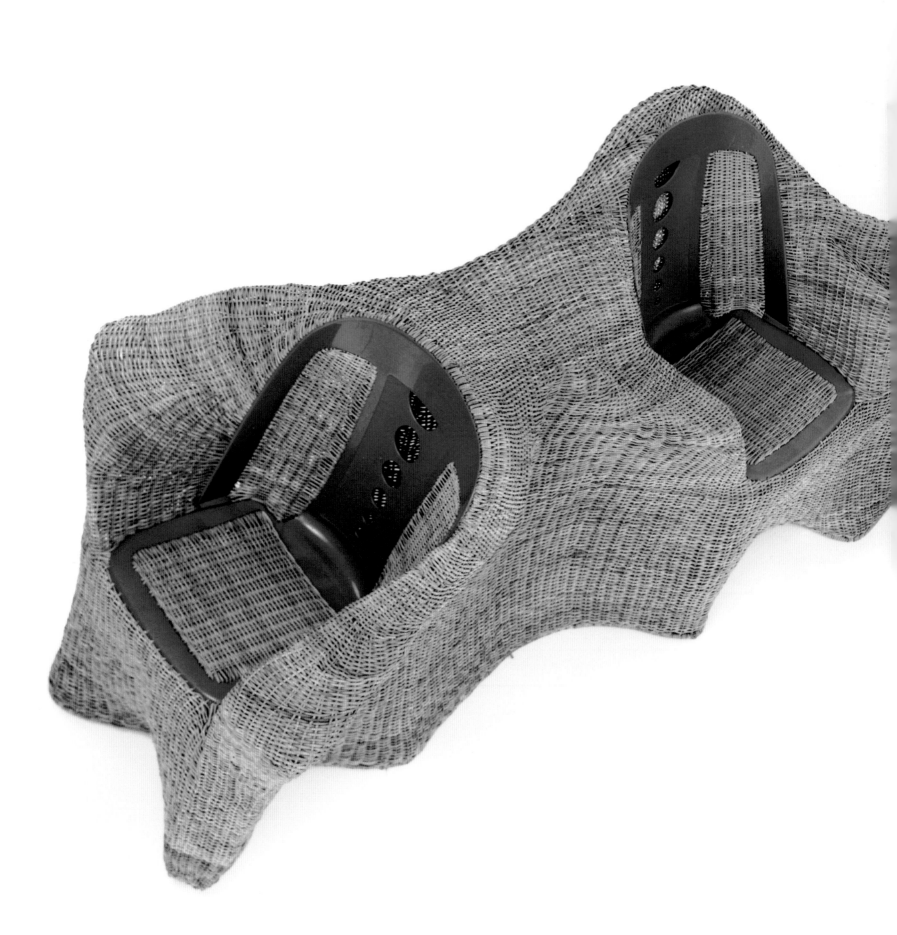

TransRock chair, 2006, plastic, iron, and natural fiber

Siwa chair, 2007, plastic, wood, leather, natural fiber, and steel

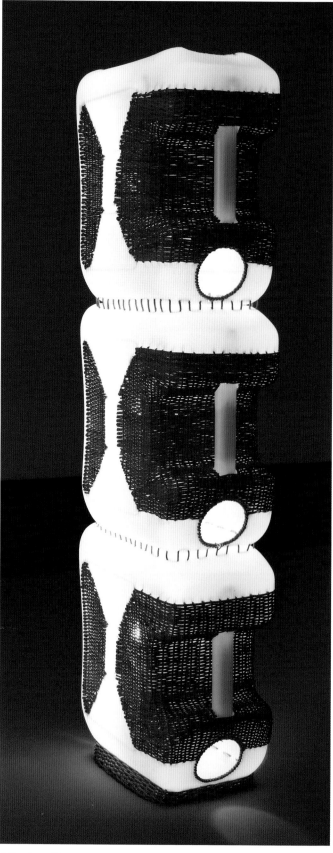

230

Gallon lamp III – phase two
2007
Plastic, natural fiber, lighting system

Gallon lamp IV – phase two
2007
Plastic, natural fiber, lighting system

Library with chair, 2007, plastic, steel, and natural fiber

At the end of 2007, the preceding research evolved organically into Cristalina (2008), a work for the Second Nature exhibition at 21_21 Design Sight in Tokyo, and Diamantina I, II, and III (2008), commissioned in honor of the Campanas receiving the prestigious Design Miami/ Designer of the Year Award 2008. Within Cristalina (named after a small Brazilian city known for the production of semiprecious stones) the vegetal world meets itself in a wicker and wood seating island. The Campanas, inspired by the nests of birds, created a large structure with branches woven into the seat. Craftsmen worked for hours to create this unusual design. Named after the Brazilian city and UNESCO World Heritage Site, the Campanas' Diamantina collection utilizes Brazilian wicker to create a number of "biomorphic islands" for Design Miami/ visitors to sit on and explore. The multi-seating units appear to have amethyst crystals emerging from within them. **"Amethyst is very present in Brazil's ecology,"** explains Humberto. **"The country is built on rock crystal—a lot of crystal! It is an element that features prominently in our lives. When we were kids we used to have crystals that our father brought for us. The Diamantina collection** **is a way of revealing the past, of bringing memories from childhood into the present and creating another vision of the materials that we used to play with when we were young."** The works can be seen as an evolution of the TransPlastic story line and perhaps its final chapter. They signify a synergy with the natural world as the amethyst emerges from within the organic material. Fernando elaborates, **"I love rock crystal and this project is an attempt to create a surprise between two different materials—crystal and wicker. We are constructing pieces that look like mountains and insert crystals into them, like something from a science fiction movie or a novel by Jules Verne."**

"Design for me is like telling a story. It has a beginning, a middle, and an end. I think a designer goes much deeper than function or form. Today, they bring emotion, because otherwise it would be really boring. I guess people like to have a relation-ship, they want to interact with design pieces, you know. And for me design is this: to bring emotion, to bring fun, and to bring joy to people."[6]

232

Gallon lamps installed at Albion Gallery, London

Coast to Coast chair
2007
Plastic, wood, leather, natural fiber, and steel

1
Humberto's remarks were quoted in "Special Video Feature: The Campana Brothers," *Dezeen*, http://www.dezeen.com/hsbc_feature.html, accessed December 2, 2008. [Adapted by author.]

2
Ibid [Adapted by author.]

3
Fernando's remarks were quoted in "Special Video Feature: The Campana Brothers," *Dezeen*, http://www.dezeen.com/hsbc_feature.html, accessed December 2, 2008. [Adapted by author.]

4
Humberto's remarks were quoted in "The Campana Brothers TransPlastic" Press Release, Albion, London [Adapted by author.]

5
Una Famiglia translates as "A family."

6
Humberto's remarks were quoted in "Special Video Feature: The Campana Brothers," *Dezeen*, http://www.dezeen.com/hsbc_feature.html, accessed December 2, 2008. [Adapted by author.]

Trans… chair, 2007, iron, natural fiber, and plastic objects

Diamantina III, 2008, iron, natural fiber, and stones

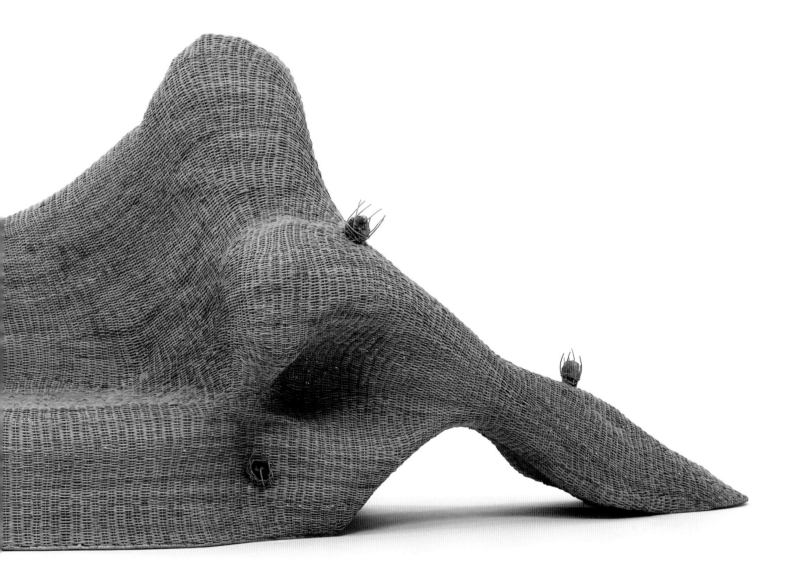

Diamantina III, 2008, iron, natural fiber, and stones

Following page: **Cristalina,** 2008, iron, natural fiber, and tree branch

SECTION 3

ESTUDIO CAMPANA

Unique and editioned pieces fabricated at the Campana brothers' studio

CATALOGUE

PROTOTYPES

Studies for Estudio Campana, industry partners, and special projects

INDUSTRY

Pieces fabricated by, and available from design industry partners

RAISONNÉ (SO FAR)

SPECIAL PROJECTS

Curated exhibitions, events, and one-off projects and commissions

1982

Humberto Campana
Brasilia sculpture
(Escultura Brasilia)

Bronze
c. 20 x 24 x 50 cm
c. 8 x 9.5 x 20 inches

1982

Humberto Campana
Labirinto sculpture
(Escultura Labirinto)

Terra-cotta
c. 35 x 25 x 20 cm
c. 14 x 10 x 8 inches

244

1982

Humberto Campana
Mirror
(Espelho)

Mirror and shells
c. 80 x 60 x 5 cm
c. 31.5 x 24 x 2 inches

1982

Humberto Campana
Untitled sculpture
(Escultura sem titulo)

Terra-cotta
c. 80 x 40 x 40 cm
c. 31.5 x 16 x 16 inches

1982

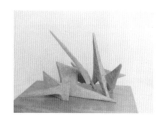

Humberto Campana
Untitled sculpture
(Escultura sem titulo)

Terra-cotta
c. 20 x 35 x 20 cm
c. 8 x 14 x 8 inches

1982

Humberto Campana
Untitled sculpture
(Escultura sem titulo)

Bronze
c. 50 x 40 x 40 cm
c. 20 x 16 x 16 inches

1987

Grelha sculpture
(Escultura Grelha)

Iron
c. 140 x 100 x 90 cm
c. 55 x 39 x 35 inches
Desconfortáveis collection

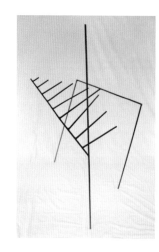

1987

Untitled sculpture
(Escultura sem titulo)

Iron
c. 110 x 15 x 100 cm
c. 43 x 6 x 39.5 inches
Desconfortáveis collection

1987

Untitled sculpture
(Escultura sem titulo)

Iron
c. 70 x 40 x 40 cm
c. 27.5 x 16 x 16 inches
Desconfortáveis collection

1987

Untitled sculpture
(Escultura sem titulo)

Iron
c. 150 x 50 x 30 cm
c. 59 x 20 x 12 inches
Desconfortáveis collection

1987

Untitled sculpture
(Escultura sem titulo)

Iron
c. 30 x 80 x 80 cm
(each piece 30 x 10 x 10 cm)
c. 12 x 31.5 x 31.5 inches
(each piece 12 x 4 x 4 inches)
Desconfortáveis collection

1987

Humberto Campana
Untitled drawing
(Desenho sem titulo)

Pastel on paper
59 x 42 cm
23.2 x 16.5 inches

1987

Humberto Campana
Untitled drawing
(Desenho sem titulo)

Pastel on paper
59 x 42 cm
23.2 x 16.5 inches

Humberto Campana
Untitled drawing II
(Desenho sem titulo II)

Pastel on paper
59 x 42 cm
23.2 x 16.5 inches

Humberto Campana
Untitled drawing III
(Desenho sem titulo III)

Pastel on paper
59 x 42 cm
23.2 x 16.5 inches

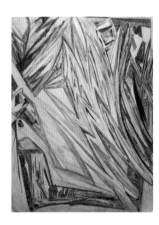

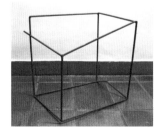

Untitled sculpture II
(Escultura sem titulo II)

Iron
c. 40 x 40 x 40 cm
c. 16 x 16 x 16 inches
Unique

Negativo chair
(Cadeira Negativo)

Iron
c. 120 x 50 x 50 cm
c. 47 x 20 x 20 inches
Desconfortáveis collection
Unique

Untitled sculpture
(Escultura sem titulo)

Iron
c. 148 x 130 x 40 cm
c. 58 x 51 x 16 inches
Unique

Positivo chair
(Cadeira Positivo)

Iron
c. 110 x 50 x 50 cm
c. 43 x 20 x 20 inches
Desconfortáveis collection
Unique

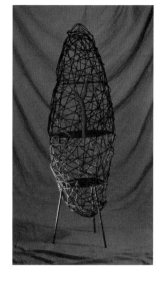

Casulo cabinet
(Armario Casulo)

Iron and jabuticabeira branch
170 x 60 x 60 cm
67 x 23.6 x 23.6 inches
Organicos series
Unique
Photo © Andrés Otero

245

Arado fruit bowl
(Fruteira Arado)

Iron
c. 20 x 30 x 30 cm
c. 8 x 12 x 12 inches
Unique
Photo © Luis Calazans

Blade chair
(Cadeira Blade)

Iron
c. 70 x 40 x 40 cm
c. 28 x 16 x 16 inches
Desconfortáveis collection
Unique
Photo © Luis Calazans

Cerca screen
(Biombo Cerca)

Iron
c. 140 x 120 x 40 cm
c. 55 x 47 x 16 inches
Desconfortáveis collection
Unique
Photo © Luis Calazans

Copper plate
(Prato de cobre)

Copper
5 x 46 x 47 cm
2 x 18.1 x 18.5 inches
Desconfortáveis collection
Unique

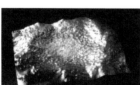

Costela chair
(Cadeira Costela)

Iron
c. 130 x 40 x 40 cm
c. 51 x 16 x 16 inches
Desconfortáveis collection
Unique
Photo © Diogo Santos

Flama chair
(Cadeira Flama)

Iron
c. 130 x 50 x 90 cm
c. 51 x 20 x 35 inches
Desconfortáveis collection
Unique
Photo © Luis Calazans

Flintstones chair
(Cadeira Flintstones)

Iron
c. 90 x 60 x 140 cm
c. 35 x 24 x 55 inches
Desconfortáveis collection
Unique
Photo © Luis Calazans

Hate 1 chair
(Cadeira Hate 1)

Iron
c. 102 x 36 x 36 cm
c. 40 x 14 x 14 inches
Desconfortáveis collection
Unique
Photo © Andreas Heiniger

Hate 2 chair
(Cadeira Hate 2)

Iron
c. 98 x 36 x 36 cm
c. 39 x 14 x 14 inches
Desconfortáveis collection
Unique
Photo © Andreas Heiniger

Hate 3 chair
(Cadeira Hate 3)

Iron
101 x 36 x 36 cm
39.8 x 14.2 x 14.2 inches
Desconfortáveis collection
Unique
Photo © Andreas Heiniger

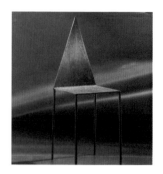

Jean Genet chair
(Cadeira Jean Genet)

Iron and copper
c. 140 x 40 x 40 cm
c. 55 x 16 x 16 inches
Desconfortáveis collection
Unique
Photo © Luis Calazans

K chair
(Cadeira K)

Iron
c. 53 x 40 x 160 cm
c. 21 x 16 x 63 inches
Desconfortáveis collection
Unique

1989

Peixe chair
(Cadeira Peixe)

Iron and copper
c. 170 x 35 x 60 cm
c. 67 x 14 x 24 inches
Desconfortáveis collection
Unique
Photo © Luis Calazans

1989

Samambaia chair
(Cadeira Samambaia)

Iron
105 x 66 x 93 cm
41.3 x 26 x 36.6 inches
Desconfortáveis collection
Unique
Photo © Andreas Heiniger

1989

Trono chair
(Cadeira Trono)

Iron and copper
c. 90 x 40 x 50 cm
c. 35 x 16 x 20 inches
Desconfortáveis collection
Unique
Photo © Diogo Santos

1989

Untitled chair
(Cadeira sem titulo)

Iron
40 x 75 x 106 cm
15.7 x 29.5 x 41.7 inches
Desconfortáveis collection
Unique
Photo © Luis Calazans

1989

Liana chair
(Cadeira Liana)

Iron
140 x 40 x 60 cm
55.1 x 15.7 x 23.6 inches
Desconfortáveis collection
Unique

1989

Untitled chair
(Cadeira sem titulo)

Iron
c. 38 x 38 x 100 cm
c. 15 x 15 x 39 inches
Desconfortáveis collection
Unique

1989

Untitled chair
(Cadeira sem titulo)

Aluminum
c. 100 x 40 x 40 cm
c. 47 x 16 x 16 inches
Desconfortáveis collection
Unique
Photo © Luis Calazans

1989

Pneu chair
(Cadeira Pneu)

Iron and car tire
c. 150 x 40 x 40 cm
c. 59 x 16 x 16 inches
Desconfortáveis collection
Unique

1989

Newman chair
(Cadeira Newman)

Iron
c. 120 x 30 x 60 cm
c. 47 x 12 x 24 inches
Desconfortáveis collection
Unique
Photo © Luis Calazans

247

1989

Untitled chair
(Cadeira sem titulo)

Iron and copper
c. 90 x 40 x 120 cm
c. 35 x 16 x 47 inches
Desconfortáveis collection
Unique
Photo © Luis Calazans

1989

Untitled fruit bowl
(Fruteira sem titulo)

Iron and screws
13 x 40 x 41 cm
5.1 x 15.7 x 16.1 inches
Desconfortáveis collection
Unique

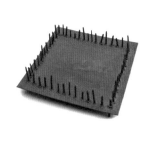

Untitled fruit bowl
(Fruteira sem titulo)

Copper and iron
c. 20 x 50 x 50 cm
c. 8 x 20 x 20 inches
Desconfortáveis collection
Unique

Yanomami chair
(Cadeira Yanomami)

Iron
c. 70 x 40 x 40 cm
c. 27.5 x 16 x 16 inches
Desconfortáveis collection
Unique
Photo © Luis Calazans

248

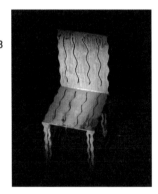

Yanomami table
(Mesa Yanomami)

Iron
c. 40 x 40 x 40 cm
c. 16 x 16 x 16 inches
Desconfortáveis collection
Unique
Photo © Luis Calazans

Zorro table
(Mesa Zorro)

Iron
c. 40 x 13 x 90 cm
c. 16 x 5 x 35 inches
Desconfortáveis collection
Unique
Photo © Luis Calazans

Martelo chair
(Cadeira Martelo)

Wood and rubber hammers
100 x 50 x 50 cm
39.4 x 19.7 x 19.7 inches
Unique
Photo © Andreas Heiniger

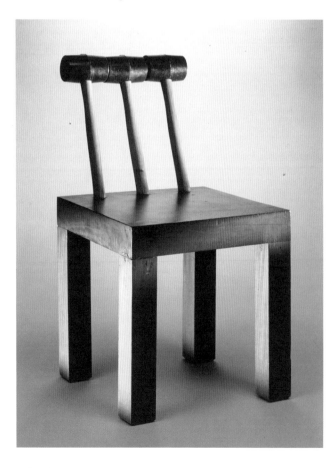

Ponte fruit bowl
(Fruteira Ponte)

Iron and nails
c. 15 x 25 x 50 cm
c. 6 x 10 x 20 inches
Unique
Photo © Luis Calazans

Untitled bench
(Banco sem titulo)

Wood and rubber
c. 80 x 80 x 140 cm
c. 31.5 x 31.5 x 55 inches
Unique

Trindade chair
(Cadeira Trindade)

Wood and rubber
c. 100 x 50 x 40 cm
c. 39 x 20 x 16 inches
Unique

Untitled chair
(Cadeira sem titulo)

Stainless steel
c. 110 x 50 x 60 cm
c. 43 x 20 x 24 inches
Unique

Untitled chair
(Cadeira sem titulo)

Copper
c. 120 x 45 x 80 cm
c. 47 x 18 x 31.5 inches
Unique

Untitled sculpture
(Escultura sem titulo)

Iron
c. 40 x 140 x 160 cm
c. 16 x 55 x 63 inches
Unique
Photo © Diogo Santos

Untitled sculpture
(Escultura sem titulo)

Iron
c. 153 x 74 x 72 cm
c. 60 x 29 x 28 inches
Unique
Photo © Romulo Fialdini

Untitled vase
(Vaso sem titulo)

Iron and screws
c. 25 x 10 x 10 cm
c. 10 x 4 x 4 inches
Unique
Photo © Luis Calazans

Via Crucis
(Candelabro Via Crucis)

Iron and barbed wire
c. 50 x 35 x 35 cm
c. 20 x 14 x 14 inches
Edition of 2
Photo © Luis Calazans

Aluminum plate
(Prato de Aluminio)

Aluminum
5 x 23 x 35 cm
2 x 9 x 13.8 inches
Organicos series
Photo © Luis Calazans

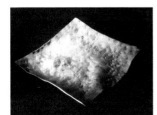

Agua chair
(Cadeira Agua)

Stainless steel, glass, and
water
c. 120 x 50 x 40 cm
c. 47 x 20 x 16 inches
Unique
Photo © Andreas Heiniger

Bola fruit bowl
(Fruteira Bola)

Wood and aluminum
c. 15 x 30 x 30 cm
c. 6 x 12 x 12 inches
Organicos series
Unique

Costela fruit bowl
(Fruteira Costela)

Die-cast aluminum and
jabuticabeira branch
54 x 21 x 22 cm
21.3 x 8.3 x 8.7 inches
Organicos series
Unique
Photo © Luis Calazans

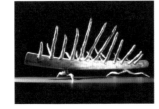

Jabuticaba fruit bowl
(Fruteira Jabuticaba)

Die-cast aluminum and
jabuticabeira branch
18 x 40 x 40 cm
7 x 16 x 16 inches
Organicos series
Unique
Photo © Luis Calazans

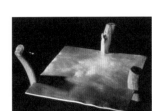

Tiranossauro container
(Estante Tiranossauro)

Wood and aluminum
180 x 60 x 45 cm
70.9 x 23.6 x 17.7 inches
Organicos series
Edition of 2
Photo © Andrés Otero

Raiz fruit bowl
(Fruteira Raiz)

Rock and aluminum
c. 15 x 40 x 40 cm
c. 6 x 16 x 16 inches
Organicos series
Unique

Untitled candleholder
(Castiçal sem titulo)

Wood and aluminum
c. 30 x 15 x 15 cm
c. 12 x 6 x 6 inches
Organicos series
Unique

Untitled fruit bowl
(Fruteira sem titulo)

Wood and aluminum
c. 5 x 10 x 25 cm
c. 2 x 4 x 10 inches
Organicos series
Unique
Photo © Diogo Santos

Untitled plate
(Prato sem titulo)

Rock and aluminum
c. 5 x 10 x 15 cm
c. 2 x 4 x 6 inches
Organicos series
Unique

250

Untitled vase
(Vaso sem titulo)

Aluminum
c. 10 x 10 x 2 cm
c. 4 x 4 x 0.8 inches
Organicos series
Unique
Photo © Luis Calazans

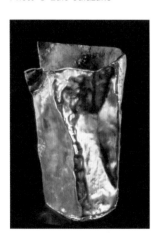

Bob chair
(Poltrona Bob)

Iron
c. 80 x 60 x 120 cm
c. 31.5 x 24 x 47 inches
Unique
Photo © Andreas Heiniger

Nervos chair
(Cadeira Nervos)

Iron
c. 130 x 55 x 100 cm
c. 51 x 22 x 39 inches
Unique
Photo © Andrés Otero

Coal candleholder
(Castiçal de carvão)

Aluminum and coal
29 x 29 x 38 cm
11.4 x 11.4 x 15 inches

Natureza Morta screen
(Biombo Natureza Morta)

Charcoal, wood, velvet,
aluminum
193 x 24 x 113 cm
76 x 9.4 x 44.5 inches
Natureza Morta series
Unique
Photo © Andrés Otero

Natureza Morta table
(Mesa Natureza Morta)

Charcoal, wood, velvet,
aluminum
70 x 60 x 60 cm
27.6 x 23.6 x 23.6 inches
Natureza Morta series
Unique
Photo © Andrés Otero

Obelisco cabinet
(Gaveteiro Obelisco)

Iron
157 x 50 x 51 cm
61.8 x 19.7 x 20.1 inches
Edition of 2

Untitled cabinet
(Estante sem titulo)

Iron and stones
157 x 57 x 55 cm
61.8 x 22.4 x 21.7 inches
Unique

Untitled vase
(Vaso sem titulo)

Aluminum
c. 10 x 10 x 2 cm
c. 4 x 4 x 0.8 inches
Amassados series
Unique

Untitled cabinet and stool
(Armário e banco sem titulo)

Wood and aluminum
Cabinet: c. 160 x 45 x 45 cm /
63 x 18 x 18 inches
Stool: c. 50 x 40 x 45 cm /
20 x 16 x 18 inches
Organicos Series
Unique

Ninho basket
(Cesta Ninho)

Aluminum
Large: 21.5 x Ø 24.5 cm /
8.5 x Ø 9.6 inches
Small: 16 x Ø 21 cm /
6.3 x Ø 8.3 inches
Ninho collection phase 1 series
Edition of c. 500

Ninho fruit bowl round tall
(Fruteira Ninho redonda alta)

Aluminum
21 x Ø 40 cm
8.3 x Ø 8.7 inches
Ninho collection phase 1 series
Edition of c. 500

Ninho vase
(Vaso Ninho)

Aluminum and glass
Large: 35 x Ø 13 cm /
13.8 x Ø 5.1 inches
Small: 26 x Ø 12 cm /
10.2 x Ø 4.7 inches
Ninho collection phase 1 series
Edition of c. 500

Ninho fruit bowl elliptical
(Fruteira Ninho Eliptica)

Aluminum
12.5 x 48.5 x 24 cm
4.9 x 19.1 x 9.4 inches
Ninho collection phase 1 series
Edition of c. 500

Ninho fruit bowl triangular
(Fruteira Ninho Triangular)

Aluminum
12.5 x 43.5 x 40 cm
4.9 x 17.1 x 15.7 inches
Ninho collection phase 1 series
Edition of c. 500
Photo © Andrés Otero

Ninho fruit bowl round small
(Fruteira Ninho redonda pequena)

Aluminum
12 x Ø 40 cm
4.7 x Ø 15.7 inches
Ninho collection phase 1 series
Edition of c. 500

Projeto ABC
(Projeto ABC)

Velvet and mixed media
Various dimensions
Four sculptures were made for
this exhibition together with
works by Nazareth Pacheco
at the Pinacoteca do Estado,
São Paulo

Favela chair
(Poltrona Favela)

Wood
110 x 100 x 110 cm
43.3 x 39.4 x 43.3 inches
Edition of 2
Photo © Andreas Heiniger

Geografica table
(Mesa Geografica)

Chipboard, epoxy resin, acrylic
paint
90 x 160 x 120 cm
35.4 x 63 x 47.2 inches
Unique
Photo © Andrés Otero

251

Discos chair
(Cadeira Discos)

Iron and wood
90 x 120 x 82 cm
35.4 x 47.2 x 32.3 inches
Unique
Photo © Andreas Heiniger

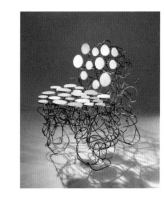

Raiz ashtray
(Cinzeiro Raiz)

Aluminum
13 x 13 x 4 cm
5.1 x 5.1 x 1.6 inches
Edition of 3
(1 aluminum and 2 stainless
steel)

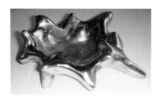

1992

Untitled lamp
(Luminária sem titulo)

Aluminum wire
c. 60 x 30 x 30 cm
c. 23.6 x 11.8 x 11.8 inches
Photo © Andrés Otero

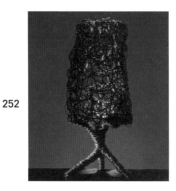

252

1992

Untitled lamp
(Luminária sem titulo)

Aluminum wire
c. 210 x 60 x 50 cm
c. 82.7 x 23.6 x 19.7 inches

1993

3 in 1 chair
(Cadeira 3 em 1)

Wood, aluminum, cotton ropes
98 x 66 x 75 cm
38.6 x 26 x 29.5 inches
Edição 93 collection
Unique
(a red version was also
produced, now destroyed)
Photo © Estudio Campana
collection

1993

Discos table
(Mesa Discos)

Wood, aluminum wires, iron
c. 90 x 150 x 150 cm
c. 35 x 59 x 59 inches
Edição 93 collection
Unique
Photo © Estudio Campana
collection

1993

Azul chair
(Poltrona Azul)

Cotton ropes and stainless
steel structure
77 x 98 x 80 cm
30.3 x 38.6 x 31.5 inches
Ropes collection
Edition of c. 5
Photo © Andreas Heiniger

1993

Verde chair
(Cadeira Verde)

Cotton ropes and stainless
steel structure
88 x 45 x 54 cm
34.6 x 17.7 x 21.3 inches
Ropes collection
Unique
Photo © Estudio Campana
collection

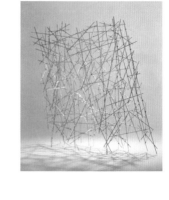

1993

Vermelha chair
(Cadeira Vermelha)

Cotton ropes and stainless
steel structure
80 x 60 x 80 cm
31.5 x 23.6 x 31.5 inches
Ropes collection
Edition of c. 5
Photo © Andreas Heiniger

1993

Escultura screen
(Biombo Escultura)

Anodized aluminum
200 x 70 x 160 cm
78.7 x 27.6 x 63 inches
Edition of 11
Photo © Andrés Otero

1993

Fios table
(Mesa Fios)

Aluminum wires, glass, iron
47 x 80 x 132 cm
18.5 x 31.5 x 52 inches
Unique
Photo © Andreas Heiniger

1993

Ciclone paper bin
(Lixeira Ciclone)

Cotton ropes and stainless
steel structure
88 x 45 x 54 cm
34.6 x 17.7 x 21.3 inches
Ropes collection
Unique
Photo © Estudio Campana
collection

1993

Fitas table
(Mesa Fitas)

Aluminum strips
c. 40 x 90 x 130 cm
c. 16 x 35 x 51 inches
Unique
Photo © Andreas Heiniger

1993

Glove vase
(Vaso Luva)

Iron and plastic glove
c. 25 x 12 x 12 cm
c. 10 x 5 x 5 inches
Edition of 100
Available from Zona D
Produced by Estudio Campana
Photo © Andrés Otero

1993

Papelão cabinet
(Armario Papelão)

Corrugated cardboard and
aluminum
c. 165 x 80 x 80 cm
c. 65 x 31.5 x 31.5 inches
Papelão collection
Unique
Photo © Andrés Otero

1993

Papelão lamp
(Luminária Papelão)

Corrugated cardboard and
aluminum
c. 40 x 20 x 20 cm
c. 16 x 8 x 8 inches
Papelão collection
Unique
Photo © Andrés Otero

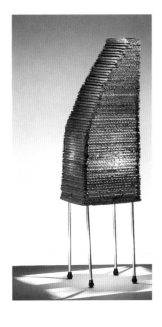

1993

Papelão lamp
(Luminária Papelão)

Corrugated cardboard and
aluminum
c. 45 x 15 x 30 cm
c. 18 x 6 x 12 inches
Papelão collection
Unique
Photo © Estudio Campana
collection

1993

Papelão lamp
(Luminária Papelão)

Corrugated cardboard and
aluminum
c. 33 x 22 x 18 cm
c. 13 x 9 x 7 inches
Papelão collection
Unique
Photo © Estudio Campana
collection

1993

Papelão lamp
(Luminária Papelão)

Corrugated cardboard and
aluminum
c. 50 x 25 x 25 cm
c. 20 x 10 x 10 inches
Papelão collection
Edition of 2
Photo © Andrés Otero

1993

Papelão screen
(Biombo Papelão)

Corrugated cardboard and
steel wire
c. 170 x 5 x 170 cm
c. 67 x 2 x 67 inches
Papelão collection
Unique
Photo © Andrés Otero

1993

Papelão screen
(Biombo Papelão)

Corrugated cardboard and
aluminum
c. 260 x 230 x 60 cm
c. 102 x 91 x 24 inches
Papelão collection
Unique

1993

Papelão sofa
(Sofá Papelão)

Cardboard and stainless steel
structure
80 x 70 x 160 cm
31.5 x 27.6 x 63 inches
Papelão collection
Edition of c. 5
Photo © Andrés Otero

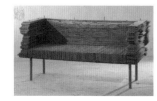

1993

Papelão table
(Mesa Papelão)

Corrugated cardboard and
aluminum
c. 40 x 35 x 35 cm
c. 16 x 14 x 14 inches
Papelão collection
Unique
Photo © Andrés Otero

1993

Papelão table
(Mesa Papelão)

Corrugated cardboard and
aluminum wires
c. 100 x 80 x 80 cm
c. 39 x 31.5 x 31.5 inches
Papelão collection
Unique
Photo © Andrés Otero

1993

Papelão table
(Mesa Papelão)

Corrugated cardboard and
aluminum wires
c. 100 x 80 x 80 cm
c. 39 x 31.5 x 31.5 inches
Papelão collection
Unique
Photo © Andrés Otero

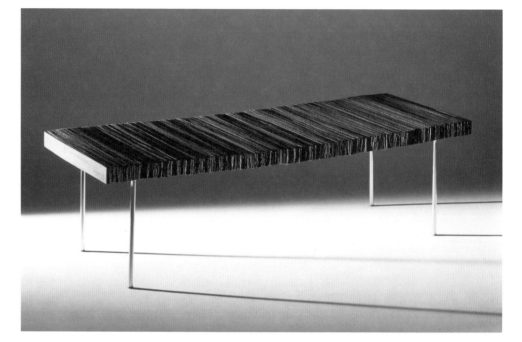

1993

Untitled cabinet
(Estante sem titulo)

Wood, aluminum, velvet
c. 175 x 40 x 40 cm
c. 69 x 16 x 16 inches
Unique
Photo © Andrés Otero

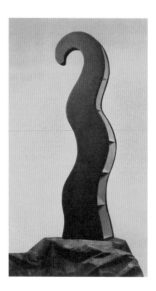

1993

Untitled chair
(Cadeira sem titulo)

Wood, aluminum, velvet
c. 110 x 40 x 90 cm
c. 43 x 16 x 35 inches
Unique
Photo © Andrés Otero

1993

Study for a chair
(Estudo para cadeira)

Iron, cotton ropes, fiber
170 x 62 x 40 cm
67 x 24.4 x 15.7 inches

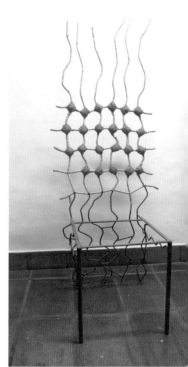

1993

Study for a table
(Estudo para mesa)

Iron, wood, fiber
44 x 50 x 60 cm
17.3 x 19.7 x 23.6 inches

1993

Untitled fruit bowl
(Fruteira sem título)

Aluminum wires
c. 10 x 30 x 50 cm
c. 4 x 12 x 20 inches

1993

Untitled table
(Mesa sem título)

Aluminum wire, iron, wood
c. 90 x 130 x 130 cm
c. 35 x 51 x 51 inches

1993

Pé de Galinha
(Pé de Galinha)

Picture – glass and chicken's foot
Produced by Estudio Campana
Photo © Andrés Otero

"This is a conceptual picture taken to register an idea that came to us during a long-awaited dinner. We wanted to make a shock, a collision between the glass and the chicken's foot—two different molecular universes!"

1994

Cerca screen
(Biombo Cerca)

Stainless steel and wicker rods
c. 180 x 50 x 60 cm
c. 71 x 20 x 24 inches
Unique
Photo © Andreas Heiniger

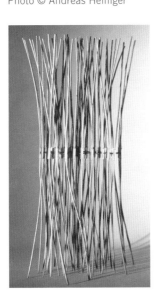

1994

Pilha screen
(Biombo Pilha)

Wicker rods, iron and metal wheels
c. 200 x 40 x 100 cm
c. 79 x 156 x 39 inches
Unique
Photo © Andrés Otero

1994

Untitled lamp
(Luminária sem título)

Iron structure and PVC threads
c. 140 x 30 x 30 cm
c. 55 x 12 x 12 inches
Edition of c. 30
Photo © Andrés Otero

1994

Vermelha stool
(Banco Vermelha)

Aluminum and cotton rope
c. 40 x 90 x 90 cm
c. 16 x 35 x 35 inches
Ropes collection
Edition of 3
Photo © Andrés Otero

1994

Small Memory Tower
(Pequena Torre de Memórias)

Corrugated cardboard and steel, aluminum, and magnets
c. 180 x 50 x 50 cm
c. 71 x 20 x 20 inches
Photo © Luis Calazans
Included in *Abitare il Tempo* – an exhibition curated by Sawaya Moroni and Vanni Pasca, Italy

1995

Bubble wrap chair
(Poltrona plastico bolha)

Plastic bubble sheet and chrome-plated iron
110 x 70 x 60 cm
43.3 x 27.6 x 23.6 inches
Edition of 3
Photo © Andreas Heiniger

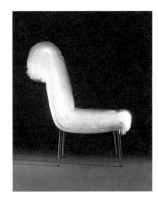

1995

Bamboo lamp
(Luminária Bambú)

Bamboo and iron
Large: c. 60 x 40 x 20 cm /
24 x 16 x 8 inches
Small: c. 43 x 16.5 x 59 cm /
17 x 6.5 x 23 inches
Edition of c. 40
Photo © Andreas Heiniger

255

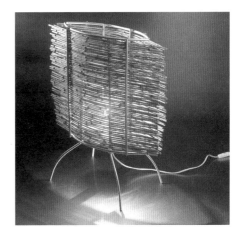

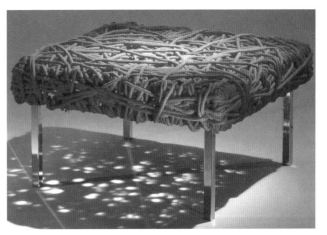

Inflatable table
(Mesa Inflável)

PVC film and anodized
aluminum
45 x 40 x 40 cm
17.7 x 15.7 x 15.7 inches
Edition of c. 100
Photo © Andrés Otero

1995

Jardim easy chair
(Poltrona Jardim)

Plastic hose and stainless steel
110 x 40 x 50 cm
43.3 x 15.7 x 19.7 inches
Hoses collection
Edition of 5
Photo © Andreas Heiniger

256

1995

Jardim chair
(Cadeira Jardim)

Plastic hose and chrome-plated
iron
90 x 60 x 60 cm
35.4 x 23.6 x 23.6 inches
Hoses collection
Small edition
Photo © Andreas Heiniger

1995

Papelão chair
(Cadeira Papel)

Corrugated cardboard and iron
87 x 40 x 52 cm
34.3 x 15.7 x 20.5 inches
Papel collection
Edition of c. 15
Photo © Andrés Otero

1995

Zig Zag screen
(Biombo Zig Zag)

Chrome-plated iron and PVC
threads
175 x 20 x 80 cm
68.9 x 7.9 x 31.5 inches
Zig Zag collection
Unique
Photo © Andrés Otero

1995

Papelão screen
(Biombo Papel)

Corrugated cardboard and iron
180 x 50 x 5 cm
70.9 x 19.7 x 2 inches
Papel collection
Edition of c. 20
Photo © Andrés Otero

1995

Untitled bench
(Banco sem titulo)

Plastic hose and painted iron
95 x 185 x 45 cm
37.4 x 72.8 x 17.7 inches
Produced by Estudio Campana
and Pedro Useche

1996

Arco chair
(Cadeira Arco)

Stainless steel, foam,
synthetic leather
c. 70 x 50 x 50 cm
c. 28 x 20 x 20 inches
Edition of 5
Photo © Estudio Campana
collection

1996

Escudo fruit bowl
(Fruteira Escudo)

Polypropylene and aluminum
structure
10 x 35 x 36 cm
3.9 x 13.8 x 14.2 inches
Escudo collection
Large-scale production by
Estudio Campana
Photo © Andrés Otero

1996

Escudo lamp
(Luminária Escudo)

Polypropylene and aluminum
structure
35 x 35 x 5 cm
13.8 x 13.8 x 2 inches
Escudo collection
Large-scale production by
Estudio Campana
Photo © Andrés Otero

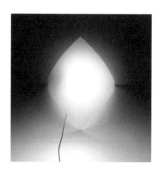

1996

Escudo magazine holder
(Revisteiro Escudo)

Polypropylene and aluminum
structure
30 x 20 x 35 cm
11.8 x 7.9 x 13.8 inches
Escudo collection
Large-scale production by
Estudio Campana
Photo © Andrés Otero

Estela lamp
(Luminária Estela)

Web stiffened with gum and
iron
40 x 25 x 30 cm
15.7 x 9.8 x 11.8 inches
Estela collection
Large-scale production by
Estudio Campana
Photo © Andreas Heiniger

Tela garbage can
(Lixeira Tela)

Chrome-plated iron and nylon
fabric
40 x 22 x 50 cm
15.7 x 8.7 x 19.7 inches
Estela collection
Edition of c. 100
Photo © Andreas Heiniger

Untitled lamp
(Luminária sem titulo)

Polypropylene and aluminum
structure
40 x 25 x 30 cm
15.7 x 9.8 x 11.8 inches

Alvo clothes holder
(Mancebo Alvo)

Iron
154 x 44 x 40 cm
60.6 x 17.3 x 15.7 inches
Edition of 3
Photo © Andrés Otero

Untitled chair
(Cadeira sem titulo)

Stainless steel and felt
c. 100 x 70 x 130 cm
c. 39 x 28 x 51 inches

Animado carpet
(Tapete Animado)

Artificial grass, leather, rubber
c. 200 x 90 cm
c. 79 x 35 inches
Photo © Andreas Heiniger

257

Estela magazine holder
(Revisteiro Estela)

Chrome-plated iron and nylon
fabric
c. 30 x 25 x 50 cm
c. 12 x 10 x 20 inches
Estela collection
Small-scale production by
Estudio Campana
Photo © Andrés Otero

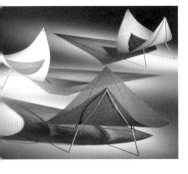

Estela tall lamp
(Luminária alta Estela)

Chrome-plated iron and nylon
fabric
100 x 30 x 70 cm
39.4 x 11.8 x 27.6 inches
Estela collection
Edition of c. 20
Photo © Andrés Otero

Untitled chaise longue
(Chaise longue sem titulo)

Bamboo
c. 80 x 50 x 150 cm
c. 31.5 x 20 x 59 inches

Cone bench
(Banco Cone)

Stainless steel and
polycarbonate sheet
c. 45 x 60 x 65 cm
c. 18 x 24 x 26 inches
Small edition

1997

Cone chair
(Cadeira Cone)

Stainless steel and
polycarbonate sheet
c. 89 x 83 x 96 cm
c. 35 x 32 x 38 inches
Edition of c. 20
Photo © Andreas Heiniger

258

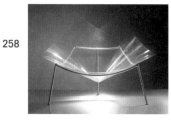

1997

Gangorra bench
(Banco Gangorra)

Iron with electrostatic paint
c. 112 x 49 x 90 cm
c. 44 x 19 x 35 inches
Unique
Photo © Andreas Heiniger

1997

Inflatable vase
(Vaso Inflável)

PVC film and PVC tube
c. 28 x 10 x 10 cm
c. 11 x 4 x 4 inches
Edition of c. 100
Photo © Andrés Otero

1997

Labirinto bookshelf
(Estante Labirinto)

Sheet of naval aluminum
c. 140 x 30 x 140 cm
c. 55 x 12 x 55 inches
Edition of 3
Photo © Andrés Otero

1997

Mais fruit bowl
(Fruteira Mais)

Polystyrene
7 x 35 x 35 cm
2.8 x 13.8 x 13.8 inches
Edition of c. 20
Photo © Andrés Otero

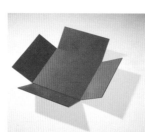
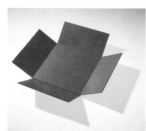

1997

Mais waste basket
(Lixeira Mais)

Aluminum and plastic sheet
40 x 25 x 25 cm
15.7 x 9.8 x 9.8 inches
Edition of c. 20
Photo © Andrés Otero

1997

Touch cushion
(Porta retrato Touch)

PVC film, gel, picture
5 x 30 x 30 cm
2 x 11.8 x 11.8 inches
Photo © Andrés Otero

1997

Trapo lamp
(Luminária Trapo)

Rubber, PVC, lamp
c. 30 x 90 cm
c. 12 x 35 inches
Photo © Andrés Otero
A flat version of the Trapo lamp
also exists.

1997

Travesseiro lamp
(Luminária Travesseiro)

Nylon fabric, polycarbonate,
acrylic blanket, fluorescent
lamp
c. 20 x 50 x 50 cm
c. 8 x 20 x 20 inches
Produced by Kika Chic, Brazil
Photo © Andrés Otero

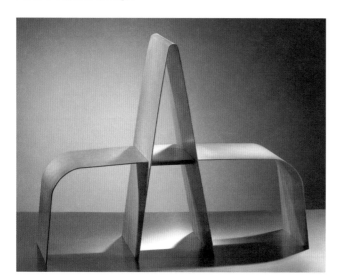

1997

Zeppelin lamp
(Luminária Zeppelin)

PVC film, lamp
c. 30 x 15 x 15 cm
c. 12 x 6 x 6 inches
Edition of c. 50
Photo © Andreas Heiniger

1997

Zig Zag fruit bowl I
(Fruteira Zig Zag I)

Aluminum and PVC wires
c. 10 x 40 x 40 cm
c. 4 x 16 x 16 inches
Zig Zag collection
Edition of c. 20
Photo © Andrés Otero

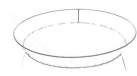

1997

Zig Zag fruit bowl II
(Fruteira Zig Zag II)

Aluminum and PVC wires
Round: c. 40 x 40 cm /
c. 16 x 16 inches
Oval: c. 35 x 50 cm /
c. 14 x 20 inches
Zig Zag collection
Small edition
Photo © Andrés Otero

1997

Estela lamp
(Luminária Estela)

Web stiffened with gum and
iron
40 x 25 x 30 cm /
15.7 x 9.8 x 11.8 inches
66 x 28 x 33 cm /
26 x 11 x 13 inches
Produced by Oluce, Italy
Photo © Oluce

1997

Carpete lamp
(Luminária Carpete)

Foam and lamp
c. 150 x 80 cm
c. 59 x 31.5 inches
Photo © Andrés Otero

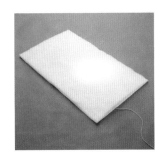

1997

Cone studies
(Estudos para a cadeira Cone)

EVA and metal
c. 15 x 10 x 18 cm
c. 6 x 4 x 7 inches

1997

Hanging shelves
(Gaveteiro Pendurado)

Wood and steel wire
c. 200 x 45 x 45 cm
c. 79 x 18 x 18 inches
Photo © Estudio Campana
collection

1997

Untitled lamp
(Luminária sem titulo)

Acrylic, lamp, nylon fabric
120 x 45 cm
47.2 x 17.7 inches

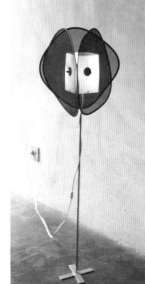

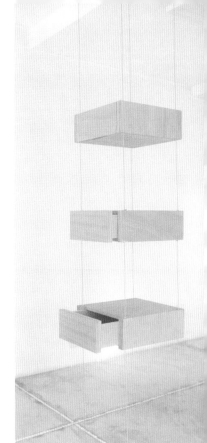

1998

Agua table
(Mesa Água)

Iron, glass, oil, colored water
c. 45 x 50 x 50 cm
c. 18 x 20 x 20 inches
Unique

259

1998

Papelão dinner table special
(Mesa Papelão Especial)

Cardboard, stainless steel,
glass
c. 70 x 150 x 150 cm
c. 28 x 59 x 59 inches
Papelão collection
Unique

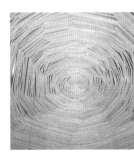

Azul chair
(Poltrona Azul)

Cotton ropes and stainless
steel structure
77 x 98 x 80 cm
30.3 x 38.6 x 31.5 inches
Ropes collection
Produced by Edra, Italy
Photo © Edra

Vermelha chair
(Cadeira Vermelha)

Cotton ropes and stainless
steel structure
77 x 58 x 88 cm
30.3 x 22.8 x 34.6 inches
Ropes collection
Produced by Edra, Italy
Photo © Edra

260

Verde chair
(Cadeira Verde)

Cotton ropes and stainless
steel structure
88 x 45 x 54 cm
34.6 x 17.7 x 21.3 inches
Ropes collection
Produced by Edra, Italy
Photo © Andreas Heiniger

Inflatable table
(Mesa Inflável)

PVC film and aluminum
45 x 40 x 40 cm
17.7 x 15.7 x 15.7 inches
Produced by MoMA, New York
Photo © Andreas Heiniger

MoMA pencil holder
(Porta-caneta MoMA)

EVA
5.5 x 6.5 x 18 cm
2.2 x 2.6 x 7.1 inches
Produced by MoMA, New York
Photo © Andreas Heiniger

Study for Jenette chair
(Estudo para cadeira Jenette)

Iron and bamboo
c. 110 x 50 x 50 cm
c. 43 x 20 x 20 inches
Mixed series

Sanfona House
Sketch

For this project, Fernando and
Humberto were invited to create
an ecological house anywhere
in the Canary Islands. After
sketching many ideas, they came
up with the solution of building
walls within walls so that mod-
ules of the house could expand
or retract, like an accordion
("sanfona" in Portuguese).

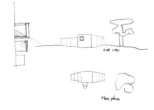

Numeros carpets
(Tapetes Numeros)

Acrylic wool
160 x 220 cm
63 x 86.6 inches
Edition of 18
Produced by Cia dos tapetes
ocidentais, Brazil
Photo © Andrés Otero

Xingu fruit bowl
(Fruteira Xingu)

Acrylic and recycled PET
threads
c. 12 x 40 x 40 cm
c. 5 x 16 x 16 inches
Small edition
Produced by Zona D
Photo © Andrés Otero

Xingu fruit bowl
(Fruteira Xingu)

Acrylic and recycled PET
threads
24.6 x 28 x 10 cm
9.7 x 11 x 3.9 inches
Small edition
Produced by Zona D
Photo © Andrés Otero

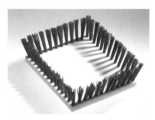

Cone chair
(Cadeira Cone)

Stainless steel and
polycarbonate sheet
77 x 85 x 97 cm
30.3 x 33.5 x 38.2 inches
Produced by Edra, Italy
Photo © Edra

Jenette chair
(Cadeira Jenette)

PVC threads, metal, wood
94 x 41 x 50 cm
37 x 16.1 x 19.7 inches
15 prototypes produced by
Estudio Campana
Photo © Andreas Heiniger

Tattoo table
(Mesa Tatoo)

Stainless steel and PVC strains
c. 75 x 80 x 160 cm
c. 29.5 x 31.5 x 63 inches
Photo © Andreas Heiniger

Study for a vase
(Estudo para vaso)

Garden hose
c. 45 x 30 x 60 cm
c. 18 x 12 x 24 inches

Zig Zag stool
(Banco Zig Zag)

Stainless steel and PVC
Large: c. 40 x 45 x 45 cm /
c. 16 x 18 x 18 inches
Small: c. 40 x 120 x 120 cm /
c. 16 x 47 x 47 inches
Zig Zag collection
Small series
Photo © Andreas Heiniger

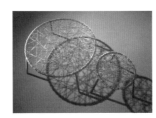

Time Capsule
(Capsula do Tempo)

Digital drawings
Produced by Fernando and
Humberto Campana
In 1999, to mark the turn of
the Millennium, *Time Magazine*
invited artists to create
capsules to be opened in
the year 3000. What would
Humberto and Fernando like
future archaeologists to dis-
cover? Rather than thinking
about the content of the
capsule, the brothers focused
on the capsule itself, devising
a multifunctional translucent
container that would remain
exposed and could also function
as a bench.

Anemona chair
(Poltrona Anemona)

Stainless steel and PVC tubes
66 x 120 x 90 cm
26 x 47.2 x 35.4 inches
Edition of c. 4
Photo © Andrés Otero

Batuque vase
(Vaso Batuque)

Glass
170 x 80 x 100 cm
67 x 31.5 x 39.4 inches
Batuque collection
Unique
Produced by QV tec, Brazil

Batuque vase
(Vaso Batuque)

Glass
c. 60 x 50 x 40 cm
c. 24 x 20 x 16 inches
Batuque collection
Unique
Produced by QV tec, Brazil
Photo © Andrés Otero

Nova fruit bowl
(Fruteira Nova)

PET sheet and aluminum
12 x 60 x 30 cm
4.7 x 23.6 x 11.8 inches
Unlimited edition
Produced by Estudio Campana
Photo © Andrés Otero

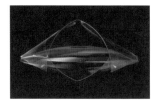

Elétrico envelope holder
(Porta cartas Elétrico)

Acrylic
11 x 45 x 30 cm /
4.3 x 17.7 x 11.8 inches
7 x 20 x 20 cm /
2.8 x 7.9 x 7.9 inches
Elétrico collection
Unlimited edition
Produced by Estudio Campana
Photo © Andrés Otero

Elétrico mirror
(Espelho Elétrico)

Acrylic and mirror
52 x 30 x 8.5 cm
20.5 x 11.8 x 3.3 inches
Elétrico collection
Unlimited edition
Produced by Acriresinas, Brazil
Photo © Andrés Otero

Elétrico photo frame
(Porta retrato Elétrico)

Acrylic and glass
23 x 27 x 9 cm
9.1 x 10.6 x 3.5 inches
Elétrico collection
Unlimited edition
Produced by Acriresinas, Brazil
Photo © Andrés Otero

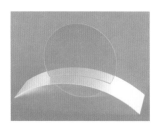

Elétrico vase
(Vaso Elétrico)

Acrylic and glass vase
28 x 12 x 5.5 cm
11 x 4.7 x 2.2 inches
Elétrico collection
Unlimited edition
Produced by Estudio Campana
Photo © Andrés Otero

Bamboo chair
(Cadeira Bambú)

Curved bamboo and acrylic
42 x 67 x 52 cm
16.5 x 26.4 x 20.5 inches
Mixed series
Unique
Photo © Andrés Otero

Shark chair
(Cadeira Shark)

Stainless steel, polycarbonate,
cane
80 x 72 x 73 cm
31.5 x 28.3 x 28.7 inches
Mixed series
Edition of c. 20
Photo © Andrés Otero

Taquaral chair
(Cadeira Taquaral)

Bamboo and iron with
electrostatic painting
93 x 50 x 42 cm
36.6 x 19.7 x 16.5 inches
Mixed series
Edition of 2
Photo © Andrés Otero

Wing chair
(Poltrona Wing)

Corrugated cardboard and
acrylic
c. 70 x 60 x 70 cm
c. 28 x 24 x 28 inches
Unique
Photo © Andrés Otero

Wing chair II
(Poltrona Wing II)

Corrugated cardboard and
acrylic
c. 70 x 60 x 70 cm
c. 28 x 24 x 28 inches
Unique

Bamboo Lamp
(Luminária Bambú)

Metal frame, plaited bamboo,
transparent cable, orange
polycarbonate
Small: 45 x 29 x 13 cm /
17.7 x 11.4 x 5.1 inches
Large: 58 x 43 x 17 cm /
22.8 x 16.9 x 6.7 inches
Produced by FontanaArte,
Brazil

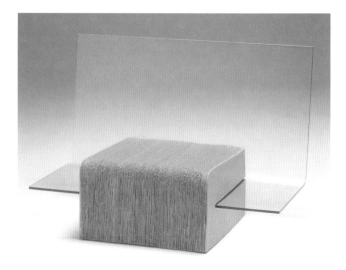

Campana pen
(Caneta Campana)

Aluminum
15 x 1 cm
5.9 x 0.4 inches
Unlimited edition
Produced by ACME, USA
Photo © Andreas Heiniger

Plastic lamp
Iron structure and PVC threads

43 x 17 x 58 cm
17 x 6.7 x 22.8 inches
29 x 13 x 17.7 cm
11.4 x 5.1 x 22.8 inches
Produced by FontanaArte, Italy
Photo © FontanaArte

Tattoo table
(Mesa Tatoo)

Stainless steel and float glass
5 sizes ranging from 40 x 100
x 100 cm / 15.7 x 39.4 x 39.4
inches to 75 x 80 x 200 cm /
29.5 x 31.5 x 78.7 inches
Produced by FontanaArte, Italy
Photo © FontanaArte

Untitled lamp
(Luminária sem titulo)

Acrylic
55 x 19 x 45 cm
21.7 x 7.5 x 17.7 inches
Photo © Andrés Otero

Untitled lamp
(Luminária sem titulo)

Acrylic
55 x 19 x 45 cm
21.7 x 7.5 x 17.7 inches
Photo © Andrés Otero

Untitled lamp
(Luminária sem titulo)

Acrylic and window shield
55 x 19 x 45 cm
21.7 x 7.5 x 17.7 inches
Photo © Andrés Otero

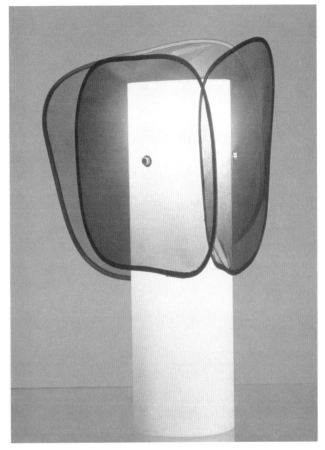

Untitled table
(Mesa sem titulo)

Stainless steel and PVC
c. 45 x 45 x 50 cm
c. 18 x 18 x 20 inches
Photo © Andrés Otero

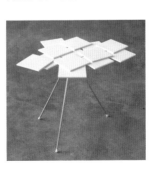

Jequitiba lamp
(Luminária Jequitibá)

Acrylic
Dimensions unknown
Unlimited edition
Produced by La Lampe, Brazil
Photo © Andreas Heiniger

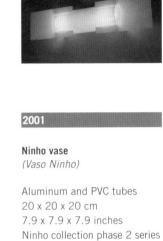

Ninho vase
(Vaso Ninho)

Aluminum and PVC tubes
20 x 20 x 20 cm
7.9 x 7.9 x 7.9 inches
Ninho collection phase 2 series
Edition of c. 180
Photo © Marcelo Spatafora

263

Jequitiba lamp
(Luminária Jequitibá)

Acrylic
55 x 19 x 45 cm
21.7 x 7.5 x 17.7 inches
Unlimited edition
Produced by La Lampe, Brazil
Photo © Andreas Heiniger

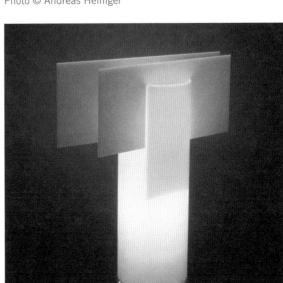

2001

Anemone chair
(Poltrona Anemone)

Stainless steel and PVC tubes
66 x 120 x 90 cm
26 x 47.2 x 35.4 inches
Unlimited edition
Produced by Edra, Italy
Photo © Edra

2001

Batuque vase
(Vaso Batuque)

Glass
c. 70 x 60 x 50 cm
c. 28 x 24 x 20 inches
Batuque collection
Unlimited edition
Produced by Capellini, Italy
Photo © Andrés Otero

2001

Box for Craft earring
(Embalagem brincos Craft)

Silicone
Various dimensions
Unlimited edition
Produced by H Stern, Brazil
Photo © H Stern

2001

Craft collection
(Coleção Craft)

Yellow gold
Limited edition
Produced by H Stern, Brazil
Photo © Fernando Laszlo
The Craft collection also includes
a bracelet and a necklace.

2001

Luz necklace
(Colar Luz)

Yellow gold
Various dimensions
Limited edition
Produced by H Stern, Brazil
Photo © Fernando Laszlo

2001

Mandala collection
(Coleção Mandala)

Yellow gold
Various dimensions
Limited edition
Produced by H Stern, Brazil
Photo © Fernando Laszlo
The Mandala collection also
includes earrings and a
necklace pendant.

2001

Mosaico collection
(Coleção Mosaico)

Yellow gold and diamond
Various dimensions
Limited edition
Produced by H Stern, Brazil
Photo © Fernando Laszlo

2001

Pantografica collection
(Coleção Pantográfica)

Stainless steel and diamonds
Various dimensions
Limited edition
Produced by H Stern, Brazil
Photo © Willy Biondani
The Pantografica collection
also includes a ring, earrings
and a fruit bowl.

2001

Scarf
(Estola)

Yellow gold
Unique
Produced by H Stern, Brazil
Photo © H Stern

2001

Slats collection
(Coleção Slats)

Yellow gold
Various dimensions
Limited edition
Produced by H Stern, Brazil
Photo © Fernando Laszlo

2001

Papel collection
(Coleção Papel)

Stainless steel structure and
corrugated cardboard
Limited edition
Produced by Edra, Italy
Photo © Edra
The collection consists of a
screen, chair, table, and sofa.

2001

Split partition
(Divisórias Split)

Acrylic
Various dimensions
Produced by Giroflex, Brazil
Photo © Nelson Kon

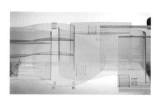

2001

Zig Zag screen
(Biombo Zig Zag)

Stainless steel and PVC tubes
190 x 40 x 180 cm
74.8 x 15.7 x 70.9 inches
Zig Zag collection
Limited edition
Produced by Edra, Italy
Photo © Edra

2001

Zig Zag stool
(Banco Zig Zag)

Stainless steel structure and
PVC tubes
Large: 40 x 100 x 100 cm /
15.7 x 39.4 x 39.4 inches
Medium: 40 x 63 x 63 cm /
15.7 x 24.8 x 24.8 inches
Small: 40 x 40 x 40 cm /
15.7 x 15.7 x 15.7 inches
Zig Zag collection
Limited edition
Produced by Edra, Italy
Photo © Edra

2001

Papel screen II
(Biombo Papel II)

Cardboard and wood
c. 180 x 50 x 5 cm
c. 71 x 20 x 2 inches
Papel collection
Produced by Estudio Campana
Photo © Andreas Heiniger

2001

Disco Zig Zag screen
(Biombo Zig Zag)

PVC wires and iron structure
with electrostatic painting
150 x 1200 x 30 cm
59 x 472.4 x 11.8 inches
Zig Zag collection
Produced by Estudio Campana
Photo © Nelson Kon
Isay Weinfeld was invited to
design the interior of the club
Disco in São Paulo, for which
the Campana Brothers created
the Disco Zig Zag screen.

2001

L´est Parisien restaurant
(Restaurante L´Est Parisien)

Paris, France
Zig Zag collection
Produced by Edra, Italy
Photo © Edra

2001

No-tech exhibition
(Exhibição No-Tech)

São Paulo, Brazil
Produced by Estudio Campana
Photo © Andrés Otero
This was an educational project
with young designers at Mube,
Museu Brasileiro de Escultura,
São Paulo. The exhibition
concept was conceived by the
Campana brothers.

265

2001

Vogue – Tactel Party
(Festa Vogue – Tactel)

Zig Zag panels, wooden
structures, PVC, felt carpet,
Lycra
Produced by Estudio Campana
Photo © Andrés Otero

2002

Ameba tray
(Bandeja Ameba)

Wood and aluminum
Large: 10 x 65 x 45 cm /
3.9 x 25.6 x 17.7 inches
Small: 10 x 55 x 40 cm /
3.9 x 21.7 x 15.7 inches
Discontinued unlimited edition
Available from Zona D

2002

Banquete chair
(Poltrona Banquete)

Stuffed toys, canvas, stainless
steel
85 x 100 x 140 cm
33.5 x 39.4 x 55.1 inches
Banquete collection
Limited edition of 150

2002

Alligator chair
(Poltrona Jacaré)

Stuffed toys, canvas, stainless
steel
85 x 100 x 140 cm
33.5 x 39.4 x 55.1 inches
Banquete collection
Limited edition of 35
Photo © Luis Calazans

2002

Dolphins and Sharks chair
(Poltrona Golfinhos e Tubarões)

Stuffed toys, canvas, stainless
steel
85 x 100 x 140 cm
33.5 x 39.4 x 55.1 inches
Banquete collection
Limited edition of 35
Photo © Luis Calazans

2002

Buriti Vase
(Vaso Buriti)

Carpet, rubber, EVA, fabric,
glass cylinder
35 x 30 x 30 cm
13.8 x 11.8 x 11.8 inches
Sushi collection
Limited edition
Photo © Design Museum,
London

2002

Sushi II chair
(Cadeira Sushi II)

Electrostatic painted iron,
carpet, EVA, fabrics
110 x 71 x 61 cm
43.3 x 28 x 24 inches
Sushi collection
Limited edition of 35
Photo © Andreas Heiniger

2002

Multidão armchair
(Poltrona Multidão)

Stainless steel and stuffed
dolls
78 x 100 x 100 cm
30.7 x 39.4 x 39.4 inches
Multidão collection
Limited edition of 35
Photo © Luis Calazans

2002

Sushi III chair
(Cadeira Sushi III)

Electrostatic painted iron, carpet,
rubber, EVA, fabric
110 x 75 x 75 cm
43.3 x 29.5 x 29.5 inches
Sushi collection
Limited edition of 35
Photo © Luis Calazans

2002

Sushi sofa
(Sofá Sushi)

Carpet, rubber, EVA, fabric,
wood, stainless steel
71 x 66 x 160 cm
28 x 26 x 63 inches
Sushi collection
Edition of 6

Sushi coffee table
(Mesa de centro Sushi)

Glass, stainless steel, rubber,
carpet, plastic
40 x 100 x 60 cm
15.7 x 39.4 x 23.6 inches
Sushi collection
Limited edition each year

Vitória Régia stool
(Banco Vitória Régia)

Carpet, rubber, EVA, fabric
Various dimensions
Sushi collection
Numbered edition each year
Photo © Luis Calazans

Curvas Chair
(Cadeira Curvas)

Stainless steel and
polycarbonate sheeting
91 x 40 x 63 cm
35.8 x 15.7 x 24.8 inches
Discontinued unlimited edition
Produced by Arredamento,
Italy
Photo © Estudio Campana

OSB panels
(Painel OSB)

OSB
122 x 244 cm
48 x 96 inches
6 prototypes
Produced by Masisa, Brazil

Boa sofa
(Sofá Boa)

Stuffed foam and velvet
60 x 350 x 190 cm
23.6 x 137.8 x 74.8 inches
Limited edition
Produced by Edra, Italy
Photo © Edra

267

Sushi fruit bowl
(Fruteira Sushi)

Fabric, felt, carpeting, web
stiffened with gum
15 x 65 x 65 cm
5.9 x 25.6 x 25.6 inches
Sushi collection
Numbered edition each year
Photo © Andreas Heiniger

Sushi table
(Mesa Sushi)

Carpet, rubber, EVA, fabric,
stainless steel
Size 1: 80 x 130 x 130 cm /
31.5 x 51.2 x 51.2 inches
Size 2: 80 x 140 x 140 cm /
31.5 x 55.1 x 55.1 inches
Size 3: 100 x 100 x 100 cm /
39.4 x 39.4 x 39.4 inches
Sushi collection
Numbered edition each year

Bolas chair
(Poltrona Bolas)

Iron and foam balls
77 x 70 x 82 cm
30.3 x 27.6 x 32.3 inches
Unlimited edition
Produced by Bozart, USA
Photo © Bozart

Labirinto bookshelf
(Estante Labirinto)

Wood
c. 140 x 30 x 140 cm
c. 55 x 12 x 55 inches
Discontinued unlimited edition
Produced by Tok & Stok, Brazil
Photo © Tok & Stok

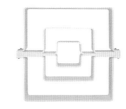

Peteca toy
(Peteca)

Rubber and synthetic feather
30 x 12 x 12 cm
11.8 x 4.7 x 4.7 inches
Unlimited edition
Produced by Magis, Italy
Photo © Estudio Campana

Sushi chair
(Cadeira Sushi)

Carpet, fabric, foam, PVC
60 x 95 x 85 cm
23.6 x 37.4 x 33.5 inches
Unlimited edition
Produced by Edra, Italy
Photo © Edra

2002

Bamboo shelter
(Cobertura Bambu)

Iron and bamboo
Large: 28 x 57 x 28 cm /
11 x 22.4 x 11 inches
Small: 20 x 49 x 20.5 cm /
7.9 x 19.3 x 8.1 inches

268

2002

Blow up prototype
(Prototipo Blow up)

Steel rods
c. 20 x 70 x 60 cm
c. 8 x 28 x 24 inches
Blow up collection
Photo © Andrés Otero

2002

Boa prototype
(Prototypo Boa)

Velvet and foam
c. 150 x 70 x 80 cm
c. 59 x 28 x 31.5 inches

2002

Sushi chair study
(Estudo cadeira Sushi)

Carpet, rubber, EVA, fabric
72 x 55 x 67 cm
28.3 x 21.7 x 26.4 inches
Sushi collection

2002

Sushi studies
(Estudos Sushi)

Carpet, rubber, EVA, fabric
c. 15 x 20 x 20 cm
c. 6 x 8 x 8 inches

2003

Novelo sofa
(Sofá Novelo)

Stainless steel wire with epoxy
paint finish
70 x 220 x 90 cm
27.6 x 86.6 x 35.4 inches
Pedra collection
Edition of 10
Photo © Luis Calazans

2003

Pedra bench
(Banco Pedra)

Stainless steel wire with epoxy
paint finish
74 x 160 x 250 cm
29.1 x 63 x 98.4 inches
Pedra collection
Edition of 10
Photo © Luis Calazans

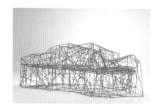

2003

Sonia Diniz chair
(Cadeira Sonia Diniz)

Electrostatic painted iron,
carpet, rubber, EVA, fabric,
wood
80 x 65 x 65 cm
31.5 x 25.6 x 25.6 inches
Sushi collection
Edition of 12
Photo © Ed Reeve

2003

Sushi IV armchair
(Poltrona Sushi IV)

Electrostatic painted iron, carpet,
rubber, EVA, fabric
90 x 100 x 100 cm
35.4 x 39.4 x 39.4 inches
Sushi collection
Limited edition of 35
Photo © Cassio Vasconcellos

2003

Favela chair
(Poltrona Favela)

Wood
67 x 74 x 62 cm
26.4 x 29.1 x 24.4 inches
Produced by Edra, Italy
Photo © Edra

2001

Sushi Upholstery fabric
(Tecido Sushi)

88% wool and 12% Polyamid
Produced by Vaveriet, Sweden
Photo © Väveriet

2003

Coconut Chair
(Cadeira Coconut)

Steel structure, coconut fiber,
black felt
110 x 70 x 94 cm
43.3 x 27.6 x 37 inches

2003

Banquete sofa
(Sofá Banquete)

Wood, steel and stuffed toys
70 x 60 x 200 cm
27.6 x 23.6 x 78.7 inches
Banquete collection
Unique

2003

Untitled sofa
(Sofá sem titulo)

Velvet with Styrofoam filling
c. 80 x 200 x 300 cm
c. 32 x 79 x 118 inches
Unique
Photo © Roberta Cosulich

2003

Untitled table
(Mesa sem titulo)

Cardboard, glass, steel
74 x 100 x 240 cm
29.1 x 39.4 x 94.5 inches
Unique

2003

**Campanas Bookmark
publication launch, Italy**

Photo © Andrés Otero

2003

Forum Parade
(Desfile Forum)

Zig Zag panels, PVC strings,
iron structure

2003

Italian Embassy
(Embaixada Italiana)

Interior design of the Italian
embassy in Brasilia

Expo Brasilia 2003

2003

Prived Oca
(Prived Oca)

Natural fiber, Swarovski
crystals, optic fiber
220 x 100 x 100 cm
86.7 x 39.4 x 39.4 inches
Unique
Produced by Estudio Campana
Photo © Swarovski

2003

SPFW mobile
(SPFW mobile)

Bienal de São Paulo
500 white stainless steel cables
Photo © Andrés Otero

2004

Black Iron chair
(Poltrona Ferro Preto)

Stainless steel wire with epoxy
paint finish
71 x 100 x 80 cm
28 x 39.4 x 31.5 inches
Iron series
Edition of 12
Photo © Luis Calazans

2004

Blue Iron chair
(Poltrona Ferro Azul)

Stainless steel wire with epoxy
paint finish
80 x 55 x 72 cm
31.5 x 21.7 x 28.3 inches
Iron series
Edition of 12
Photo © Luis Calazans

269

2004

Vermelha Iron armchair
(Poltrona Ferro Vermelha)

Stainless steel wire with epoxy
paint finish
80 x 100 x 82 cm
31.5 x 39.4 x 32.3 inches
Iron series
Edition of 12

2004

Yellow Iron armchair
(Poltrona Ferro Amarela)

Stainless steel wire with epoxy
paint finish
90 x 100 x 120 cm
35.4 x 39.4 x 47.2 inches
Iron series
Unique

2004

Cactus lamp
(Luminária Cactus)

Iron, bamboo, lamp
40 x 100 x 40 cm
15.7 x 39.4 x 15.7 inches
Unique
Photo © Andrés Otero

2004

Volcano lamp
(Luminária Volcano)

Iron, bamboo, lamp
Large: 180 x base Ø 60 cm /
70.9 x base Ø 23.7 inches
Small: 120 x base Ø 40 cm /
47.3 x base Ø 15.8 inches
Photo © Andrés Otero

2004

Galho vase
(Vaso Galho)

Glass
25 x 70 x 20 cm
9.8 x 27.6 x 7.9 inches
Edition of 150
Photo © Estudio Campana

2004

Harumaki chair
(Cadeira Harumaki)

Electrostatic painted iron,
carpet, EVA, fabric
80 x 47 x 45.5 cm
31.5 x 18.5 x 17.9 inches
Sushi collection
Numbered edition each year
Photo © Luis Calazans

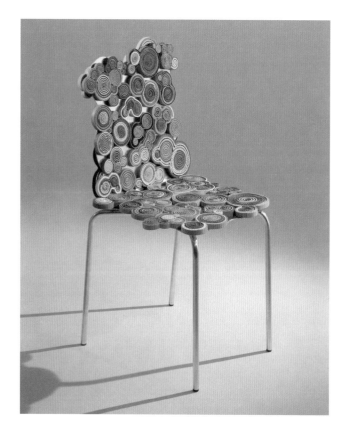

2004

Teddy Bear chair
(Poltrona Ursos)

Stuffed toys, canvas, stainless
steel
85 x 100 x 140 cm
33.5 x 39.4 x 55.1 inches
Banquete collection
Edition of 20

2004

Blow up centerpiece
(Centro de mesa Blow up)

Stainless steel
14.5 x 67.5 x 64.5 cm
5.7 x 26.6 x 25.4 inches
Blow up collection
Unlimited edition
Produced by Alessi, Italy
Photo © Alessi

2004

Blow up citrus basket
(Cesto Blow up)

Stainless steel
31.5 x 35 x 36 cm
12.4 x 13.8 x 14.2 inches
Blow up collection
Unlimited edition
Produced by Alessi, Italy
Photo © Alessi

2004

Blow up placemat
(Descanso Blow up)

Stainless steel
40.5 x 39.5 cm
15.9 x 15.6 inches
Blow up collection
Unlimited edition
Produced by Alessi, Italy
Photo © Alessi

2004

Celia buffet
(Aparador Celia)

OSB wood
30 x 18 x 50 cm
11.8 x 7.1 x 19.7 inches
Celia collection
Unlimited edition
Produced by Habitart, Brazil
Photo © Pierre Yves Refalo

2004

Celia chair
(Cadeira Celia)

OSB wood
90 x 40 x 44 cm
35.4 x 15.7 x 17.3 inches
Celia collection
Unlimited edition
Produced by Habitart, Brazil
Photo © Pierre Yves Refalo

2004

Corallo chair
(Cadeira Corallo)

Steel wire with epoxy paint
finish
90 x 140 x 100 cm
35.4 x 55.1 x 39.4 inches
Unlimited edition
Produced by Edra, Italy
Photo © Edra

2004

Celia dinner table
(Mesa Celia)

OSB wood
74 x 100 x 100 cm
29.1 x 39.4 x 39.4 inches
Celia collection
Unlimited edition
Produced by Habitart, Brazil
Photo © Pierre Yves Refalo

2004

Celia side table
(Mesa de centro Celia)

OSB wood
30 x 150 x 50 cm
11.8 x 59.1 x 19.7 inches
Celia collection
Unlimited edition
Produced by Habitart, Brazil
Photo © Pierre Yves Refalo

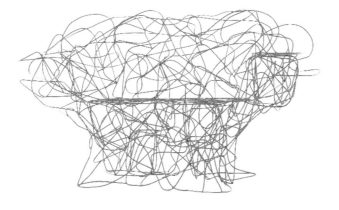

2004

Infinito
(Infinito)

Ceramic plant pots
Size 1: 34 x 30 x 57 cm /
13.4 x 11.8 x 22.4 inches
Size 2: 34 x 35 x 81 cm /
13.4 x 13.8 x 31.9 inches
Size 3: 34 x 33 x 80 cm /
13.4 x 13 x 31.5 inches
Produced by Teracrea, Italy
Photo © Teracrea

2004

Labirinto
(Labirinto)

Ceramic plant pots
Large: 34 x 60 x 60 cm /
13.4 x 23.6 x 23.6 inches
Small: 34 x 60 x 26 cm /
13.4 x 23.6 x 10.2 inches
Produced by Teracrea, Italy
Photo © Teracrea

2004

Green fruit basket
(Fruteira Verde)

Aluminum sheet and plastic
fabric
2 x 50 x 50 cm
0.8 x 19.7 x 19.7 inches

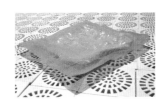

2004

Janice stool
(Banco Janice)

Stainless steel and cotton
handmade dolls
c. 45 x 50 x 50 cm
c. 18 x 20 x 20 inches

2004

Pendant lamp
(Luminária Pendente)

Wood and lamp
60 x 53 x 12 cm /
23.6 x 20.8 x 4.7 inches
Small edition
Photo © Andrés Otero

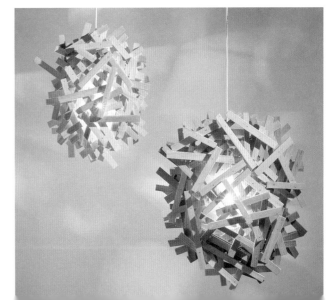

2004

Rock coffee table
(Mesa de centro Pedra)

Aluminum frame, paper, glue
Dimensions variable

2004

Corallo tree
(Árvore Corallo)

Iron with electrostatic paint
c. 210 x 100 x 100 cm
c. 83 x 39 x 39 inches
Unique
Produced by Estudio Campana
for Moss, New York

2004

Favela tree
(*Árvore Favela*)

Brazilian pine, steel frame,
screws
290 x 183 cm
114 x 72 inches
Unique
Produced by Estudio Campana
for Moss, New York
Photo © Moss

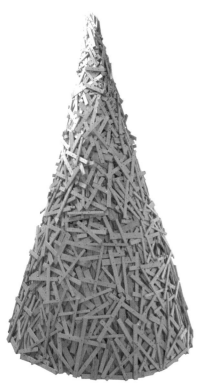

2004

D&D Preview
(*D&D Preview*)

PVC tubes and PVC frames
Produced by Estudio Campana

2004

Iluminar Exhibition
(*Exposição Iluminar*)

Copper, plastic, and lamps
from the Centre Pompidou and
the Musée des Arts Décoratifs,
Paris
Produced by Estudio Campana
Photos © Fernando Silveira

2004

Ideal House
(*Ideal House*)

Cologne Design Fair, Germany
Wood, natural plants, fiber,
iron, furniture
Produced by Estudio Campana

2004

Glass garden
(*Jardim de Vidro*)

Drawing for future glass piece
for Droog Design
Produced by Estudio Campana

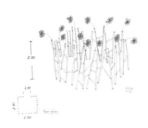

2004

Loucos por design – exhibition
(*Loucos por design – exposição*)

São Paulo, Brazil
Paper, nylon, light
Produced by Estudio Campana

2004

Favela wall
(*Painel Favela*)

Moss Gallery, New York
Wooden strips nailed and
stuck together
c. 600 x 800 cm
c. 236 x 315 inches
Produced by Estudio Campana
Photo © Andrés Otéro

2004

Zest for Life – exhibition
(*Zest for Life – exposição*)

Design Museum, London,
England
Produced by Estudio Campana

2004

London London
(London London)

Aluminum wire with epoxy
paint finish
c. 80 x 100 x 80 cm
c. 31.5 x 39 x 31.5 inches
Unique
Produced by Estudio Campana
Photo © Fernando Campana
Made for the Design Museum,
London

2005

Blow up magazine holder
(Revisteiro Blow up)

Stainless steel
45.5 x 28.5 x 35 cm
17.9 x 11.2 x 13.8 inches
Blow up collection
Unlimited edition
Produced by Alessi, Italy
Photo © Alessi

2005

Blow up umbrella holder
(Porta guarda-chuva Blow up)

Stainless steel
50 x 33 x 33 cm
19.7 x 13 x 13 inches
Blow up collection
Unlimited edition
Produced by Alessi, Italy
Photo © Alessi

2005

Brasilia table
(Mesa Brasilia)

Stainless steel and glass
Various dimensions
Unlimited edition
Produced by Edra, Italy
Photo © Edra

2005

Panda Banquete chair
(Poltrona Banquete Panda)

Stainless steel and stuffed toys
85 x 100 x 140 cm
33.5 x 39.4 x 55.1 inches
Banquete collection
Edition of 25
Photo © Luis Calazans

2005

Blow up mirror
(Espelho Blow up)

Stainless steel
74.5 x 11 x 86.5 cm
29.3 x 4.3 x 34 inches
Blow up collection
Unlimited edition
Produced by Alessi, Italy
Photo © Alessi

2005

Blow up vase
(Vaso Blow up)

Stainless steel
33.5 x 18.5 x 18.5 cm
13.2 x 7.3 x 7.3 inches
Blow up collection
Unlimited edition
Produced by Alessi, Italy
Photo © Alessi

2005

Jenette chair
(Cadeira Jenette)

Rigid polyurethane and PVC
stalks
94 x 41 x 50 cm
37 x 16.1 x 19.7 inches
Available in 6 colors
Unlimited edition
Produced by Edra, Italy
Photo © Edra

273

2005

Blow up candleholder
(Candelabro Blow up)

Stainless steel
16.5 x 17.5 x 19 cm
6.5 x 6.9 x 7.5 inches
Blow up collection
Unlimited edition
Produced by Alessi, Italy
Photo © Alessi

2005

Blow up side table
(Mesa Blow up)

Stainless steel and glass
44 x Ø 45 cm
17.3 x Ø 17.7 inches
Blow up collection
Unlimited edition
Produced by Alessi, Italy
Photo © Alessi

2005

Blow up wall clock
(Relógio Blow up)

Stainless steel
6 x Ø 65 cm
2.4 x Ø 25.6 inches
Blow up collection
Unlimited edition
Produced by Alessi, Italy
Photo © Alessi

2005

Melissa Zig Zag – bag and sandals
(Melissa Zig Zag – Bolsa e sapatilha)

PVC
Dimensions variable
Melissa + Campana collection
Unlimited edition
Produced by Grendene, Brazil
Photo © Grendene

2005

Melissa Zig Zag – tennis shoe
(Melissa Zig Zag – Tenis)

PVC
Dimensions variable
Melissa + Campana collection
Unlimited edition
Produced by Grendene, Brazil
Photo © Grendene

274

2005

Sushi chair with Swarovski
(Cadeira Sushi com Swarovski)

Cotton, foam, elastic,
Swarovski crystals
65 x 85 x 95 cm
25.6 x 33.5 x 37.4 inches
Diamond collection
Produced by Edra, Italy
Photo © Edra

2005

Aster Papposus – Research I
(Aster Papposus – Pesquisa I)

Canvas covered with Styrofoam
filling
50 x 162 x 162 cm
19.7 x 63.8 x 63.8 inches
Study for Historia Naturalis
collection for Edra
Produced by Estudio Campana

2005

Aster Papposus – Research II
(Aster Papposus – Pesquisa II)

Canvas covered with Styrofoam
filling
58 x 166 x 166 cm
22.8 x 65.4 x 65.4 inches
Study for Historia Naturalis
collection for Edra
Produced by Estudio Campana

2005

Unstructured sofa study
(Estudo para Sofá Deconstruido)

Canvas covered with Styrofoam
filling
16 x 70 x 43 cm
6.3 x 27.6 x 17 inches
Study for Historia Naturalis
collection for Edra
Produced by Estudio Campana

2005

Unstructured sofa study
(Estudo para Sofá Deconstruido)

Canvas covered with Styrofoam
filling
16 x 73 x 42 cm
6.3 x 28.7 x 16.5 inches
Study for Historia Naturalis
collection for Edra
Produced by Estudio Campana

2005

Unstructured sofa study
(Estudo para Sofá Deconstruido)

Canvas covered with Styrofoam
filling
60 x 90 x 170 cm
23.6 x 35.4 x 67 inches
Study for Historia Naturalis
collection for Edra
Produced by Estudio Campana

2005

Kaiman Jacaré – Historia Naturalis research
(Jacaré Kaiman – Pesquisa Historia Naturalis)

Canvas covered with Styrofoam
filling
Dimensions variable
Study for Historia Naturalis
collection for Edra
Produced by Estudio Campana

2005

Unstructured sofa
(Sofá Desconstruido)

Natural canvas and Styrofoam
balls
Dimensions variable
Study for a private collector

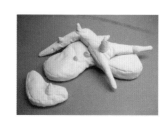

2005

Castelo sofa
(Sofá Castelo)

Paper pulp
Dimensions unknown
Papier-mâché study collection
for Vitra
Produced by Estudio Campana

2005

Green screen
(Biombo Verde)

EVA and papier-mâché model
24 x 114 x 8.5 cm
9.4 x 44.9 x 3.3 inches
Papier-mâché study collection
for Vitra
Produced by Estudio Campana

2005

Pink screen
(Biombo Rosa)

EVA and papier-mâché model
24 x 60 x 8 cm
9.4 x 23.6 x 3.1 inches
Papier-mâché study collection
for Vitra
Produced by Estudio Campana

2005

Red screen
(Biombo Vermelho)

EVA and papier-mâché with
texturized structure
24 x 60 x 1.5 cm
9.4 x 23.6 x 0.6 inches
Papier-mâché study collection
for Vitra
Produced by Estudio Campana

2005

Paper bin
(Lixeira de Papel)

Paper
45 x 30 x 30 cm
17.7 x 11.8 x 11.8 inches
Papier-mâché study collection
for Vitra
Produced by Estudio Campana

2005

Papier-mâché bed
(Cama Papel Machê)

Cardboard, papier-mâché,
foam
25 x 10 x 8 cm
9.8 x 3.9 x 3.1 inches
Papier-mâché study collection
for Vitra
Produced by Estudio Campana

2005

Papier-mâché bench
(Banco Papel Machê)

Papier-mâché and 3D rendering
Papier-mâché study collection
for Vitra
Produced by Estudio Campana

2005

Papier-mâché bookshelf
(Estante Papel Machê)

EVA and papier-mâché model
17 x 13 x 2.5 cm
6.7 x 5.1 x 1 inches
Papier-mâché study collection
for Vitra
Produced by Estudio Campana

2005

Papier-mâché Sofa
(Sofá Papel Machê)

Papier-mâché and iron structure
23 x 39 x 24 cm
9.1 x 15.4 x 9.4 inches
Papier-mâché study collection
for Vitra
Produced by Estudio Campana

2005

Papier-mâché office desk
(Mesa de trabalho Papel Machê)

Acrylic, papier-mâché, and
freehand sketch
26 x 15 x 10 cm
10.2 x 5.9 x 3.9 inches
Papier-mâché study collection
for Vitra
Produced by Estudio Campana

2005

Papier-mâché screen
(Biombo Papel Machê)

Papier-mâché and digital
rendering
Papier-mâché study collection
for Vitra
Produced by Estudio Campana

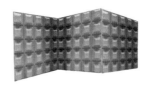

2005

Papier-mâché stool / side table
*(Banco / Mesa de canto Papel
Machê)*

Papier-mâché with metallic
mesh structure
c. 30 x 40 x 50 cm
c. 12 x 16 x 20 inches
Papier-mâché study collection
for Vitra
Produced by Estudio Campana

2005

Coal fruit bowl
(Fruteira de Carvão)

Coal over thin metal sheet
Ø 12 x 50 cm
Ø 4.7 x 19.7 inches

2005

Cobogó tile table
(Mesa de tijolos Cobogó)

Brick tiles and cement
35 x 89 x 78 cm
13.8 x 35 x 30.7 inches
Cobogó collection

2005

Hibrido
(Hibrido)

Natural fiber, plastic, wood
77 x 30 x 30 cm
30.3 x 11.8 x 11.8 inches
Studies for TransPlastic
collection

2005

Mirror fabric
(Tecido de espelho)

Dimensions variable

2005

Ring prototype
(Prototipo para anel)

Leather and Brazilian stone
Dimensions variable

275

2005

Favela / Sushi sofa
(Sofá Favela / Sushi)

Wood and EVA
c. 90 x 200 x 60 cm
c. 35 x 79 x 24 inches

2005

Campane di Campana
(Campane di Campana)

Exhibition at Moss, New York
Mouth-blown glass
Dimensions variable
Campane di Campana collection
Limited edition of 195 of
various designs
Produced by Venini, Italy
Photo © Moss

2005

Drop
(Gota)

Welded iron rods with
electrostatic paint
c. 1,800 x 100 x 110 cm
c. 708 x 39 x 43 inches
Unique

2005

Okachimaki
(Okachimaki)

Aluminum and carpet tiles
60 x 45 x 100 cm
23.6 x 17.7 x 39.4 inches
Pen Magazine commission
Unique

2005

Pencil sculpture
(Escultura de Lapis)

Wooden pencils
c. 50 x 50 x 20 cm
c. 20 x 20 x 8 inches
Unique
Commissioned by Faber Castel

2005

Pinocchio
(Pinocchio)

Exhibition for Case da Abitare
Aluminum
Dimensions unknown
Produced by Estudio Campana

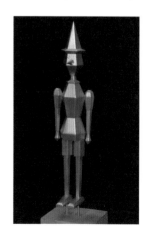

2005

Reflexes
(Reflexos)

Mosaic of reflective acrylic
pieces
Unique
Designed by Fernando Campana
Produced by Estudio Campana
for *Casa Brutus* magazine,
Tokyo, Japan

2005

Tokyo Garden
(Tokio Garden)

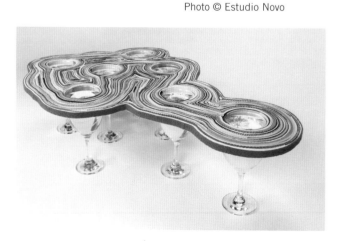

2006

Corallo table
(Mesa Corallo)

Stainless steel wire with epoxy
paint finish and glass
70 x 90 x 93 cm
27.6 x 35.4 x 36.6 inches
Unique

Wine glasses, carpet, rubber,
EVA, fabric
30 x 85 x 55 cm
11.8 x 33.5 x 21.7 inches
Unique
Designed by Humberto Campana
Produced by Estudio Campana
for *Casa Brutus* magazine,
Tokyo, Japan
Photo © Estudio Novo

2006

Fragmentos sofa
(Sofá Fragmentos)

Velvet covered foam cubes
Various dimensions
Unique

2006

Multidão Mulata armchair
(Poltrona Multidão Mulata)

Stainless steel and stuffed dolls
78 x 100 x 100 cm
30.7 x 39.4 x 39.4 inches
Multidão collection
Unique
Photo © Luis Calazans

2006

Jatobá side table
(Mesa de canto Jatobá)

Stainless steel structure, glass,
EVA, rubber, carpet
c. 45 x 55 x 55 cm
c. 18 x 22 x 22 inches
Sushi collection
Unique

Café chair
(Cadeira Café)

Plastic chair, natural fiber, iron
structure
87 x 62 x 76 cm
34 x 24 x 30 inches
TransPlastic collection
Unique

Children's chairs
(Cadeiras de Criança)

Plastic chair and wicker
From left to right:
82 x 36 x 36 cm /
32.3 x 14.2 x 14.2 inches
65 x 36 x 36 cm /
25.6 x 14.2 x 14.2 inches
56 x 40 x 42 cm /
22 x 15.7 x 16.5 inches
TransPlastic collection
Unique
Photo © Ed Reeve
Courtesy of Albion, London

Double chair
(Cadeira Dupla)

Plastic chair and synthetic fiber
80 x 60 x 132 cm
31.5 x 23.6 x 52 inches
TransPlastic collection
Unique
Photo © Ed Reeve

Gallon lamp I – phase one
(Luminária Galão I – fase um)

Plastic water gallon,
wickerwork, lighting system
184 x 16 x 34 cm
72.4 x 6.3 x 13.4 inches
TransPlastic collection
Unique
Photo © Fernando Laszlo

Gallon lamp II – phase one
(Luminária Galão II – fase um)

Plastic water gallon,
wickerwork, lighting system
91 x 16 x 34 cm
35.8 x 6.3 x 13.4 inches
TransPlastic collection
Unique
Photo © Ed Reeve
Courtesy of Albion, London

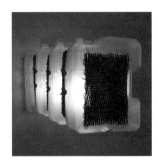

Gallon lamp III – phase one
(Luminária Galão III – fase um)

Plastic water gallon,
wickerwork, lighting system
91 x 16 x 80 cm
35.8 x 6.3 x 31.5 inches
TransPlastic collection
Unique
Photo © Ed Reeve
Courtesy of Albion, London

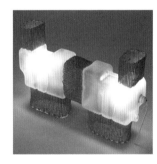

Gallon lamp IV – phase one
(Luminária Galão IV – fase um)

Plastic water gallon,
wickerwork, and lighting system
54 x 16 x 29 cm
21.3 x 6.3 x 11.4 inches
TransPlastic collection
Unique
Photo © Ed Reeve
Courtesy of Albion, London

Gallon lamp V – phase one
(Luminária Galão V – fase um)

Plastic water gallon, wicker-
work, lighting system
55 x 16 x 34 cm
21.7 x 6.3 x 13.4 inches
TransPlastic collection
Unique
Photo © Ed Reeve
Courtesy of Albion, London

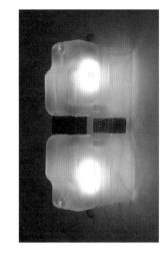

TransRock chair
(Cadeira TransRock)

Plastic chairs, natural fiber,
iron structure
90 x 203 x 382 cm
35 x 80 x 150 inches
TransPlastic collection
Unique

Una Famiglia chair
(Cadeira Una Famiglia)

Plastic chair, natural fiber, iron
structure
78 x 87 x 140 cm
30.7 x 34.3 x 55.1 inches
TransPlastic collection
Unique

277

Aster Papposus
(Aster Papposus)

Velvet and foam
86 x 330 x 330 cm
34 x 130 x 130 inches
Historia Naturalis collection
Unlimited edition
Produced by Edra, Italy
Photo © Edra

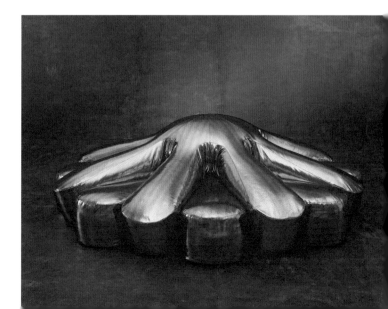

Kaiman Jacaré
(Kaiman Jacaré)

Foam and leather
Dimensions ranging from
100 x 450 x 260 cm to
100 x 700 x 500 cm /
39 x 177 x 102 inches to
39 x 276 x 197 inches
Historia Naturalis collection
Unlimited edition
Produced by Edra, Italy
Photo © Edra

Brasilia table colored
(Mesa Brasilia Colorida)

Glass and stainless steel
Dimensions ranging from
42 x 60 x 50 cm to
73 x 270 x 150 cm /
16.5 x 23.6 x 19.7 inches to
28.7 x 106 x 59 inches
278 Brasilia collection
Unlimited edition
Produced by Edra, Italy
Photo © Edra

Melissa Carioca
(Melissa Carioca)

PVC
Dimensions variable
Melissa + Campana collection
Unlimited edition
Produced by Grendene, Brazil
Photo © Grendene

Melissa Zig Zag
(Melissa Zig Zag)

PVC
Various dimensions
Melissa + Campana collection
Unlimited edition
Produced by Grendene, Brazil
Photo © Grendene

Brown chair
(Cadeira Marrom)

Plastic chair and synthetic fiber
80 x 60 x 65 cm
31.5 x 23.5 x 25.5 inches
Study for TransPlastic collection

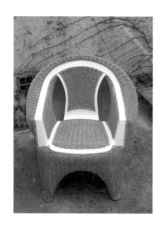

White chair
(Cadeira Branca)

Plastic chair and synthetic fiber
c. 80 x 60 x 65 cm
c. 31.5 x 23.6 x 25.6 inches
Study for TransPlastic collection

Tire and wicker centerpiece
(Centro de mesa em pneu e vime)

Rubber tire and natural fiber
c. 8 x Ø 35 cm
c. 3.2 x Ø 14 inches
Study for TransPlastic collection

Coconut fiber stool
(Banquinho de fibra de coco)

Wood and natural fiber
40 x 36 x 36 cm
15.7 x 14.2 x 14.2 inches

Fruit bowl
(Fruit bowl)

Plastic doll limbs and glue
c. 22 x 47 x 48 cm
c. 9 x 18.5 x 19 inches
Nazareth centerpiece prototype

Green screen
(Biombo Verde)

Aluminum structure and fabric
277 x 235 x 40 cm
109 x 92.5 x 15.7 inches

Wall Pocket
(Bolso de parede)

Aluminum structure and fabric
c. 120 x 130 cm
c. 47 x 51 inches
Prototype for Drosera Wall Pocket

Yellow screen I
(Biombo Amarelo I)

Aluminum structure and fabric
225 x 160 x 30 cm
89 x 63 x 12 inches
(each module)

Yellow screen II
(Biombo Amarelo II)

Aluminum structure and fabric
225 x 160 x 30 cm
89 x 63 x 12 inches
(each module)

Leather carpet studies
(Estudos para tapete couro)

Leather
Various sizes

2006

Leather carpet studies II
(Estudos para tapete couro II)

Leather
65 x 40 cm
25.6 x 15.7 inches

2006

Leather purse
(Bolsa de couro)

Leather and wicker patchwork
study
Synthetic leather and natural
fiber
4 x 37 x 52 cm
1.6 x 14.6 x 20.5 inches

2006

Leatherworks chair prototype
*(Prototipo da Cadeira
Leatherworks)*

Metal chair upholstered in
leather patchwork
87 x 43 x 52 cm
34.3 x 17 x 20.5 inches

2006

Mandacaru Formiga
(Mandacaru Formiga)

Fabric, synthetic foam, aluminum
structure, plastic buttons
305 x 290 x 30 cm
120 x 114 x 12 inches

2006

Mandacaru Girafa
(Mandacaru Girafa)

Fabric, synthetic foam filling,
plastic buttons
530 x 230 x 140 cm
209 x 91 x 55 inches

2006

Unstructured pieces
(Peças Desestruturadas)

Fabric and synthetic foam filling
Dimensions variable
Five two-piece prototypes
Studies for desk objects

2006

Paper screen
(Biombo Papel)

Cardboard and paper
120 x 70 x 10 cm
47 x 27.6 x 3.9 inches
Papier-mâché study collection
for Vitra
Produced by Estudio Campana

2006

Papier-mâché chair
(Cadeira Papel Machê)

Corrugated cardboard
90 x 50 x 73 cm
35.4 x 19.7 x 28.7 inches
Papier-mâché study collection
for Vitra
Produced by Estudio Campana

2006

Papier-mâché children's chair
(Cadeira infantil Papel Machê)

Corrugated cardboard
72 x 60 x 22 cm
28.3 x 23.6 x 8.7 inches
Papier-mâché study collection
for Vitra
Produced by Estudio Campana

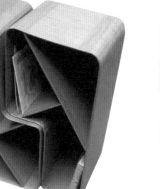

2006

Papier-mâché wall segment
(Parede Papel Machê)

Corrugated cardboard
80 x 63 x 35 cm
31.5 x 24.8 x 13.8 inches
Papier-mâché study collection
for Vitra
Produced by Estudio Campana

2006

Rug
(Tapete)

Fabric and cotton strings
135 x 140 cm
53 x 55 inches

2006

Screen
(Biombo)

Polystyrene covered in adhesive
kraft paper
c. 200 x 160 x 40 cm
c. 79 x 63 x 16 inches

279

2006

Suede tall stool
(Banco alta em camurça)

Wooden stool, suede patchwork,
synthetic foam filling
71 x 33 x 33 cm
28 x 13 x 13 inches

Triple suede chair
(Cadeira tripla em camurça)

Plastic chair covered in suede
patchwork
c. 50 x 85 x 115 cm
c. 20 x 33.5 x 45 inches

Aalto's vase
(Vaso Aalto)

Epoxy painted brass
Dimensions unknown
Unique
Produced by Estudio Campana
Special commission to celebrate
the 90th anniversary of Alvar
Aalto's vase

Banzé
(Banze)

Wicker and plastic
45 x 34 x 56.5 cm
17.7 x 13.4 x 22.25 inches
Unique
Part of the Puppy Love project
for 2006 edition of the
Luminaire fund-raiser

Camper Shop Berlin
(Loja da Camper em Berlin)

Billboard misprints
345 x 900 x 1,540 cm
136 x 354 x 606 inches
Camper together with Campana
– Torn Left Over store
Produced by Estudio Campana
Photo © Camper
As part of "Together," Camper's
ongoing series of collaborations
with artists, designers and
architects, the Campana brothers
were invited to design a new
temporary store in Ku'damm,
Berlin. "The concept needed
to be strong but low budget,
easy, and quick to build… what
is on the walls are printing
errors—paper used for color
calibration in printing machines
which are then thrown away.
Here visual waste is pasted to
the wall, becoming art."

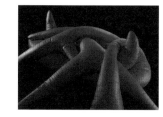

Disco Mirror screen
(Painel Disco)

Polycarbonate, iron, aluminum
150 x 1,200 x 30 cm
59 x 472 x 11.8 inches
Unique
Produced by Estudio Campana
Photo © Estudio Campana
Five years after the inauguration
of Disco club in São Paulo, the
owner decided to renovate the
venue and hired Isay Weinfeld
and the Campanas, the same
duo as before, to refurbish it.
Isay wanted to work with reflective surfaces and the Campanas
came up with the shattered
silver mirror panel to cover
the 10-meter-long bar wall.

Kaiman Jacaré Rosso
(Kaiman Jacaré Rosso)

Foam and leather
c. 406 x 470 x 130 cm
c. 160 x 185 x 51 inches
Historia Naturalis collection
Unique piece for Luminaire
fund-raising auction
Produced by Edra, Italy
Photo © Edra

Favela screen
(Painel Favela)

Wooden bars, nails, acrylic
paint
Size 1: 215 x 640 cm /
85 x 252 inches
Size 2: 170 x 660 cm /
67 x 260 inches
Size 3: 315 x 550 cm /
124 x 217 inches
Edition of 3
Produced by Estudio Campana
Photo © Estudio Campana
Special commission for JWT
ad agency in São Paulo as part
of their renovation program.
Three Favela screens were
built: reception (natural wood),
a corridor alongside the
conference rooms (white),
and a conference room.

Parasol
(Parasol)

Metallic structure and
wickerwork
365 x 525 x 360 cm
144 x 207 x 142 inches
Produced by Estudio Campana
This project was a study to
create portable sunshades for
a museum.

Special banquete
(Banquete Especial)

Stuffed toys, canvas, stainless
steel
85 x 100 x 140 cm
33.5 x 39.4 x 55.1 inches
Banquete collection
Unique

T logo
(Logo T)

Carpet, rubber, EVA, fabric,
glass cylinder
32 x 24 x 1.5 cm
12.6 x 9.4 x 0.6 inches
Logo for *The Times Magazine*
Produced by Estudio Campana

Zig Zag screen
(Biombo Zig Zag)

Iron with electrostatic paint
and PVC strings
300 x 250 x 35 cm
118 x 98.4 x 13.8 inches
Zig Zag collection
Unique
Produced by Estudio Campana
Photo © Vitra Design Museum,
Germany
Courtesy of Vitra Design
Museum

Black Café chair
(Cadeira Café Preta)

Plastic chair, natural fiber, iron
structure
87 x 62 x 76 cm
34.3 x 24.4 x 30 inches
TransPlastic collection
Unique
Photo © Fernando Laszlo

Coast to Coast chair
(Cadeira Costa a Costa)

Plastic chair, wood and leather
stool, and wicker on steel
structure
82 x 74 x 135 cm
32.3 x 29.1 x 53.1 inches
TransPlastic collection
Unique
Photo © Fernando Laszlo

Gallon lamp I – phase two
(Luminária Galão I – fase dois)

Plastic water gallon, wicker-
work, lighting system
32 x 170 x 62 cm
12.6 x 67 x 24.4 inches
TransPlastic collection
Edition of 3
Photo © Ed Reeve
Courtesy of Albion, London

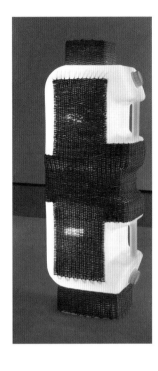

Gallon lamp III – phase two
(Luminária Galão III – fase dois)

Plastic water gallon, wickerwork,
lighting system
30 x 90 x 90 cm
11.8 x 35.4 x 35.4 inches
TransPlastic collection
Unique
Photo © Fernando Laszlo

Gallon lamp II – phase two
(Luminária Galão II – fase dois)

Plastic water gallon, wicker-
work, lighting system
35 x 122 x 103 cm
13.8 x 48 x 40.6 inches
TransPlastic collection
Unique
Photo © Ed Reeve
Courtesy of Albion, London

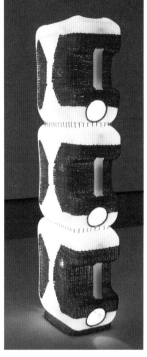

Gallon lamp IV – phase two
(Luminária Galão IV – fase dois)

Plastic water gallon, wickerwork,
lighting system
16 x 45 x 24 cm
6.3 x 17.7 x 9.4 inches
TransPlastic collection
Unique
Photo © Ed Reeve
Courtesy of Albion, London

281

Island
(Ilha)

Steel frame, wickerwork,
plastic globes, lighting system
350 x 300 x 220 cm
137.8 x 118.1 x 86.6 inches
TransPlastic collection
Unique
Photo © Ed Reeve
Courtesy of Albion, London

Library with table
(Biblioteca com mesa)

Plastic table, steel frame,
wickerwork
194 x 210 x 250 cm
76.4 x 82.7 x 98.4 inches
TransPlastic collection
Unique
Photo © Ed Reeve
Courtesy of Albion, London

282

2007

Meteor
(Meteoro)

Steel frame, wickerwork,
plastic globes, lighting system
Large: 240 x 280 x 300 cm /
94.5 x 110.2 x 118.1 inches
Medium: 100 x 170 x 220 cm /
39.4 x 67 x 86.6 inches
Small: 95 x 165 x 205 cm /
37.4 x 65 x 80.7 inches
TransPlastic collection
One of each size
Photo © Ed Reeve
Courtesy of Albion, London

2007

TransCloud
(TransCloud)

Steel frame, wickerwork, plastic
globes, lighting system

Size 1: 37 x 130 x 160 cm /
14.6 x 51.2 x 63 inches
Size 2: 200 x 137 x 50 cm /
78.7 x 53.9 x 19.7 inches
Size 3: 200 x 160 x 30 cm /
78.7 x 63 x 11.8 inches
Size 4: 200 x 180 x 82 cm /
78.7 x 70.9 x 32.3 inches
Size 5: 70 x 270 x 330 cm /
27.6 x 106.3 x 130 inches

TransPlastic collection
One of each size
Photo © Ed Reeve
Courtesy of Albion, London

2007

Library with chair
(Biblioteca com cadeira)

Plastic chair, steel frame,
wickerwork
19 x 200 x 190 cm
7.5 x 78.7 x 74.8 inches
TransPlastic collection
Unique
Photo © Ed Reeve
Courtesy of Albion, London

2007

Siwa chair
(Cadeira Siwa)

Plastic chair, wood and leather
stool, and wicker on steel
structure
112 x 102 x 253 cm
44.1 x 40.2 x 99.6 inches
TransPlastic collection
Unique
Photo © Ed Reeve
Courtesy of Albion, London

2007

Harumaki bench
(Banco Harumaki)

Stainless steel, EVA, fabric,
rubber
45 x 120 x 60 cm
17.7 x 47.2 x 23.6 inches
Sushi collection
Edition of 25

2007

Leatherworks chair
(Cadeira Leatherworks)

Metal and leather
55 x 60 x 84 cm
21.6 x 23.6 x 33 inches
Materialismi collection
Unlimited edition
Produced by Edra, Italy
Photo © Edra

Leatherworks armchair
(Poltrona Leatherworks)

90 x 85 x 75 cm
35.4 x 33.5 x 29.5 inches
Materialismi collection
Unlimited edition
Produced by Edra, Italy
Photo © Edra

Leatherworks small armchair
*(Poltrona Leatherworks
pequena)*

78 x 75 x 78 cm
30.7 x 29.5 x 30.7 inches
Materialismi collection
Unlimited edition
Produced by Edra, Italy
Photo © Edra

Nuvem – citrus basket
(Fruteira Nuvem)

Aluminum
24 x 23 x 23 cm
9.4 x 9.1 x 9.1 inches
Nuvem series
Unlimited edition
Produced by Alessi, Italy
Photo © Alessi

Nuvem – flower vase
(Vaso para flores Nuvem)

Aluminum
17 x 10 x 10 cm
6.7 x 3.9 x 3.9 inches
Nuvem series
Unlimited edition
Produced by Alessi, Italy
Photo © Alessi

Nuvem – bowl
(Cesto Nuvem)

Aluminum
Large: 12 x 30 x 30 cm /
4.7 x 11.8 x 11.8 inches
Medium: 9 x 24 x 24 cm /
3.5 x 9.4 x 9.4 inches
Small: 6.5 x 15 x 15 cm /
2.6 x 5.9 x 5.9 inches
Nuvem series
Unlimited edition
Produced by Alessi, Italy
Photo © Alessi

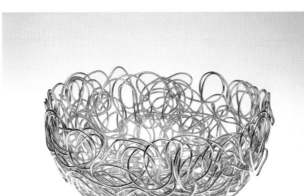

Nuvem – oven to table
(Travessa Nuvem)

Aluminum
7.5 x 27 x 27 cm
3 x 10.6 x 10.6 inches
Nuvem series
Unlimited edition
Produced by Alessi, Italy
Photo © Alessi

Nuvem – wire mat
(Descanso de mesa Nuvem)

Aluminum
43 x 37 cm
16.9 x 14.6 inches
Nuvem series
Unlimited edition
Produced by Alessi, Italy
Photo © Alessi

TransNeomatic centerpiece
(Centro de mesa TransNeomatic)

Rubber tire and natural fiber
65 x 65 cm
25.6 x 25.6 inches
Unlimited edition
Produced by Artecnica, USA
Photo © Ed Reeve

Aguapé chair
(Prototipo cadeira Aguapé)

Leather
112 x 86 x 68 cm
44.1 x 33.9 x 26.8 inches

Café chair
(Cadeira Café)

Plastic, iron, natural fiber
c. 82 x 74 x 80 cm
c. 32 x 29 x 31.5 inches
TransPlastic collection

283

Café chair small
(Cadeira Café pequena)

Plastic, iron, natural fiber
c. 74 x 65 x 65 cm
c. 29 x 25.5 x 25.5 inches
TransPlastic collection

2007

Chandelier study
(Estudo para Candelabro)

Marble
Dimensions variable
Assembled by Fernando and
Humberto Campana during a
visit to a marble company in
Cairo, Egypt

2007

Fragmentos table
(Mesa Fragmentos)

Wood model
24 x 8 x 6 cm
9.5 x 3.2 x 2.4 inches

2007

Leather basket I
(Cesto de couro I)

Leather
36 x 28 x 28 cm
14.2 x 11 x 11 inches

2007

Leather basket II
(Cesto de couro II)

Leather
36 x 28 x 28 cm
14.2 x 11 x 11 inches

2007

Leather basket III
(Cesto de couro III)

Leather
55 x 30 x 34 cm
21.7 x 11.8 x 13.4 inches

2007

Leather cube
(Dado de couro)

Wood, coconut fiber, leather
c. 50 x 50 x 50 cm
c. 20 x 20 x 20 inches

2007

Leather fruit bowl I
(Fruteira couro I)

Leather
16 x 50 x 52 cm
6.3 x 19.7 x 20.5 inches

2007

Leather fruit bowl II
(Fruteira couro II)

Leather
12 x 35 x 38 cm
4.7 x 13.8 x 15 inches

2007

Squared basket
(Cesto quadrado)

Leather
13 x 24 x 31 cm
5.1 x 9.4 x 12 inches

2007

Mandacaru family studies
(Estudo para Familia Mandacaru)

Various dimensions
Iron skeleton, synthetic fabric,
foam filling
Mandacaru Family collection
Emerging from the Unstructured
works in 2006, the Mandacaru
pieces are toys for children of
all ages! They are inspired by

characters from a Brazilian folk
story whose family name is
Mandacarú, which is also the
name of a plant that is typical
of the arid regions of Northeastern Brazil. Mandacaru
Formiga was the first to be
designed in 2006 and, with
the exception of one prototype
(Mandacaru Iara) the
Mandacaru Family collection
went into production with
Alessi in 2008.

2007

Melissa Pump – Bag
(Melissa Pump – Bolsa)

Aluminum wire
Dimensions variable
Melissa + Campana collection

2007

Melissa Pump – Shoe
(Melissa Pump – Sapatilha)

Aluminum wire
Dimensions variable
Melissa + Campana collection

2007

Blow up Architecture
(Arquitetura Blow up)

Aluminum tubes
400 x 400 x 8,000 cm
157 x 157 x 3,150 inches
Sculpture built in the atrium
of a residential building in
São Paulo
Produced by Estudio Campana

Campanas in the Garden
V&A Vitoria Regia stool

Stainless steel, coconut, fiber,
EVA, rubber net
45 x 150 x 150 cm
17.7 x 59 x 59 inches
Sushi collection
Produced by Estudio Campana
Installation featuring Vitoria
Regia stools and bamboo
structures in the gardens of
the V&A, London

Cartoon chair
(Cadeira Cartoon)

Stuffed Disney toys, fabric,
stainless steel
80 x 120 x 70 cm
31.5 x 47.2 x 27.6 inches
Banquete collection
3 types in an edition of 35 (each)
The 3 types of the Cartoon
chair are: Mickey chair, Mickey
and Minnie chair, and Mickey,
Minnie, and Pluto chair
Photo © Ed Reeve
Courtesy of Albion, London

Drosera wall pocket
(Drosera Bolso de parede)

Copper, fabric, aluminum
c. 150 x 130 x 40 cm
c. 59 x 51 x 16 inches
Edition of 2 twelve-piece sets
Produced by Vitra Design
Museum, Germany
Photo © Nichole Bachmann

FAD trophy
(Troféu FAD)

Esperança dolls sewn over a
stainless steel structure
43 x 25 x 25 cm
17 x 9.8 x 9.8 inches
Multidão collection

Fruit bowl
(Fruteira)

Wicker and marble
10 x 60 x 60 cm
3.9 x 23.6 x 23.6 inches
Edition of 3
Produced by Haaz, Istanbul
Photo © Ali Beckman
Haaz Gallery invited several
international artists and designers to take part in an exhibition
called Block. The main goal
was to come up with innovative
uses for marble—a traditional
and popular material in Turkey.

JWT Garden Landscape
(Jardim JWT)

Various species of plants
Produced by Estudio Campana
Photo © JWT
As part of the renovation of the
JWT ad agency in São Paulo,
the Campana brothers were
invited to redesign the garden.
Fernando and Humberto took
the opportunity to reintroduce
native vegetation.

285

Métamorphoses
(Metamorphoses)

Various materials
Produced by the Ballet National
de Marseille
Photo © Pino Pipitone
In 2007 the brothers were
invited by Frédéric Flamand to
design the sets and costumes
for his ambitious staging of
Métamorphoses at the Ballet
National de Marseille, France.
"The development took almost
a year. We went to supermarkets
and shops around Marseille,
sourcing plastic, canvas hose,
costume jewellery, Velcro and
all sorts!"

2007

Costume study I
(Estudo para figurino I)

PVC threads
Dimensions variable
Produced for the Marseille
ballet by Estudio Campana
One of a number of studies
and sketches produced by
Humberto and Fernando
for Métamorphoses

2007

Terrastool
(Terrastool)

Ceramic stool with carpet,
rubber, EVA, fabric
46 x 46 x 46 cm
18.1 x 18.1 x 18.1 inches
Sushi collection
Edition of 26
Produced by Galerie Kreo
Photo © Galerie Kreo

2007

TOP 21 trophy
(Troféu TOP 21)

Fabric doll with silver covering
35 x 10 x 10 cm
13.8 x 3.9 x 3.9 inches
Edition of 21
Produced by Estudio Campana

2008

Cake stool
(Banco Cake)

Stuffed toys, canvas, stainless
steel
55 x 120 x 120 cm
21.7 x 47.2 x 47.2 inches
Stool collection
Edition of 150

2008

Multidão stool
(Banco Multidão)

Stuffed toys, canvas, stainless
steel
70 x 66 x 57 cm
27.6 x 26 x 22.4 inches
Stool collection
Edition of 35
Photo © Ed Reeve

2008

Carvalho stool
(Banco Carvalho)

Stuffed toys, canvas, stainless
steel
67 x 56 x 52 cm
26.4 x 22 x 20.5 inches
Stool collection
Edition of 35
Photo © Ed Reeve

2007

My Home exhibition
(Exposição My Home)

Raffia fiber, wood floor,
lighting system
Unique
Produced by Vitra Design
Museum, Germany
Photos © Thomas Dix
This was a group exhibition
in which each designer was
invited to reflect on different
aspects of houses. Fernando
and Humberto were interested
in exploring the addition of
volume into the geometrical
architecture of Frank Gehry,
which they achieved by means
of piaçava—a species of
Brazilian raffia.

2007

Trans... chair
(Cadeira trans...)

Iron structure, wicker, plastic
objects
84 x 90 x 110 cm
33.1 x 35.4 x 43.3 inches
Unique
Produced by Estudio Campana
and presented at the Cooper
Hewitt National Design
Museum, New York, in February
2008
Photo © Andrew Garn

2008

Flamboyant
(Flamboyant)

Stuffed toys, canvas, stainless
steel
75 x 55 x 55 cm
29.5 x 21.7 x 21.7 inches
Stool collection
Edition of 35

2007

TransPlastic exhibition
(Exposição TransPlastic)

Albion Gallery, London
Photo © Ed Reeve
Courtesy of Albion, London

Samambaia
(Samambaia)

Stuffed toys, canvas, stainless
steel
78 x 52 x 60 cm
30.7 x 20.5 x 23.6 inches
Stool collection
Edition of 35

Blow up centerpiece
(Centro de mesa Blow up)

Bamboo
Ø 70 cm
Ø 27.6 inches
Blow up Bamboo collection
Unlimited edition
Forthcoming – prototype
produced by Alessi, Italy
Photo © Alessi

Aguapé chair
(Cadeira Aguapé)

Leather and stainless steel
68 x 86 x 112 cm
26.8 x 33.9 x 44.1 inches
Unlimited edition
Designed by Estudio Campana
Produced by Edra, Italy
Photo © Edra

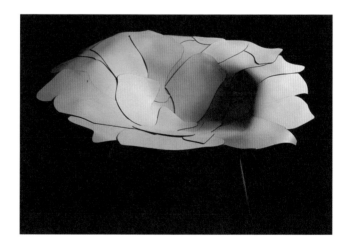

Blow up side table
(Mesa Blow up)

Bamboo
44 x Ø 45 cm
17.3 x Ø 17.7 inches
Blow up Bamboo collection
Unlimited edition
Forthcoming – prototype
produced by Alessi, Italy
Photo © Alessi

Blow up citrus basket
(Cesto de Frutas Blow up)

Bamboo
40 x Ø 35 cm
15.7 x Ø 13.8 inches
Blow up Bamboo collection
Unlimited edition
Forthcoming – prototype
produced by Alessi, Italy
Photo © Alessi

Mandacaru Curupira
(Mandacaru Curupira)

Pose-able fabric puppet
22 x Ø 38 cm
8.7 x Ø 15 inches
Available in two colors/fabrics
Produced by Alessi, Italy
Photo © Alessi

Mandacaru Boto
(Mandacaru Boto)

Pose-able fabric puppet
35 x 55 x 8 cm
13.8 x 21.7 x 3.1 inches
Available in two colors/fabrics
Produced by Alessi, Italy
Photo © Alessi

Mandacaru Formiga
(Mandacaru Formiga)

Pose-able fabric puppet
32 x 19 x 7 cm
12.6 x 7.5 x 2.8 inches
Available in two colors/fabrics
Produced by Alessi, Italy
Photo © Alessi

Mandacaru Saci
(Mandacaru Saci)

Pose-able fabric puppet
29 x 49 x 6 cm
11.4 x 19.3 x 2.4 inches
Available in two colors/fabrics
Produced by Alessi, Italy
Photo © Alessi

287

Mandacaru Tatá
(Mandacaru Tatá)

Pose-able fabric puppet
23 x 43 x 8 cm
9.1 x 16.9 x 3.1 inches
Available in two colors/fabrics
Produced by Alessi, Italy
Photo © Alessi

Melissa + Campana bag
(Bolsa Melissa + Campana)

PVC with up to 30% recycled
materials
28.4 x 7.2 x 42 cm
11.2 x 2.8 x 16.5 inches
Unlimited edition
Melissa + Campana collection
Inspired by the Corallo chair
Designed by Estudio Campana
Produced by Melissa, Brazil
Photo © Melissa

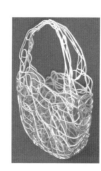

2008

Melissa + Campana shoes
(Sapatilha Melissa + Campana)

PVC with up to 30% recycled
materials
Various sizes
Melissa + Campana collection
Unlimited edition
Inspired by the Corallo chair
Designed by Estudio Campana
Produced by Melissa, Brazil
Photo © Melissa

2008

Blue chair
(Cadeira Azul)

Plastic chair and synthetic
wicker
72 x 50 x 77 cm
28.3 x 19.7 x 30.3 inches
Study for TransPlastic series

2008

Cobogó center table
(Mesa de centro Cobogó)

Cobogó tiles and cement
Dimensions unavailable
Ceramic series
Cobogó collection

2008

Doll basket
(Cesto de Bonecas)

Plastic doll limbs
63 x 55 x 46 cm
24.8 x 21.7 x 18.1 inches
Study for Nazareth collection

2008

Espelhos ceiling lamp
(Lustre Espelhos)

Acrylic mirror on steel structure
120 x 115 x 25 cm
47.2 x 45.3 x 9.8 inches

2008

Floor lamp
(Luminária de Piso)

Wood and iron
185 x Ø 76 cm
72.8 x 29.9 inches
2 prototypes

2008

Fragmentos chair
(Cadeira Fragmentos)

Pinewood on steel structure
50 x 49 x 96 cm
19.7 x 19.3 x 37.8 inches
Study for Fragmentos series
Prototype produced by
Habitart, Brazil
Photo © Estudio Campana

2008

Fragmentos dinner table
(Mesa Fragmentos de Jantar)

Pinewood on steel structure
300 x 100 x 77 cm
118 x 39.4 x 30.3 inches
Study for Fragmentos series
Prototype produced by
Habitart, Brazil
Photo © Estudio Campana

2008

Fragmentos square table
(Mesa Fragmentos quadrada)

Pinewood on steel structure
150 x 120 x 77 cm
59 x 47.2 x 30.3 inches
Study for Fragmentos series
Prototype produced by
Habitart, Brazil
Photo © Estudio Campana

2008

Fruit bowl
(Fruteira)

Steel structure and stainless
steel mesh
185 x 179 x 650 cm
72.8 x 70.5 x 25.6 inches

2008

Fruit bowl
(Fruteira)

Wicker and thin stainless steel
mesh
Dimensions unavailable

2008

Fruit bowl
(Fruteira)

Wicker and thin stainless steel
mesh
Dimensions unavailable

2008

Fruit bowl
(Fruteira)

Wicker and thin stainless steel
mesh
Dimensions unavailable

2008

Fruit bowl
(Fruteira)

Wicker and thin stainless steel
mesh
Dimensions unavailable

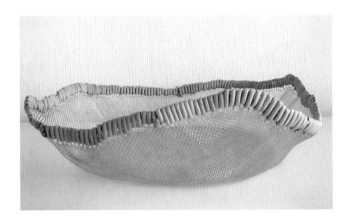

2008

Imã necklace
(Colar Imã)

Aluminum sheet, leather,
magnet
23 x 20 x 0.5 cm
9.1 x 7.9 x 0.2 inches

2008

Leather cabinet
(Armário em couro)

Wood, aluminum wires, leather
80 x 85 x 210 cm
31.5 x 33.5 x 82.7 inches

2008

Leather hammock
(Rede de Couro)

Leather on steel structure
240 x 320 cm
94.5 x 126 inches
Study for Leather series

2008

Leather fruit bowl
(Fruteira Couro)

Leather patchwork
15 x Ø 38 cm
5.9 x Ø 15 inches
Study for Leather series

2008

Leather fruit bowl
(Fruteira Couro)

Leather patchwork
15 x Ø 38 cm
5.9 x Ø 15 inches
Study for Leather series

2008

Leather fruit bowl
(Fruteira Couro)

Wood, aluminum wires, latex
leather
50 x 40 x 16 cm
19.7 x 15.7 x 6.3 inches
Study for Leather series

2008

Leather vessel
(Vaso de Couro)

Latex leather
29 x 18 cm
11.4 x 7.1 inches
Study for Leather series

2008

Leather vessel
(Vaso de Couro)

Natural leather
16 x 12 cm
6.3 x 4.7 inches
Study for Leather series

2008

Leather vessel
(Vaso de Couro)

Latex leather
14 x 12 cm
5.5 x 4.7 inches
Study for Leather series

2008

Leather vessel
(Vaso de Couro)

Natural leather
29 x 18 cm
11.4 x 7.1 inches
Study for Leather series

2008

Leather waste basket
(Lixeira de Couro)

Synthetic leather
38 x 36 x 53 cm
15 x 14.2 x 20.9 inches
Study for Leather series

289

2008

Multidão chair – unfinished study
*(Cadeira Multidão – estudo
inacabado)*

Plastic chair, fabric, Esperança
dolls
60 x 51 x 92 cm
23.6 x 20.1 x 36.2 inches
Multidão collection

2008

Necklace
(Colar)

Leather and magnet
33 x 25 cm
13 x 9.8 inches

2008

Ninho table
(Mesa Ninho)

Aluminum wire structure with
epoxy paint finish and glass
75 x Ø 82 cm
29.5 x Ø 32.3 inches

290

2008

Sushi buffet
(Buffet Sushi)

Wood, EVA, rubber, carpet
40.4 x 180 x 70 cm
15.9 x 70.9 x 27.6 inches
Sushi collection

2008

Screen
(Biombo)

Amethyst and clear glass
81 x 10 x 200 cm
31.9 x 3.9 x 78.7 inches

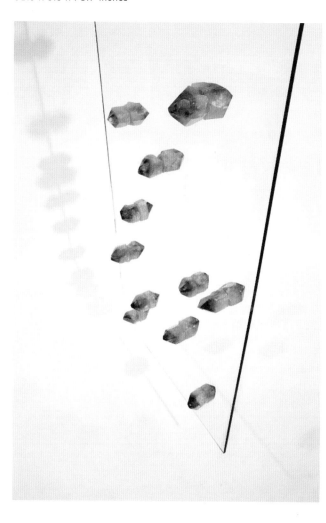

2008

Table lamp study
*(Estudo para Luminária de
Mesa)*

Piaçava and aluminum wire
structure
55 x Ø 30 cm
21.7 x Ø 11.8 inches

2008

Telha lamp I
(Luminária Telha I)

Hard paper and wicker
40 x 23 x 50 cm
15.7 x 9.1 x 19.7 inches
Study for Ceramic series

2008

Telha lamp II
(Luminária Telha II)

Ceramic tile and wicker
36 x 25 x 39 cm
14.2 x 9.8 x 15.4 inches

2008

Telha lamp III
(Luminária Telha III)

Ceramic tile and wicker
29 x 16 x 46 cm
11.4 x 6.3 x 18.1 inches

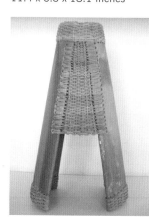

2008

Untitled ceramic table I
*(Mesa em ceramica sem
titulo I)*

Ceramic and pinewood
49 x Ø 50 cm
19.3 x Ø 19.7 inches
Ceramic series
Produced by Olaria Pajé
Photo © Estudio Campana
Study for Pagé table produced
by Skitsch, Italy

2008

Untitled ceramic table II
*(Mesa em ceramica sem
titulo II)*

Ceramic
46 x 46 x 49 cm
18.1 x 18.1 x 19.3 inches
Ceramic series
Produced by Olaria Pajé
Photo © Estudio Campana

Untitled lamp I
(Luminária sem titulo I)

Wood, nylon mesh, wicker
42 x 25 x 54 cm
16.5 x 9.8 x 21.3 inches

**Camper together with Campanas –
Florence**
*(Camper together with
Campanas – Florença)*

Produced by Estudio Campana
Photo © Camper

Diamantina I
(Diamantina I)

Iron, natural fiber, precious
stones
160 x 450 x 180 cm
63 x 177.2 x 70.9 inches
TransPlastic collection
Unique
Produced by Estudio Campana
Photo © James Harris
Courtesy of Design Miami/

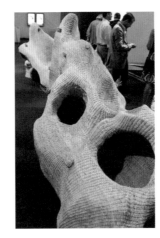

**HSBC Private Bank lounge at
Design Miami/**
As Designers of the Year,
Fernando and Humberto were
invited to design a special lounge
for the fair's main sponsor.
Photo © James Harris
Courtesy of Design Miami/

Wall lamp
(Arandela)

Aluminum wire and nylon mesh
75 x 116 x 30 cm
29.5 x 45.7 x 11.8 inches

Cristalina
(Cristalina)

Iron, natural fiber, tree branch
150 x 450 x 170 cm
59.1 x 177.2 x 66.9 inches
TransPlastic collection
Unique
Especially designed for the
Second Nature Exhibition,
Tokyo
Produced by Estudio Campana
Photo © Masaya Yoshimura
Courtesy of 21_21, Tokyo

Diamantina III
(Diamantina III)

Iron, natural fiber, precious
stones
142 x 433 x 169.5 cm
56 x 170.5 x 66.7 inches
TransPlastic collection
Unique
Produced by Estudio Campana
Photo © Fernando Laszlo
Courtesy of Vitra Design
Museum, Germany

Favela bookshelf
(Estante Favela)

Wood
260 x 700 cm
102.4 x 275.6 inches
Photo © Maíra Acayaba

291

Diamantina II
(Diamantina II)

Iron, natural fiber, precious
stones
160 x 450 x 180 cm
63 x 177.2 x 70.9 inches
TransPlastic collection
Unique
Produced by Estudio Campana
Photo © James Harris
Courtesy of Design Miami/

Wicker chandelier
(Lustre em Vime)

Stainless steel, wicker, plastic
5 sizes:
183 x 243 x 43 cm /
72 x 95.7 x 17 inches
202 x 171 x 58 cm /
79.5 x 67.3 x 22.8 inches
203 x 175 x 66 cm /
79.9 x 68.9 x 26 inches
244 x 138 x 44 cm /
96.1 x 54.3 x 17.3 inches
192 x 139 x 62 cm /
75.6 x 54.7 x 24.4 inches
TransPlastic collection

Wicker armchair
(Banco em Vime)

Wicker on steel structure
185 x 179 x 65 cm
72.8 x 70.5 x 25.6 inches

Nazareth centerpiece
(Centro de mesa Nazareth)

Porcelain with bronze glaze
19 x 36 x 42 cm
7.5 x 14.2 x 16.5 inches
Limited edition of 100 in
10 colors
Produced by Bernardaud, France
Photo © Bernardaud
Also fabricated without glaze

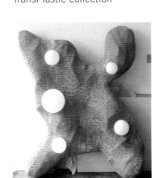

Papier-mâché fruit bowl
(Fruteira de Papel Machê)

Papier-mâché
55 x 47 x 9 cm
21.7 x 18.5 x 3.5 inches
Papier-mâché collection studies
for Vitra Design Museum
Produced by Estudio Campana
Photo © Estudio Campana

Peter and the Wolf
(Pedro e o Lobo)

As part of the cultural program
of the Guggenheim Museum,
Fernando and Humberto were
invited to create the set design
for the musical tale of *Peter
and the Wolf*. Fashion designer
Isaac Mizrahi narrated live
performances of Sergei
Prokofiev's children's classic,
accompanied by the Juilliard
ensemble.

Vertical garden
(Jardim Vertical)

Digital rendering of an iron
shelf
Produced by Estudio Campana

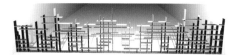

Sushi fruit bowl
(Fruteira Sushi)

EVA, felt, rubber, rug
8 x Ø 30 cm / 3.2 x Ø 11.8
inches
Unlimited edition
Sushi collection
This piece was first presented
at the MoMA Destination
Brazil exhibition, 2009.

Cardboard fruit bowl
(Fruteira Papelão)

Painted cardboard
c. 30 x 7 cm
c. 11.8 x 2.8 inches

Cipria sofa
(Sofá Cipria)

Metal tube frame, Gellyfoam®,
Dacron, ecological fur
222 x 128 x 84 cm
87.4 x 50.4 x 33.1 inches
Shining collection
Unlimited edition
Produced by Edra, Italy
Photo © Edra

Miraggio
(Miraggio)

Colored reflective acrylic and
nylon strips
6 x 107 x 187 cm
2.3 x 42.1 x 73.6 inches
Shining collection
Unlimited edition
Produced by Edra, Italy
Photo © Edra

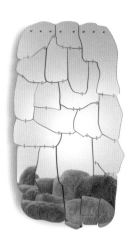

Scrigno
(Scrigno)

Reflective acrylic in gold,
silver, and other colors
47 x 135 x 115 cm
18.5 x 83.1 x 45.2 inches
Shining collection
Unlimited edition
Produced by Edra, Italy
Photo © Edra

Segreto
(Segreto)

Steel and aluminum frame,
shiny painted leather panels,
colored acrylic
85 x 73 x 205 cm
33.4 x 28.7 x 80.7 inches
Shining collection
Unlimited edition
Produced by Edra, Italy
Photo © Edra

2009

Cobogó table
(Mesa Cobogó)

Terra-cotta, resin, steel
137 x 125 x 74 cm
53.9 x 49.2 x 29.1 inches
Edition of 21
Produced by Plusdesign, Italy
Photo © Plusdesign

2009

Table lamp
(Luminária de Mesa)

Bamboo, metal
c. 50 x 62 cm
c. 20 x 24 inches

2009

Ceiling lamp II
(Luminária de Teto II)

Acrylic
70 x Ø 60 cm
27.6 x Ø 23.6 inches

2009

Untitled Tray
(Bandeja sem título)

Stainless steel
40 x 38 cm
15.7 x 15 inches
Produced by Riva
Photo © Romulo Fialdini

2009

2 in 1 Table
(Mesa 2 em 1)

Pine
c. 160 x 76 x 80 cm /
62.9 x 29.9 x 31.4 inches
(closed)
c. 250 x 76 x 80 cm /
98.4 x 29.9 x 31.4 inches
(extended)
Produced by Habitart, Brazil
Photo © Estudio Campana

2009

Apuí chair
(Cadeira Apuí)

Apuí
c. 90 x 48 x 87 cm
c. 35 x 19 x 34 inches

2009

Blow up lamp study
(Estudo para Luminária Blow up)

Stainless steel
Ø 36 cm / 14.2 inches

293

2009

Wood floor lamp
(Luminária Wood Floor lamp)

Wood
170 x Ø 72 cm
67 x Ø 28.3 inches
Unlimited edition
Produced by Skitsch, Italy
Photo © Skitsch

2009

Bamboo chair
(Cadeira Bambú)

Metal structure and bamboo
c. 50 x 53 x 80 cm
c. 20 x 21 x 31.5 inches

2009

Ceiling lamp I
(Luminária de Teto I)

Piaçava and cardboard
88 x Ø 70 cm
34.7 x Ø 27.6 inches

2009

Cupboard
(Armário)

Wood, piaçava
c. 165 x 155 x 65 cm
c. 65 x 61 x 25.6 inches

Favela table study
(Estudo para Mesa Favela)

Wood
140 x 111 x 79 cm
55.1 x 43.7 x 31.1 inches

Square container
(Cesto quadrado)

Aluminum wire
Nuovi Nuvem collection
Prototype produced by Alessi
for the Square container.
Photo © Alessi

Palha Piacava chair
(Cadeira Palha Piacava)

Metal structure, piaçava
c. 63 x 68 x 81 cm
c. 25 x 27 x 32 inches

Fruit bowl
(Fruteira)

Cardboard
Dimensions unknown

Paper lamp I
(Luminária Papel I)

Drawing, paper off-cuts, cotton
thread
37 x 30 x 88 cm
14.6 x 11.8 x 34.6 inches
Photo © Fernando Laszlo

Flip Flop study
(Estudo para Chinelo)

Plastic alligators
Dimensions variable

294

Basket
(Lixeira)

Cardboard
Dimensions unknown

Fruit bowl
(Fruteira)

Cardboard
8 x Ø 40 cm
3.1 x Ø 15.7 inches

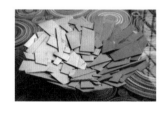

Paper lamp II
(Luminária Papel II)

Drawing, paper off-cuts, cotton
thread
78 x Ø 20 cm
30.7 x Ø 7.9 inches
Photo © Fernando Laszlo

Metal lampshade study
*(Estudo para cúpula de
luminária)*

Metal
Ø 45 cm / 17.7 inches

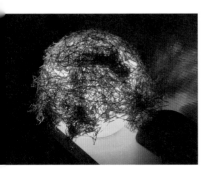

Metal chair
(Cadeira de Metal)

Welded iron
50 x 55 x 90 cm
19.6 x 21.6 x 35.4 inches

Basket
(Lixeira)

Cardboard
20 x 23 x 33 cm
7.9 x 9.1 x 13 inches

Tray
(Bandeija)

Cardboard
48 x 35 x 2 cm
18.9 x 13.8 x 0.8 inches

Sofa study
(Estudo Sofá)

Fabric and foam
50 x 23 x 10 cm
19.6 x 9 x 3.9 inches

Sofa study
(Estudo Sofá)

Fabric and foam
70 x 150 x 109 cm
27.5 x 59 x 43.3 inches

Sofa study
(Estudo Sofá)

Fabric and foam
23 x 74 x 70 cm
9 x 29.1 x 27.5 inches

Straw Pendant lamp
(Luminária Pendente de Palha)

Straw place mats, metal
structure
c. 77 x 75 cm
c. 30 x 29.5 inches

Tall Tile lamp
(Luminária Alta de Telhas)

Clay tile and wicker
c. 65 x 50 x 130 cm
c. 25.5 x 20 x 51 inches
Ceramics series

Tall Tile lamp
(Luminária Alta de Telhas)

Clay tile and wicker
c. 65 x 50 x 117 cm
c. 25.5 x 20 x 46 inches
Ceramics series

Tile lamp
(Luminária de Telhas)

Clay tile and wicker
c. 55 x 30 x 45 cm
c. 22 x 12 x 18 inches
Ceramics series

Tile lamp
(Luminária de Telhas)

Clay tile and wicker
c. 27 x 15 x 55 cm
c. 11 x 6 x 22 inches
Ceramics series

Tile lamp
(Luminária de Telhas)

Clay tile and wicker
c. 34 x 17 x 88 cm
c. 13 x 7 x 35 inches
Ceramics series

Transparent hybrid
(Transparent Hibridi)

Glass and scotch tape
Dimensions variable

Mirror wall study
(Estudo para Parede Espelhada)

Cardboard and acrylic mirror
82 x 47 x 37 cm
32.3 x 18.5 x 14.6 inches

Table lamp
(Luminária de Mesa)

Wicker and steel structure
70 x Ø 40 cm
27.6 x Ø 15.7 inches

**Installation created for the
Antibodies exhibition at Vitra
Design Museum**
*(Instalação criada para a
exposição Antibodies no Vitra
Design Museum)*
Plastic bottles
Photos © Thomas Dix

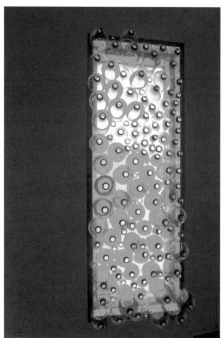

Corkscrew
(Saca-rolhas)

Aluminum
14 x 13 cm
5.5 x 5.1 inches
Special commission for Ibravin
Brazilian Institute for Wine
Produced by Ibravin, Brazil

**Destination Brazil logo for
MoMA, NY**
*(Logo para o Destination Brazil
no MoMA, NY)*

DESTINATION
BRAZIL
MoMA Design Store Presents New Brazilian Design

Garrafa exhibition
(Exposição Garrafa)

Plastic bottle installation
Dimensions variable
Centre d'Art de Versailles,
France
Illustration © Estudio Campana

Jardim de Infância – exhibition
*(Jardim de Infância –
exposição)*

Photo © Rochelle Costi
Exhibition curated by Fernando
and Humberto for the Museu
de Arte Moderna (MaM) in São
Paulo. "Jardim de infância"
translates as "kindergarten"
in English.

Baby bed
(Berço)

Wood crib, stuffed toy animals,
leather
c. 85 x 130 x 100 cm
c. 33.5 x 51 x 39 cm
Banquete collection
Unique

Lacoste Polo limited edition, Liana female and Anavilhana male
(Edição Limitada da Polo Lacoste, Liana feminina e Anavilhana masculina)

Various sizes
Holiday collector's edition
Produced by Coopa Roca
Photo © Lacoste

Lacoste Polo special edition, female and male
(Edição Especial da Polo Lacoste, feminina e masculina)

Various sizes
Holiday collector's edition
Produced by Lacoste
Photo © Lacoste

Special Edition packaging
(Embalagem da Edição Especial)

26 x Ø 13 cm
10.2 x Ø 5.1 inches
Natural straw and natural canvas
Collection Lacoste + Campanas
Produced by Lacoste
Photo © Lacoste

Lacoste Polo super limited edition, female and male
(Edição Super Limitada da Polo Lacoste, feminina e masculina)

Made only from Lacoste logos
Various sizes
Holiday collector's edition
Produced by Coopa Roca
Photo © Lacoste

Mandacaru Blow up
(Mandacaru Blow up)

Welded stainless steel place mats and epoxy paint
c. 148 x 240 cm
c. 58 x 94.5 inches
Unique
Special commission from Alessi SPA, Italy
Photo © Alessi NY
This image shows the piece installed in the window of Harrods, London, as part of the London Design Festival, 2009.

2009

Nazareth candleholder
(Castiçal Nazareth)

Porcelain
8 x 35 cm
3.1 x 13.8 inches
Nazareth collection
Unlimited edition
Produced by Bernardaud,
France
Photo © Bernardaud

298

2009

Nazareth bookends
(Separador de livro Nazareth)

Porcelain
14 x 26 cm
5.5 x 10.2 inches
Nazareth collection
Unlimited edition
Produced by Bernardaud,
France
Photo © Bernardaud

2009

Ring the Bells
Blown Murano glass, ropes

Dimensions variable
Produced by Venini
Photo © Archivio fotographico
Venini S.p.A

2009

Nazareth paper holder
(Peso de Papel Nazareth)

Porcelain
7 x 23 cm
2.8 x 9.1 inches
Nazareth collection
Unlimited edition
Produced by Bernardaud
Photo © Bernardaud

2009

Untitled candlestick
(Castiçal sem titulo)

Metal
Height: 39 cm
(base: 15 x 12 cm;
top: 3.5 x 5 cm)
Height: 15.4 inches
(base: 5.9 x 4.7;
top: 1.4 x 2 inches)
Special commission for
MAD Museum, New York

Humberto & Fernando Campana / The Estudio Campana

The Estudio Campana is a collaboration between brothers Humberto Campana (b. 1953) and Fernando Campana (b. 1961). Based in São Paulo, the Estudio Campana is constantly investigating new conceptual and productional possibilities for unexpected and everyday materials, creating bridges and dialogues where the exchange of information is also a source of inspiration. Their work incorporates the ideas of transformation and reinvention, elevating poor, day-to-day materials to high design, a technique that the Campana brothers identify as quintessentially Brazilian.

Born in Brazil, the Campanas' Italian heritage comes from their great-grandfathers, who emigrated to Brazil in the 19th century to work on coffee plantations. The Campanas were raised in Brotas, a lush, idyllic small town, and São Paulo, Brazil's largest metropolis. The duality of their childhood's countryside background and urban excursions highly informed their youth and adulthood. "How to make the transition between the two has been our most precious learning experience," the Campanas have stated.

As children Humberto and Fernando learned to appreciate and respect the natural landscape from their father, Alberto Campana, an agronomic engineer, who often took them along to survey the farms in Brotas. This experience with the countryside has inspired them to plant over ten thousand native trees on the land they have inherited from their family. Their mother, Celia Piva Campana, was a primary school teacher who taught a generation of children in the 1950s and 1960s, including the Campana boys.

Humberto Campana studied law at University of São Paulo from 1972 to 1977. Fernando Campana studied architecture at the São Paulo School of Fine Arts from 1979 to 1981. After Humberto's graduation from law school he opened a sculpture and jewelry studio, where he started producing wicker baskets to support his artistic creations. The desire to make things with his own hands spurred Humberto's investigations into handcraft works and techniques. During a very busy season he called Fernando to give him a helping hand. "From that day on we started, spontaneously, to make experiments and put together ideas that were in our unconscious. This happened in 1983 and we have been working together ever since," according to Humberto.

Their first true artistic collaboration resulted in a collection of iron chairs called Desconfortáveis, in 1989. The first chair, made of heavy iron plates, was called Negativo (negative), and its inspiration came to Humberto in a dream. From the leftover scraps of the Negativo Fernando created a new chair, called Positivo (positive), which was lighter and more functional. "Forty other chairs followed them, exploring the artistic potential of discomfort, the poetry of the distorted and the error," explains Fernando.

In 1993 *Domus* published the first international article on the Campanas, a four-page story filled with images of their works. With the production of the Vermelha Chair in 1998, they sealed their first partnership with a high-end contemporary design manufacturer, Edra, in Italy. From then on, each year new products and concepts are launched in collaboration with national and international companies such as Grendene, Edra, Alessi, and Artecnica for their unlimited edition pieces.

In 1998, Paola Antonelli invited them to exhibit at the Museum of Modern Art in New York, their first international show. The idea of the exhibition, "Project 66", was to pair two design studios of distinctly different backgrounds that shared the same poetics. The Campanas were paired with Ingo Maurer, the German lighting designer.

In 2002, the Estudio Campana officially started crafting its own line of editions and unique pieces handmade at the studio in São Paulo, with international galleries, including the Albion in London and Moss in New York, representing these special editions.

The Campana brothers' works are in the permanent collections of renowned cultural institutions such as MoMA in New York, the Centre Georges Pompidou in Paris, the Vitra Design Museum in Weil am Rhein, Germany, and the Museum of Modern Art in São Paulo. In 2008 they were honored with the Designer of the Year award by Design Miami/.

Bibliography

Selected Publications and Catalogues

Antonelli, Paola (Ed.). *Workspheres: Design and Contemporary Work Styles.* New York: The Museum of Modern Art, 2002

Antonelli, Paola, Joshua Siegel, and Kirk Varnedoe. *Modern Contemporary: Aspects of Art at MoMA Since 1980.* New York: Harry N. Abrams, 2000

Borges, Adélia. *Cartas a um jovem designer.* São Paulo: Campus-Elsevier, 2009

Borges, Adélia et al. *Design brasileiro hoje: Fronteiras.* São Paulo: Museu de Arte Moderna de São Paulo, 2009

Botha, Nadine, Fiona Zerbst, and Fatima Salie. *Design Indaba All Stars.* Cape Town, South Africa: Interactive Africa, 2008

Branzi, Andrea. *Il Design Italiano: 1964–2000.* Milan: La Triennale di Milano, 2008

Bueno, Patricia. *Design Furniture.* Barcelona: Atrium Group De Ediciones Y Publicaciones, 2002

Byars, Mel. *50 Chairs: Innovations in Design and Materials.* Hove, England: RotoVision, 1996

———. *50 Lights: Innovations in Design and Materials.* Hove, England: RotoVision, 1997

———. *50 Tables: Innovations in Design and Materials.* Hove, England: RotoVision, 1997

———. *50 Products: Innovations in Design and Materials.* Hove, England: RotoVision, 1998

Byars, Mel (Ed.). *Tropical Modern: The Designs of Fernando and Humberto Campana.* New York: Acanthus Press, 1998

Campana, Fernando and Humberto. *Campanas.* São Paulo, Brazil: Bookmark, 2003

Campana, Fernando and Humberto. *The Campana Brothers: Complete Works (So Far).* New York: Rizzoli, and London: Albion, 2010

Chiarella Vignon, Sarah, and Stéphane Corréard. *Iluminar: Design da Luz – Design et Lumière: 1920–2004.* São Paulo: Fundação Armando Alvares Penteado, 2004

Conran, Terence, and Max Fraser. *Designers on Design.* London: Conran Octopus, 2004

Couturier, Élisabeth. *Le Design Hier, Aujourd'hui, Demain: Mode D'emploi.* Paris: Filipacchi, 2006

Dixon, Tom (Ed.). *International Design Yearbook 19.* London: Laurence King Publishing, 2004

Fiell, Charlotte and Peter. *Designing the 21st Century.* Cologne: Taschen, 2001

———. *Design Now: Designs for Life.* Cologne: Taschen, 2007

Fuad-Luke, Alastair. *The Eco-Design Handbook: A Complete Sourcebook for the Home and Office.* London: Thames & Hudson, 2002

Hanks, David A., and Anne Hoy. *Design for Living: Furniture And Lighting 1950–2000.* Paris: Flammarion, 2000

Hudson, Jennifer. *1000 New Designs and Where to Find Them: A 21st-Century Sourcebook.* London: Laurence King Publishing, 2006

Linley, David, Charles Cator, and Helen Chislett. *Star Pieces: The Enduring Beauty of Spectacular Furniture.* London: Thames & Hudson, 2009

Lloyd Morgan, Conway, Jennifer Hudson, and Philippe Starck (Eds.). *International Design Yearbook 12.* London: Laurence King Publishing, 1997

Lovegrove, Ross (Ed.). *International Design Yearbook 17.* London: Laurence King Publishing, 2002

Lovell, Sophie. *Limited Edition: Prototypes, One-Offs and Design Art Furniture.* Basel, Switzerland: Birkhäuser, 2009

MAM. *Entre o design e a arte: Irmãos Campana, entre a arte e o design: Acervo do MAM.* São Paulo: Museu de Arte Moderna, 2000

———. *Jardim de infância: Os irmãos Campana visitam o MAM.* São Paulo: Museu de Arte Moderna, 2009

McKinlay, Sophie. *Zest for Life: Fernando and Humberto Campana.* London: The Design Museum, 2004

Morozzi, Cristina. *Oggetti Risorti.* Milan: Costa & Nolan, 1998

Morisson, Jasper (Ed.). *International Design Yearbook 14.* London: Laurence King Publishing, 1999

Nichols, Sarah. *Aluminum by Design.* New York: Harry N. Abrams, 2000

Pedersen, B. Martin (Ed.). *Graphis Product Design 3.* New York: Graphis, 2003

Phaidon Press. *Spoon.* London: Phaidon Press, 2002

Saville, Laurel. *Design Secrets: Furniture.* Beverly, Massachusetts: Rockport Publishers, 2006

Schwartz-Clauss, Mathias (Ed.). *Scoprire Il Design, Adventures with Objects: La collezione Alexander von Vegesack.* Milan: Electa, 2008

Van Cauwelaert, Karolien (Ed.). *Design/Art Limited Editions.* Netherlands: Stichting Kunstboek, 2009

Von Vegesack, Alexander, and Mathias Schwartz-Clauss. *Fernando and Humberto Campana 1989–2009: Antibodies.* Germany: Vitra Design Museum, 2009

Williams, Gareth. *Furniture Machine: Furniture Design Since 1990.* London: V&A Publications, 2006

Yelavich, Susan. *Design for Life: Our Daily Lives, the Spaces We Shape and the Ways We Communicate, As Seen Through the Collections of the Cooper Hewitt National Design Museum.* New York: Rizzoli, 1997

Ying, Yeh. *A Designer's Map: Navigation with 21+1 Industrial Designers.* Taipei: Garden City Publishers, 2006

Selected Articles: Magazines and Journals

"Bagdá & Brasilia." *Revista da Folha*, vol. 14, no. 666 (April 2005)

"Ballet de Marseille by Campana." *Arc Design*, no. 59 (March/April 2008)

Bernstein, Fred A. "21 for the 21st Century." *Metropolitan Home*, (March/April 1999)

Bitzer, Philipp. "Estudio Campana." *Wohnrevue*, no. 9 (2006)

Borges, Adélia. "Irmãos Campana Brasileiros e Universais." *Board Magazine*, no. 17 (August 1998)

Bossi, Laura. "Le Gioie Dell'ordinario." *Domus*, no. 844 (January 2002)

"Brutas, belas e loucas." *Vip Exame*, (August 1995)

Cabral, Nicolás. "Fernando y Humberto Campana: Una Pasión Mineral." *Arquine*, no. 32 (Summer 2005)

Campana, Fernando and Humberto. "A Contatto con gli Artigiani, In Contact with Artisans." *Domus*, no. 903 (May 2007)

Campana, Humberto. "The Campanas: Designing Objects with Tropical Influences and Universal Appeal." *Architectural Record*, 192, no. 4 (April 2004)

"The Campana Brothers Give Beauty to São Paulo." *Axis,* 111, no. 10 (October 2004)

"The Campana Brothers – Taking Inspiration from Brazil's Street Culture." *Domus,* no. 860 (June 2003)

Casciani, Stefano and Marco Romanelli. "End of the Century: Findings/Objects/Projects – Fernando e Humberto Campana, Fruteria." *Abitare*, no. 357 (December 1996)

Clayton, Richard. "Brazilian Rope Tricks." *Time*, 170, no. 19 (November 2007)

"Código genético." *Casa Vogue*, no. 264 (August 2007)

"Com uma lente nos detalhes." *Arc Design*, no. 14 (January/February 2000)

"Consciência com leveza." *Audi*, no. 71 (June 2008)

"Cover Interview / Humberto and Fernando Campana." *Axis*, 121, no. 6, (June 2006)

"De Brotas para o Mundo." *Casa Vogue*, 162, no. 11 (November 1998)

"Design – Humberto et Fernando Campana: Toute L'âme du Brésil." *Cimaise*, no. 286 (June/July/August 2007)

"Design: What Gets Me Going / Campana Brothers." *DAM,* no. 11 (May/June 2007)

Dokul IL, Heidi. "In the Studio with Fernando and Humberto Campana." *Monument, Architecture & Design,* no. 87 (October/November 2008)

"Entre o design e a arte." *Bravo*, no. 31 (April 2000)

"Entrevista com os designers brasileiros – Irmãos Campana." *Swisscam Brasil*, no. 48 (2007)

"Estética do bom humor." *Arte & Decoração*, (November 1996)

Estrada, Maria Helena. "Subjetos, Ou a Tentativa de Reverter Valores." *Arch Design*, no. 3 (December 1997/January 1998)

"Uma expressão dramática." *Casa Vogue*, no. 3 (March 1989)

"Faces and Places: q&a Marco Antonio Nakata: Brazilian Talent is shining off the soccer pitch." *Metropolis*, no. 603 (October, 2005)

Fairs, Marcus. "The Campana Brothers." *Icon*, no. 14 (July/August 2004)

Finessi, Beppe. "Bouroullec, Campana, Grcic, Rashid: Case Ideali." *Abitare*, no. 437 (March 2004)

Fitoussi, Brigitte. "Intérieurs Portrait: Fernando et Humberto Campana Designers Brésiliens." *L'Architecture d'aujord'hui*, no. 302 (December 1995)

"Flash back, de sola no mercado, trash chic, neo realismo, tirando o atraso." *Journal design*, no. 18 (2005)

Gomes, Edward M. "Insites: Indigenous Design." *Metropolis*, (March 1993)

Hirst, Arlene. "Editors Choice: Milan 2005." *Metropolitan Home*, (June 2005)

"Irmãos Campana." *Arc Design*, no. 53 (March/April 2007)

"Irmãos Campana." *Casa Claudia*, 20, no. 244 (May 2008) Special collectors' edition

"Irmãos Campana – brasileiros e universais." *Viaje Bem*, no. 17 (1998)

"Irmãos comemoram dez anos de design com mostra no Rio." *Tribuna da Imprensa*, (May, 2005)

"Jóias de vestir." *Veja*, (June 2001)

Kronowitz, Debra. "Campana Brothers Named 'Designer of the Year' 2008 by Design Miami." *Design District: Art+Design+Entertainment*, (Winter 2008)

"Laboratório de idéias." *Kaza*, vol. 4, no. 38 (2006)

Lang Ho, Cathy. "Brothers of Invention." *I.D.*, 50, no.4 (June 2003)

Lehmann, Werner und von Dorothee, "Salone del 2008 Visionen und Stilrecycling." *Raum und wohnen*, (May 2008)

"Loucos por design." *Arc Design*, no. 39 (November/December 2004)

"Modernidade tropical." *Arc Design*, no. 8 (January/February 1999)

Madison, Lucy. "Second Helpings." *Surface*, 68 (2007)

Moreno, Shonquis. "A Tale of Two Cities." *Surface*, 71 (2008)

Morteo, Enrico. "Brasile: Humberto e Fernando Campana." *Interni*, no. 482 (July/August 1998)

"Móveis bossa-nova." *Veja,* (November 1998)

Muniz, Vik. "Campana Brothers." *Bomb*, no. 102 (Winter 2008)

"Na fase dos espaços virtuais." *Casa & Jardim*, no. 505 (February 1997)

"PAC Pólo Arte Contemporânea." *Revista Nossa,* (October 2001)

"Para ver a metamorfose do mobiliário." *O Globo*, (May 1999)

Picchi, Francesca, and Cristina Tommasini. "Design Morbido." *Domus*, no. 848 (May 2002)

Pulfer, Rachel. "Urbane Sprawl." *Azure*, (May/June 2004)

"Quirky Massimo capitalises on design talent." *Design Indaba*, (2nd Quarter 2005)

Ribeiro, Airton. "Designers no Mube." *Projeto Design*, no. 214 (November 1997)

Romanelli, Marco. "5 + 9 Pezzi Speciali al Salone del Mobile di Milano." *Abitare*, no. 420 (September 2002)

_____. "Designs from 1991 to 1994." *Domus*, no. 757 (February 1994)

_____. "Il Disegno del Mobile Brasiliano: Appunti di viaggio." *Domus*, no. 728 (June 1991)

_____. "Fernando e Humberto Campana: Trans-Plastic ovvero infettare il sintetico con protesi naturali." *Abitare*, no. 467 (December 2006)

_____. "Milano 2004: Cercare L'eccellenza." *Abitare*, no. 440 (June 2004)

_____. "Nomen Omen: Le Campane dei Campana." *Abitare*, no. 460 (April 2006)

_____. "Salone del Mobile 2002." *Abitare*, no. 419 (July/August 2002)

_____. "Telegrammi da Milano 03." *Abitare*, no. 429 (June 2003)

Roux, Caroline. "The Campana Brothers: Favela Chic, Plastic Fantastic, and Fraternal Love with Humberto and Fernando Campana." *Blue Print*, no. 257 (August 2007)

Rozzo, Mark. "Waxing Brazilian." *Men's Vogue*, (May 2008)

Rubinstein, Dan. "Poster Boys." *Surface*, 64 (2007)

Scarzella, Patrizia. "Nhow & Thun." *Surface*, 66 (2007)

"Signés Humberto et Fernando Campana." *Marie Claire Maison*, (May 2008)

Spencer, Amy. "A Fashionable Life: Kanye West & Alexis Phifer." *Harper's Bazaar*, (June 2008)

"Summer of Art." *Art Review*, no. 12 (June 2007)

"A toca do alquimista." *Arc Design*, No. 61 (July/August 2008)

"Todas as luzes. A luz." *Arc Design*, no. 35 (March/April 2004)

"Universo em sintonia: a transformação dos materiais." *Arc Design*, no. 20 (January/February 2001)

"Walk of Fame." *Wohnrevue*, no. 1 (2006)

Wolff, Laetitia. "Creature Comfort." *Surface*, 60 (2006)

Selected Articles: Newspapers

Blackburn, Janice. "Designers with a flair for home truths." *Financial Times*, 21 May 2004

_____. "Pushing the limited." *Financial Times*, 25 March 2006

_____. "The thrill of the chairs." *Financial Times*, 29 September 2006

"Brincos que acendem ou feitos de ralos na coleção de Jóias Campana." *O Globo*, 16 May 2001

Chaplin, Julia. "An Old Friend of Ancient Wood." *The New York Times Magazine*, 6 March 2008

"Coleção Campana H. Stern." *O Estado do Paraná*, 23 June 2002

Crafti, Stephen. "Chairmen of our material world." *The Australian Financial Review*, 17 October 2008

"O design da escassez." *O Globo*, 28 November 1998

"O design dos Campana chega ao MoMa" *Gazeta Mercantil*, 25 November 1998

"Designers do caos artesanal." *Jornal do Brasil*, 12 June 1999

"Designers paulistas expõem criações em Nova York." *O Estado de São Paulo*, 8 December 1998

"Diálogo sutil entre o Brasil e o Japão." *O Estado de São Paulo, Caderno 2*, 10 April 2008

Hales, Linda. "Sitting Pretty." *The Washington Post*, 24 September 2006

"Irmãos Campana conquistam a Inglaterra." *O Estado de São Paulo, Caderno 2*, 29 June 2004

"Irmãos Campana criam jóia conceitual." *O Estado do Paraná*, 5 July 2001

"Irmãos Campana expões suas obras na Inglaterra." *A Gazeta Cuiabá/MT*, 30 June 2004

Kahn, Eve. "Selected Museum Pieces With a Woven Theme." *The New York Times*, 14 February 2008

"Keeping it in the family: sibling partnerships." *Financial Times*, 23 August 2008

Lyttle, Bethany. "Shopping: Textiles." *The New York Times*, 9 December 2005

McKee, Bradford. "Louche Life." *The New York Times*, 13 April 2006

"As metamorfoses dos irmãos Campana." *Valor*, 23–25 November 2007

Morgan-Griffiths, Lauris. "Fraternity, Fun, and Furniture." *Financial Times*, 9 March 2007

"MoMA exibe Tropical Modern dos Campana." *Folha de São Paulo, Ilustrada*, 24 November 1998

"O mundo fantástico dos irmãos Campana." *O Estado de São Paulo, Casa & especial*, 30 April 2006

"No bazar com os Campana." *Jornal da Tarde*, 17 July 2004

"Um objeto dos irmãos Campana pode ser jóia." *Jornal da Tarde*, 17 June 2001

O'Flaherty, Mark C. "Brothers of Invention." *Financial Times*, 1 January 2008

"Ouro à flor da pele." *O Estado do Paraná*, 27 June 2002

"Os papas." *Diário 10!*, 14 September 2008

"O poder de uma cor." *O Estado de São Paulo, Casa &*, 20 July 2008

"Poesia e humor de dois irmãos." *O Estado de São Paulo, Casa &*, 06 April 2008

"O Rio dos Campanas." *O Globo, Caderno Ela*, 30 August 2008

"Sinos dos Campana dobram em Nova York." *Folha de São Paulo, Ilustrada*, 28 October 2005

Sunshine, Becky. "Edgy, secret and slightly illicit." *Financial Times*, 26 January 2008

Tang, Syl. "The New Russia Houses." *Financial Times*, 28 June 2008

Underwood, Paul. "Contributors." *The New York Times Magazine*, 8 October 2006

Viladas, Pilar. "Style: Designing Men." *The New York Times Magazine*, 27 July 2003

Wainwright, Jean. "The Campana Brothers on Design." *The Art Newspaper*, December 2007

Wennberg, Per. "Bygga bo." *Skona Hem*, 28 October 2008

Image Credits

Li Edelkoort essay: 14 Fernando Laszlo (FL)

Stephan Hamel essay: 20 FL (church in Brotas); 20 Fernando and Humberto's personal archives; 21 FL; 23 Andréas Heiniger (AH); 24 Rafael Assef (drain cover); 24 FL (Mosaico bracelet); 25 Luis Calazans (LC) (Liana chair); 25 Ed Reeve (ER) (Multidao armchair). Courtesy of Albion, London; 26 Estudio Campana; 27 Rhett Butler (water lilies); 27 Estudio Campana (VR at V&A); 27 Estudio Campana (Jabuticabeira tree); 27 AH (Jabuticaba fruitbowl)

Cathy Lang Ho essay: 28 FL; 29 Estudio Campana; 30 FL (homeless shelter); 30 Estudio Campana collection (Papelao sofa); 30 Estudio Campana collection (Vitoria Regia stool); 30 Andrés Otero (AO) (Anemona chair); 31 Stefan Jonot (SJ) (plastic doll basket); 31 SJ (Leather patchwork vase); 32 Estudio Campana (Banquete chair); 32 SJ (Humberto and shopkeeper); 32 Zanotta Spa, Italy (Stella stool); 33 Gerard van Hees. Courtesy of Droog, Amsterdam (85 Lamps); 33 Gerard van Hees. Courtesy of Droog, Amsterdam (Chest of drawers); 33 Estudio Campana (mirror); 33 Fernando and Humberto's personal archives (Fernando on tractor); 35 SJ; 36 Edra, Italy; 38 SJ; 39 FL (the Estudio Campana); 39 SJ (Esperança doll)

Deyan Sudjic essay: 40 FL; 41 Collection Alexander von Vegesack; 42 V&A Images, Victoria and Albert Museum, London (Sottsass typewriter); 42 Bitossi Ceramiche, Italy (Sottsass Totem); 42 National Museum of Ireland (Eileen Gray prototype); 43 Galerie Jacques De Vos, Paris (Chareau table lamp); 43 Photo: Tom Vack. Courtesy of Ron Arad Associates, London; 44 Ingo Maurer GmbH, Munich; 46 Nelson Kon; 47 Nelson Kon

Photo essay: 48–64 Fernando Laszlo

Chapter 1: 66 AH; 68 LC; 70 LC (Costela chair); 70 AH (Samambaia chair); 71–75 LC; 76 AH; 77 LC (Flama chair); 78 Photo: Peter Wood. Courtesy of Danny Lane, London (Stacking chair); 78 Collection of Corning Museum of Glass, New York. Courtesy of Corning Museum and Danny Lane (Etruscan chair); 79 AH; 80 AH

Chapter 2: 82 AH; 84 AH; 85 FL; 86 AO; 87 Edra (Papel collection); 87 AO (Papelão lamp, table, and cabinet); 88 FL (paper cart); 88 Courtesy of Vitra Design Museum, Germany (Grandpa Beaver chair); 88 Photo: Hans Hansen. Courtesy of Vitra Design Museum, Germany (Wiggle side chair); 89 AH; 90 AH; 91 AO (Papel table); 91 AH (Papel sofa); 92 AO; 93 AH; 94 AO; 95 AO; 96 Edra; 97 Edra; 98 Photo: Pierre Yves Refallo. Courtesy of Habitart, Brazil; 99 SJ; 100 Photo: Pierre Yves Refallo. Courtesy of Habitart, Brazil; 101 Skitsch Italy; 102 Maíra Cayaba; 103 Bernardaud, France; 104 Lacoste

Chapter 3: 106 Fernando Campana; 108 AH; 110 AO; 111 Fernando Campana; 112 Edra; 114–119 LC; 120 AH; 121–123 Alessi, Italy; 124 AH

Chapter 4: 126 AH 129 Edra; 130 Edra; 131 AH; 132 AH; 133 AO; 134 AO; 135 AH; 136 AH; 137 AH; 138 AO; 139 Edra; 140 Edra; 141–145 Melissa / Grendene, Brazil

Chapter 5: 146 Edra; 148 Edra; 149 Starck Network; 149 Photo: Walter Gumiero. Courtesy of Jasper Morrison Ltd., London; 150 Nelson Kon; PP.152–156 AO; 157 Estudio Campana; 158 Moss, New York; 159 Swarovski

Chapter 6: 160 Ed Reeve (ER); 163 Edra; 164 Edra; 166 LC; 167 AH; 168–171 ER; 172 LC; 173–177 ER; 179 Estudio Campana; 180 AH; 181 ER; 182–187 LC; 188–192 ER; 194–197 Edra

Chapter 7: 198 Edra; 201 AO; 202 Romulo Fialdini; 203 Nicole Bachmann; 204–211 Edra

Chapter 8: 212 ER; 215 Artecnica, Los Angeles; 216 ER; 217 ER; 218 FL; 219 FL; 220 ER; 221 ER; 222–227 FL; 228–232 ER; 233 FL; 234 Andrew Garn; 235 Andrew Garn; 236–239 FL. Courtesy of Vitra Design Museum, Germany; 240 Masaya Yoshimura

Acknowledgements

Charles Miers (Rizzoli, New York) and Michael Hue-Williams (Albion, London) would like to thank everyone involved in this publication, without whose time, expertise, effort and generosity it would not have been possible.

Fernando and Humberto Campana

Text: Darrin Alfred

Essays: Li Edelkoort, Stephan Hamel, Cathy Lang Ho, and Deyan Sudjic

Commissioned photography: Stefan Jonot, Fernando Laszlo, and Ed Reeve

Designers: Herman Lelie and Stefania Bonelli

Editors: Matt Price, Dung Ngo, and Lelia Arruda

UK editorial assistant: Sarah Smiley

Archive research: Roberta Cosulich

Bibliography compilation: Estudio Campana, Darrin Alfred, and Wendy Smith

Proofreaders: Jennifer Milne and William Lambie

Production: Kaija Markoe and Maria Pia Gramaglia

The Estudio Campana team: Luiza Albuquerque, Dorival Barbosa Pereira, Claudio Campana, Cristina Esther, Leo Kim, Diogo Matsui, Debora Ribeiro dos Santos, Julia dos Santos Ribeiro, Ana Paula Moreno, Silvia Prada, and Eduardo Wolk

The Albion team: Alia Al-Senussi, Ed Brunning, Grant Eldridge, Gemma Harrison, Matthew Langton, Antony Parkes, and Sophie de Poulpiquet

Special thanks to:

Alessi, Italy; Ron Arad; Bernardaud; Marilene Bittencourt (Habitart); Luis Calazans; Benedetta Cerutti (Edra); Katherine Cocke and Genevieve Beddard (Swarovski); Rochelle Costi; Alain Degobert and Miryon KO (21_21 Design Sight); Design Miami/; Droog Amsterdam; Edra, Italy; Philip Fimmano (Li Edelkoort); Concetta Gallo; Frank Gehry; Franklin Getchell and Murray Moss (Moss); Dianella Gobbato, Daniela De Ponti, Clara Buoncristiani (Castiglioni); Hans Hansen; Thomas Happel (Ingo Maurer); Andreas Heiniger; Galerie Kreo; Nelson Kon; Marina Neder (Estúdio 321); Andrés Otero; Danny Lane; Clodagh Latimer (Ron Arad Associates); Fiona Meldrum (Danny Lane Ltd.); Melissa; Giampaolo Moonti (Bitossi Ceramiche); Jasper Morrison; PlusDesign; Skitsch, Italy; SNP, Hong Kong; Philippe Stark; Swarovski; Teracrea; Rahel Ueding; Alexander von Vegesack, Marianne Goebl, Andreas Nutz, Mathias Schwartz-Clauss (Vitra Design Museum); Venini; Masaya Yoshimura; Marina Zanetta (Alessi); Zona D